Using Art for Social Transformation

Social arts are manifold and are initiated by multiple actors, spaces, and direction from many directions and intentions, but generally they aim to generate personal, familial, group, community or general social transformation which can maintain and enhance personal and community resilience, communication, negotiation, and transitions, as well as help with community building and rehabilitation, civic engagement, social inclusion, and cohesion. Occurring via community empowerment, institutions, arts in health, inter-ethnic conflict, and frames of lobbying for social change, social art can transform and disrupt power relations and hegemonic narratives, destigmatize marginalized groups, and humanize society through creating empathy for the other.

This book provides a broad range of all of the above, with multiple international examples of projects (photo-voice, community theater, crafts groups for empowerment, creative place-making, arts in institutions, and arts-based participatory research) that is initiated by social practitioners and by artists – and in collaboration between the two. The aim of this book is to help to illustrate, explore, and demystify this interdisciplinary area of practice.

With methods and theoretical orientation as the focus of each chapter, the book can be used both in academic settings and for training social and art practitioners, as well as for social practitioners and artists in the field.

Eltje Bos (PhD) is Professor Emerita of Cultural and Social Dynamics at the University of Applied Sciences Amsterdam. Also trained as a drama teacher, she focused and focuses in her work on the use of arts and creativity in social work as well as on strategies of collaboration to increase personal empowerment and livability in the city.

Ephrat Huss (PhD) is Professor of Social Work and Art Therapy at Ben-Gurion University of the Negev. She heads an innovative MA social work specialization that integrates arts in social practice and has 40 students doing social arts projects per year. She has a background in fine arts. Her areas of research are the interface between arts and social practice and arts-based research: using arts as a way of accessing the voices of marginalized populations.

Routledge Advances in Social Work

Social Work, Social Welfare, Unemployment and Vulnerability Among Youth
Edited by Lars Uggerhøj, Vibeke Bak Nielsen, Ilse Julkunen and Petra Malin

Boys' Stories of Their Time in a Residential School
'The Best Years of Our Lives'
Mark Smith

Social Work and Climate Justice
International Perspectives
Edited by Devendraraj Madhanagopal and Bala Raju Nikku

Social Work and Human Services Responsibilities in a Time of Climate Change
Country, Community and Complexity
Amanda Howard, Margot Rawsthorne, Pam Joseph, Mareese Terare, Dara Sampson and Meaghan Katrak-Harris

Revolutionary Social Work
Promoting Systemic Changes
Edited by Masoud Kamali

Using Art for Social Transformation
International Perspective for Social Workers, Community Workers and Art Therapies
Edited by Eltje Bos and Ephrat Huss

For more information about this series, please visit: www.routledge.com/Routledge-Advances-in-Social-Work/book-series/RASW

Using Art for Social Transformation

International Perspective for Social Workers, Community Workers and Art Therapists

Edited by Eltje Bos and Ephrat Huss

LONDON AND NEW YORK

Designed cover image: © Getty Images

First published 2023
by Routledge
4 Park Square, Milton Park, Abingdon, Oxon OX14 4RN

and by Routledge
605 Third Avenue, New York, NY 10158

Routledge is an imprint of the Taylor & Francis Group, an informa business

British Library Cataloguing-in-Publication Data
A catalogue record for this book is available from the British Library

Library of Congress Cataloging-in-Publication Data
Names: Bos, Eltje, editor. | Huss, Ephrat, editor.
Title: Using art for social transformation : international perspective for social workers, community workers and art therapists / edited by Eltje Bos and Ephrat Huss.
Description: Abingdon, Oxon ; New York, NY : Routledge, 2023. | Series: Routledge advances in social work | Includes bibliographical references and index.
Identifiers: LCCN 2022030077 (print) | LCCN 2022030078 (ebook) | ISBN 9780367615239 (hbk) | ISBN 9780367615185 (pbk) | ISBN 9781003105350 (ebk)
Subjects: LCSH: Social sciences—Study and teaching. | Arts and society—Study and teaching. | Social change—Study and teaching. | Community development—Study and teaching.
Classification: LCC H62 .U637 2023 (print) | LCC H62 (ebook) | DDC 300.71—dc23/eng/20220919
LC record available at https://lccn.loc.gov/2022030077
LC ebook record available at https://lccn.loc.gov/2022030078

ISBN: 978-0-367-61523-9 (hbk)
ISBN: 978-0-367-61518-5 (pbk)
ISBN: 978-1-003-10535-0 (ebk)

DOI: 10.4324/9781003105350

Typeset in Sabon
by Apex CoVantage, LLC

Contents

Figures

Tables

Contributors

Nesrien Abu Ghazaleh (PhD) is a social psychologist. She is a senior researcher at the Amsterdam University of Applied Sciences; she teaches there and also at the University of Amsterdam. Her research focuses on young people (future plans, preventing loneliness, or coaching), social and work integration (e.g. refugee and minority groups), and the use of arts-based research methods.

Arjen Barel is the director and coach of the Storytelling-Centre Amsterdam where he teaches storytelling and delivers training for professionals to use storytelling in community work in various places in the world. Recently he published two books about how sharing stories can contribute to personal growth and social impact.

Noa Barkai-Kra (PhD) is a social worker and a lecturer in the social work department at Ben-Gurion University of the Negev. Over the last ten years, along with teaching at the academy, Noa has been conducting workshops and courses for Arab-Jewish conflict/dialogue groups on behalf of The School for Peace in Wahat a-Salam – Neve Shalom, including short-term and long-term workshops for youth, teachers, adults, and social activists, using creative tools.

Michal Bat Or is an art-therapist in private practice, a senior lecturer at the University of Haifa, and Researcher in the Emili Sagol Creative Arts Therapies Research Center (https://catrc.haifa.ac.il/). Her area of research includes working alliance in art-= therapy, the Open Studio art-therapy approach, art therapy for trauma and loss, community-based art therapy, and art-based assessments. She is also an author and illustrator of children's books

Diana Betzler (PhD) has 20 years of experience in teaching, research, and consulting within the arts and cultural sectors. She holds a PhD in social sciences and economics. She has evaluated arts programs, projects, and institutions on the behalf of Swiss Cantons and State Authorities for more than ten years. Link: www.dianabetzler.ch.

Beata Bigaj-Zwonek is an active artist (painter, graphic) and associate professor (PhD) at the Jesuit University Ignatianum in Krakow (AIK). Her scientific research includes art, history of art, aesthetics, and cultural studies. She particularly deals with the issues of expression in art, social art, engaged art, and Polish culture.

Eva Bojner Horwitz (PhD) is Professor of Music and Health at the Royal College of Music in Stockholm and a researcher at the Department of Clinical Neuroscience Karolinska Institute (KI). She specializes in psychosomatic medicine and the creative arts; she is co-founder of the Center for Social Sustainability (CSS), KI and anchored in interdisciplinary research, focusing on flow, benevolence, music, and health.

Eltje Bos (PhD) is Professor Emerita of Cultural and Social Dynamics at the University of Applied Sciences Amsterdam. Also trained as a drama teacher, she focused and focuses in her work on the use of arts and creativity in social work as well as on strategies of collaboration to increase personal empowerment and the livability in the city.

Artist/educator **Paola de Bruijn** is a teacher/researcher at the Academy of Social Studies at the HAN University of Applied Sciences in The Netherlands. She is currently conducting her PhD study at Maynooth University in Ireland. Her ambition is to explore how students in social work can be sufficiently prepared to utilize visual arts in working with older people.

Sander van Bussel is a social artist. With his collective, Tilburg Cowboys (Netherlands), he has been working since 2001 on many projects in the field of engaged/social design and participatory art. His long-running project *Human Rights Tattoo* started in 2012; Van Bussel also is curator of Kaapstad Tilburg – an annual, three-day artistic takeover of the city center – and lecturer at AKV St. Joost, School of Art and Design, Breda.

Shelley Cohen Konrad, (PhD, LCSW, FNAP) is a professor at University of New England School of Social Work and Director of the Center for Excellence in Collaborative Education. Her publications focus on relational practice, interprofessional education, and arts and experiential learning in the health professions.

Luis Garcia (EdD) is a clinical social worker, social-service administrator, and re-entry advocate with over two decades of non-profit, public systems administrative experience, working with populations who have histories of complex trauma. He holds a Doctorate of Educational Leadership for Social Justice from Loyola Marymount University.

Juan Carlos Gauli Pérez holds a PhD in audiovisual communication and is the director of the Audiovisual Design and Illustration Program at ESNE University School of Design, Innovation and Technology. He is a member of several editorial boards and editorial committees and founder of the scientific society Icono14. https://icono14.net/ojs/index.php/icono14

Tami Gavron (PhD) is an art psychotherapist, supervisor, and researcher. She is the coordinator of the graduate Art Therapy Program at Tel-Hai College, Israel. She is a lecturer at the Graduate School of Creative Art Therapies at the University of Haifa. She has a private practice in the north of Israel.

Jolanta Gisman-Stoch is a lecturer in art and cultural education, socio-cultural animation, and arts therapy at the University of Silesia in Katowice. Art teacher, socio-cultural animator, and certified arts therapist, she works with various groups staying in a long-term collaboration with cultural, educational, and therapy institutions in Poland.

Emilio J. Gómez-Ciriano (PhD) is an associate professor at Castilla-La Mancha University. He conducts his research as director of Alter-Acción team. His main interest areas are migration and human rights. He is currently the secretary of ESWRA and responsible for Human Rights of Justice and Peace Spain (on a voluntary basis).

Dave Gussak, (PhD, ATR-BC) is Professor in the Florida State University's Graduate Art Therapy Program and the project coordinator for the FSU/FDC Art Therapy in Prisons program. He has presented and published extensively internationally and nationally on forensic art therapy and art therapy in forensic settings. He is the co-editor and contributing author for *The Wiley Handbook of Art Therapy*.

Mel Gray (PhD) is Professor Emerita of Social Work in the School of Humanities and Social Science at the University of Newcastle in New South Wales, Australia. Her research interests include social work, social policy, social development, knowledge production, research use, and evidence-based practice in social work and the human services.

Tero Heinonen is preparing a PhD at the University of Helsinki, Faculty of Theology, on organizational interventions based on collective and self-transcending emotions for fine artwork and for academic communities.

Ephrat Huss (PhD) is Professor of Social Work and Art Therapy at Ben-Gurion University of the Negev. She heads an innovative MA social work specialization that integrates arts in social practice and has 40 students doing social arts projects per year. She has a background in fine arts. Her areas of research are the interface between arts and social practice and arts-based research: using arts as a way for accessing the voices of marginalized populations.

Catherine Hyland Moon is Professor Emerita in the Art Therapy Department at the School of the Art Institute of Chicago. She is the author of *Studio Art Therapy: Cultivating the Artist Identity in the Art Therapist* and editor of *Materials and Media in Art Therapy*.

Rebecca Jackson works as the director of Cameo House for the Center on Juvenile and Criminal Justice in San Francisco, California, supporting justice-involved women and their children as they heal. As a 49-year-old African American woman and mother who spent half her life in difficult-to-escape cycles, she now serves as a role model of hope and change.

Erik Jansen (PhD) is Associate Professor of Capabilities in Care and Wellbeing at the Academy for Social Studies at HAN University of Applied Sciences in The Netherlands. His primary research interest is in issues regarding the contextual and situational influences on wellbeing and quality of life.

Debra Kalmanowitz (PhD) is Co-editor in Chief of the Journal CAET (http://caet.inspirees.com/) and works in the context of humanitarian aid, disaster relief, political violence, refugees, and social change. She is a practicing artist and art therapist, assistant professor at the Academic College of Society and the Arts (ASA), as well as supervisor and psychosocial facilitator for an international humanitarian organization (NGO),

Brian L. Kelly (PhD, MSW, CADC) is an associate professor at Loyola University Chicago, School of Social Work. His research explores current and historical uses of recreational, art, and music-based activities in social work. He holds an associate degree in audio engineering and incorporates audio documentary and other audio-based, ethnographic methodologies.

Maria Kint is currently Impact Manager for Human Rights Tattoo Foundation (www.humanrightstattoo.org) and a board member of *ZAM Magazine*, Contemporary Creative Viewpoint on Africa (www.zammagazine.com). Her awards include the 2014 Knight in the Order of Oranje Nassau by King Willem Alexander of the Netherlands and 2015 Companion (S) in the Order of OR Tambo by the president of South Africa.

Marián López Fdz. Cao (PhD) is Professor of Art Education and Art Therapy at the Complutense University of Madrid, Spain. She holds a PhD in social art and is an art therapist. She is the vice president of ECARTE, European Consortium of Arts Therapies Education. She received a Research Award in 2020 from the Spanish Association of Art Therapy and First Prize 2017 for Transfer in Research in Social Sciences and Humanities for her mobile application "Madrid, city of women."

Jacquelyn McCroskey is John Milner Professor of Child Welfare and Children's Data Network Co-Director at the University of Southern California Suzanne Dworak-Peck School of Social Work. She uses linked administrative data to inform children's programs and policies, particularly in the areas of early care and education, child welfare, and juvenile justice.

Hugh McLaughlin is Professor Emeritus at Manchester Metropolitan University. He was a practitioner for 22 years before entering academia. His research interests include service user involvement in education and research and critical professional practice.

Ignacio (Nacho) Moreno Segarra is Postdoctoral Researcher in the Universitat Rovira i Virgili of Tarragona. He holds a PhD in journalism from the Universidad Complutense of Madrid and a masters in gender and feminist studies. His research focuses on gender, communication, and subaltern, buried micro-histories.

Siebren Nachtergaele holds an MA in social pedagogy, is a lecturer in culture and politics at Ghent University of Applied Sciences and Arts, and is a researcher at the research center eCO – CITY (Hogeschool Gent). His research interests include collaborative and collective making processes, dramaturgy, and processes of art mediation.

Elizabeth Odom is an art therapist, a former art educator, and a current PhD student studying art therapy at Florida State University. She completed her master's thesis research focusing on art therapists' use of personal art making. Her research interests include collage processes in art, research, and therapy, art therapists' identities, arts-based research, and post perspectives.

Inspired by the symbiotic vision of the world by Sahelian peasant traditions, the painter and graphic artist **Blaise Patrix** has worked for 30 years to develop"socia(B)le art" methods to promote creative social ties on the path of culture for and by all. Creations of socia(B)le art, carrying a strong message of solidarity with which participants, viewers, or users easily identify, have to this day reached hundreds of thousands of citizens.

Anne Birgitta Pessi (PhD) is Professor of Church and Social Studies (University of Helsinki). She also holds the title of a Docent in Sociology (University of Eastern Finland). Pessi has directed various interdisciplinary research projects on themes such as compassion, altruism, and civil society, as well as religiosity and emotions.

Nina Poluektova (PhD in psychology) is an associate professor at the Department of Social Work of St. Petersburg State University (retired) and a practicing psychologist and art therapist.

Oto Potluka (PhD) is a senior researcher at the Center for Philanthropy Studies, University of Basel (Switzerland). He conducts evaluations in regional and economic development, labor and social affairs, civil society, and social governance. He is a member of the European Evaluation Society (board of directors) and the American Evaluation Association.

Reineth Prinsloo (PhD) is a professor at the Department of Social Work and Criminology, Faculty of Humanities, University of Pretoria, South Africa where she teaches group work as intervention method in social work. She currently serves as vice president of the International Association for Social Work with Groups (IASWG). She is a researcher with international recognition from the National Research Foundation (NRF).

Izumi Sakamoto, PhD, MSW, MA, MS is an associate professor at the Factor-Inwentash Faculty of Social Work and an Academic Fellow at the Centre for Critical Qualitative Health Research at the University of Toronto. Izumi has expertise in arts-based research, community-based participatory research, qualitative research, critical immigration studies, cultural identities, anti-oppressive practice, and critical consciousness.

Gregory Sale is a socially engaged artist and Arizona State University associate professor. Sale works with communities to co-create artistic responses to the challenges of mass incarceration in the US. His projects including *Future IDs at Alcatraz* and *It's not just black and white* (2011) have been supported by Creative Capital, the Rainin Foundation, and the Andy Warhol Foundation.

Leanne Schubert (PhD) is an artist and social worker in private practice. Affiliated with the University of Newcastle in New South Wales, Australia, she has worked as a research associate. Her research interests include the relationship between social work and art, community practice, and domestic and family violence and how these are influenced by the contemporary sociopolitical context.

Anna Smirnova (PhD Soc) is an associate professor at the Department of Social Work of St. Petersburg State University. She uses arts-based methods in teaching social work and investigating the problem of developing identity and agency in young people.

Evie Soape, ATR, LMHC, is an art therapist with the Art Therapy in Prisons Program of the of the Florida State University and the Florida Department of Corrections. She obtained a master's in art therapy at Florida State University. She enjoys bringing the benefits of art therapy to individuals housed within Florida's carceral system, as well as contributing to the knowledge base on the efficacy of art therapy in forensics.

Tine Vanthuyne holds a master's degree in educational sciences (Ghent University) and is lecturer in social work at Ghent University for Applied Sciences and Arts and researcher at the research center eCO – CITY (Hogeschool Gent). Her research and teaching interests are focused on processes of urbanization and community development, community-based social work, co-creation, and living labs.

Griet Verschelden (PhD) is Head of the Department of Social Work at the Ghent University for Applied Sciences and Arts and Researcher at the research center eCO – CITY (Hogeschool Gent). Her research and teaching interests are on community arts and participatory art practices, adult education, youth work, community development, child-friendly cities, and urban renewal.

Monica Worline (PhD) holds a lectureship at the Ross School of Business, University of Michigan, and she is part of the core faculty at the Center for Positive Organizations as well as being a research scientist at Stanford University's Center for Compassion and Altruism Research and Education.

Introduction

Eltje Bos and Ephrat Huss

In a world facing rapid social change, with our societies becoming ever more diverse, fluid, and divided, the impact of arts on social transformation is a rapidly expanding field of interest.

When we think of art for social transformation, as the title of this book suggests, we intend to illustrate how the use of art can enhance social resilience by manifesting and, holding resistant and also hopeful methodologies and meanings, emerging from both social practitioners and artists.

Art for social transformation, also referred to as "social art", is used in a wide variety of contexts to help maintain and enhance personal growth, community resilience, community building and rehabilitation, civic engagement, social inclusion, and cohesion. Social art can emerge from multiple actors, spaces, and directions. This area is relatively new and still very much developing. Art for social transformation can be based on a spectrum of social and psychological theories and can occur in arts or non-arts settings and in private, semi-public, and public spaces (Dokter et al., 2011; Huss, 2015; Huss & Bos, 2019).

Our aim in this book is to help canonize this fluid, bottom-up, and undefined phenomena as a theoretical and methodological field for social practitioners, artists, and artist-practitioners, each of whom may be involved in social arts while utilizing different methods and theories and perhaps even having different aims.

Psychological theories see art as a therapeutic activity in itself and focus on the effects of the process of making art and the results (Huss, 2012). In psychodynamic approaches art is seen to offer a bridge to unconscious desires and aims while humanistic theories define art as a path to the authentic self (Huss, 2015). Theories of phenomenological and embodied aesthetic experience deal with the experiences of daily life to activate cognition, recognition, and affect in an embodied, relational manner (Chemero, 2011). While pursuing arts activities,

DOI: 10.4324/9781003105350-1

theorized as "flow", participants' deep engagement in an intermediary zone of play, creativity, or meditation achieves a lifted psychic state and also can be related to mindfulness (Bell & Robbins, 2007; Csikszentmihalyi, 1990).

As for social theories, we have noticed the term "social arts" increasingly used in social and community practices that bring out silenced experiences and connect them to social contexts that enhance empathy, tolerance, creative problem solving, resilience etc. (Huss, 2012; Huss & Bos, 2019; Landy & Montgomery, 2012).

Social practitioners utilize arts in the fields of (community) empowerment, humanization of institutions, professional education, arts in (mental) health, interethnic conflict, lobbying for social change, and civic engagement to tempt the people they work with, who often are in precarious circumstances, into transformational processes. These can be aimed at healing (shifting focus from victimhood to coping); at personal, group, and community empowerment; at strengthening resilience, at developing new perspectives of the future; and/or at challenging existing local power systems.

Social artists tend to use arts more in order to disrupt hegemonic narratives, destigmatize marginalized groups, and humanize society (Belfiori & Bennett, 2010; Bishop 2006, 2012; Sachs Olsen, 2019; Schruers & Olson, 2020). Some artists actively engage people in the process of creating an artwork, and others create an artwork with the intent to address a certain social issue and expect the artwork through its expressive powers and locality, to speak for itself to the public. Bishop (2012) suggests that the art itself always keeps a promise for improvement. The artwork, then, is seen as an entity with agency, as is expressed in the Actor Network Theory (ANT) (De Mol, 2010; Latour, 2005).

The literature on social engagement by artists has also been referred to as Socially Engaged Art Practices, Socially Engaged Art and Social Practice Art, or Relational Aesthetics (Schruers & Olson, 2020). We will use the term "Social Arts" as we feel it more explicitly includes both art practices for social transformation by social professionals and by professional artists and by artist-professionals who combine these professions. Often the two groups, social artists and social practitioners using arts, do not define their aims in the same language and so miss opportunities for integrating their skills to work together.

Some of the inherent characteristics of the arts are helpful for Social Art projects. First, the dynamic relationship between form and content come into play by deciding what will be depicted – or pronounced – and then give it shape. Arts can have impact on people, groups, and communities in various ways. They can help individuals, groups, and communities to excavate and make heard silent facets of experience due to trauma, taboos, or marginalization. Second, the arts can embody the connection between micro and macro aspects of experiences through the aesthetic tension between elements, like actor and stage, figure and background (Huss & Bos, 2019), which is helpful in order to see personal experiences in social contexts. The arts offer the possibility for expression in a nonlinear, metaphorical way – which is a third characteristic. It provides a rich form to give shape to what is difficult to put in discursive linear texts, because it is contradictory, complex, traumatic, or in some cases too difficult for people with mental challenges. From the perspective of shared cultural contexts, collective symbols (metaphors) can help people express who they are, gain strengths, and thus enhance resilience from creating, revisiting, and reliving collective symbols. Fourth, the improvisational character of the arts helps people and groups to deal with and act more freely in complex social situations (Bertinetto & Ruta, 2021).

Engaging in an arts activity means one enters an actual and symbolic safe place (Huizinga, 1938, Sutton-Smith, 1997). This free space is where the rules of daily life are paused and people engage in the arts with some distance from the "real" and from ordinary life; a space where individuals, groups, and communities can express emotions in a nonlinear and metaphorical way. In this symbolic space automatic thinking is disrupted, and the artforms are used to provide a canvas or stage, beyond the linearity of discursive language, for the many contradictions, ambiguities, secrets, and fears of our lives.

Art provides a safe environment not only for individuals and groups – in more therapeutical activities – but also for the encounter and connection between groups that otherwise avoid each other due to tension or conflict. The arts can help to enhance exchange and understanding by creating a space and connection by engagement in the arts, by sharing life stories (Bar-On & Kassem, 2004; Cobb, 2013; Frühmann et al., 2021). In the context of more political activities such as this playful setting combined with the metaphorical nature of art forms, power relations can be mitigated as the parties engage not in "the real" but in the safe space the arts provides. This also protects those without power from power holders.

In addition, we now know from positive psychology and brain research that when people experience repeated positive emotions by having positive experiences they tend to feel better about themselves, thus empowering themselves and becoming more open to their environment (Fredrickson, 1998, 2000; Heiser, 2020; Huss & Bos 2019; Seligman &

Csikszentmihalyi, 2000; Wilkinson & Chilton, 2013). This emphasis on what is positive, on strengths that exist, helps to change the focus from what was/is wrong and looking back to a focus on coping and on possibilities, to integrate past and present and to create new perceptions of the future (Antonovsky, 1987; Eriksson, 2017; Simon, 2005).

The arts are particularly well equipped to provide these positive experiences, since they often provide pleasant experiences (Lomas, 2016; Matarasso, 1997, 2019). Arts are even more impactful as they affect the "old brain" region, which controls our emotions. Juslin and Sloboda (2010) found that being engaged in music and/or performing art stimulates certain brain stem reflexes and the interplay of parts that form the reward system, like the amygdala, the hippocampus, and the prefrontal cortex. This causes a pleasurable experience and a pattern of input and reward – such that people want to repeat the experience (Berridge & Kringelbach, 2015; Juslin & Sloboda, 2010; Salimpoor et al., 2018). Recently more research has been conducted on how arts stimulate new paths in the human brain that seem to enable people to change thinking and behavioral patterns (Altenmüller et al., 2020).

This book emerges from the positionality of the editors as social practitioners and also includes perspectives of artists and those who are both social practitioners and artists. Our main aim is to provide a broad descriptive set of multiple international examples of projects initiated by social practitioners and by artists – and by collaboration between the two – in varied settings and domains. This will help to demystify this interdisciplinary area that is theorized through different lenses by showing what people are doing and through focusing on their methods. The aim of this book is to provide an umbrella description of social arts to help all types of social artists better define their aims, theoretical orientation methods, and ways of evaluating their intervention. Also, this book is intended to provide inspiration for the practice of social professionals, artists, social change advocates, and policy makers. Furthermore, we aim to acknowledge the multidisciplinary nature of this area of practice.

This book contains a broad set of case studies, methods, and ideas including social practitioners, social artists, cultural policy makers, academics, and arts-based participatory research. We have aimed for a smorgasbord of varied international examples emerging from social practitioners (social workers, community workers, social change advocates, art therapists, psychologists, human geographers), social artists, (fine art, performing art, visual culture, visual anthropology, art history), and cultural and social policy makers. What is common to them all is that they aim to utilize arts as a method to transform society, directly or indirectly. Through this, we hope to inspire and guide all of the aforementioned groups on the theoretical, academic, training, and practice levels.

There were various possibilities for how to organize this book, including by the use of art disciplines, by whether they took place in an organizational or non-organizational context, or by whether the emphasis was on the empirical practice or on a more theoretical approach. All of those arrangements felt somewhat artificial, so we decided not to do so. Thirty-eight authors with extensive experience contributed to this book. We are grateful to them and mention their names and chapters shortly in the following paragraphs (mentioning them according to the order of the chapters); after that we capture the chapters (in alphabetical order of the first author) in a table for an overview and some reflections.

In the chapter by Debra Kalmanowitz, artist and art therapist (PhD), Michal Bat Or (art therapist, senior lecturer, PhD), and Tami Gavron (art psychotherapist, researcher, PhD), arts therapy was combined with social action, in a moving art studio, during the Palestinian Israeli unrest in May 2021, using visual arts and also recycling trash into art.

Arjen Barel (storyteller, author, MA) and Nesrien Abu Gazaleh (senior researcher and lecturer, PhD) described how the use of photographic material and storytelling in a European project helped to connect youth of groups with a tense or conflictual relationship in Estonia, Lithuania, North Macedonia, The Netherlands, and Spain.

Noa Barkai-Kra (social worker, lecturer, PhD) studied art as a tool for contact theory, as she brought together Bedouin Arab and Jewish children using arts, crafts, and the creation of a Facebook page.

Artist and professor Beata Bigaj-Zwonek and art lecturer Jolanta Gisman-Stock explain how art, especially visual arts and theatre, contributed to the development of democracy since 1980 in Poland. Their historical reflections are illustrated by examples of past and present projects.

The artist and associate professor Gregory Sale, Rebecca Jackson (Director Cameo House), Luis Garcia (clinical social worker, PhD), and Jacquelyn McCroskey (professor) engaged in a conversation and described through their reflections the Future IDs project in California. They shared how creating future IDs enabled inmates to create a new identity and life for themselves for their return from incarceration to society; the IDs are both created and exhibited.

Professor Reineth Prinsloo explored how non deliberative groupwork in a safe environment enabled personal and social growth. In South Africa, she has used arts and crafts with elderly women from townships, homeless men and domestic workers, and social work students from various backgrounds, enabling them to build connection and to gain some income through a newly developed skill.

Professor David Gussak, Elisabeth Odom (BFA, MS), and Evie Soape (art therapist) researched how with the visual arts, in therapeutic arts sessions with prison inmates in Tallahassee (U.S.A.), demonstrate how art therapy helped to create positive self-appraisal, to create new labels, and to assist in establishing new, healthy identities, contributing to personal and social transformation.

The painter Blaise Patrix shares from his long experience in Burkina Faso how the use of symbols and creation of collective artworks in processes of spontaneous co-creation where participants are equal helped to see oneself and the other. Blaise Patrix works in many countries, with a variety of mostly underprivileged people and communities, e.g. with women in shelters and youth in the West Bank.

Erik Jansen (associate professor) and Paola de Bruijn (artist and PhD candidate) investigate the importance of improvisation in complex social contexts and describe a process of improvisation during mask making by refugees with an addiction in a residential care home in Nijmegen, Netherlands.

Anna Smirnova (associate professor) explored the effect of social arts on identity formation and spheres of recognition and taught social work students in St. Petersberg, Russia how the use of art, photovoice, and creative genograms enable individuals and groups who are disrespected to empower themselves.

Eva Bojner Horwitz (professor), Tula Heinonen (PhD candidate), Anne Birgitta Pessi (professor), and Monica Worline (PhD, lecturer) developed a deeper insight in embodied compassion and have examined the particular power of arts-based interventions to foster embodied skills, such as compassion. They make a case for embodied compassion in future leadership.

Catherine Hyland Moon (art therapist, professor emerita) explored the role of community art practice to mitigate the impact of social inequality. She addressed the aims and challenges of Artworks, a location open to all in Chicago (U.S.), which reimagined public space as a site to challenge assumptions about socio-cultural divisions, to provide for preventive and restorative healthcare, and to enhance care for each other.

Emilio Gómez-Ciriano (associate professor) and Hugh Fraser (professor emeritus) described their experience in a European project that explored approaches to enhance the cooperation between artists and social professionals using various art forms such as dance, photographic representations, and liberarte activities. The project was carried out in Finland, the UK, Estonia, and Spain.

Shelley Cohen Konrad (professor) and Izumi Sakamoto (associate professor) make a case for the integration of the arts in human service education as a means to strengthen relational learning and enhance critical consciousness. They explored the relational learning theory and the approach of critical consciousness in anti-oppressive practice. They described their approaches through case examples of applied art productions by students and communities, examining how the use of arts advances transformational learning.

Brian Kelly (associate professor) revisited three of his studies that explored the use of music-based activities with young adults who experience homelessness and other forms of unstable housing in Chicagoland (U.S.). The studies showed useful practices of how participants can benefit from the provision of structure, mentoring, and support in their music-related goals. An important aspect of the work is the acknowledgement of participants as artists, musicians, DJs, poets, and dancers.

Marián López Fdz. Cao (professor), Juan Carlos Gauli (PhD, audiovisual communication), and Nacho Moreno Segarra (PhD, researcher) explored feminist and emotional geography as well as the concept of artivism and how this concept served as a narrative driver for the project "Madrid, City of women". The project aims to gather and share new narratives on the city to recover the lost geographies from the female perspective, resulting in an itinerary and an interactive map of life stories.

Leanne Schubert (artist, PhD) and Mel Gray (professor emerita) explored the complexities and the "entanglement" of socially engaged art practices and present two case studies that demonstrate collaborative artworks designed to generate insight into and transform awareness of a community issue and ethical dilemmas in entangled community-based art models. They examined the core concepts of Socially Engaged Art Practices (SEAP), showing theoretical attempts to explain SEAP's intent and ways to evaluate its impact.

Siebren Nachtergaele (lecturer, researcher), Tine Vanthuyne (lecturer, researcher), and Griet Verschelden (professor) reflected on the political and agonistic potential of participatory processes of participatory art practices. From various forms of art practices, mainly theater, they scrutinize how, in which way, and why participatory arts emphasize the sociopolitical aspects in their work. Also, they have concluded when participative art processes do have political and agonistic potency.

Diana Betzler (evaluator, PhD) and Oto Potluka (senior researcher) have written a chapter about evaluation of the social impact of arts projects and programs. They created an inventory of thirteen published evaluations. The developments of existing evaluation practices are discussed, and they present suggested approaches for future practices.

Sander van Bussel (artist) and Maria Kint (manager) share their experiences with their world-wide body-art project on the Universal Declaration of Human Rights.

We captured the chapters in the following table:

Table 0.1 Chapter overview

Author	*Arts used*	*Theories and methods*	*Population*	*Setting*	*Emphasis*	*Impact level*
Barel, Arjen et al.	Storytelling, photography, toolkit, and website	Social identity theory, self-categorization theory and the similarity-attraction paradigm, empathic exchange	Individuals of 10 groups in 5 countries, living separately/live in conflict	Five processes of encounter in neutral spaces, European project Estonia, Latvia, Spain, the Netherlands	Method development	Increase empathy between individuals/ groups
Barkai-Kra, Noa	Various arts, crafts, creating a Facebook page	Arts as a contact method	Jewish and Arab children in Israel (groups in conflict)	Neutral encounter spaces, visiting each other's houses in Israel	Coping with Arab-Israeli conflict on educational and social level	Increase empathy between individuals/ groups
Betzler, Diana and Potluka, Oto	Evaluation of social impact practices of art projects	Various evaluation practices	Description and analysis of 13 evaluation practices		Evaluation project	Increase knowledge on measuring social impact
Bigaj-Zwonek, Beata and Jolanta Gisman-Stock	Emphasis on visual arts, theater arts, theater performances	Elitist and egalitarian approach of the arts. Art as dynamic complementarity of opposites. Dialectical character of the arts Stróżewski. Social role of artists in Poland. Ross, Baumann a.o.	Polish people, society since 1980s.	Arts initiatives in various contexts	Role of art in Polish democracy	Impact of arts on the process of democratization Polish society

Bojner-Horwitz, Eva et al.	Music, dance, theatre art (theoretical or other studies)	Embodiment, embodied compassion, 5 steps approach	Leaders in workplaces	Various workplaces	Method, approach for embodied empathy in workplaces	Increase of embodied compassion in workplaces
Cohen-Conrad, Shelly and Sakamoto, Izumi	Classroom as a laboratory for modeling and experiencing. (as if space)	Relational learning theory, critical consciousness in anti-oppressive practice Critical Consciousness Conceptual Model	Social work students	Classroom Social work school	Method, model to enhance critical consciousness	Behavior of future social workers
Gomez, Emilio and Fraser, Hugh	Dance, a concept card game to identify the formula for effective interprofessional work, designing occupational maps, photographic representations, liberarte activity	Development of approaches of cooperation between artists and social professionals ACCES, CAST-models	Social work students and artists in various countries cooperation in the arts.	European project of encounters between artists and social professionals. Finland, UK, Estonia, and Spain	Develop methods to enhance cooperation	Enhance cooperation between artists and social professionals
Gussak, David, et al.	Visual arts	Labeling theory. Symbolic Interaction, reverse societally and institutionally assigned identities	People in correctional institutions	Art Therapy sessions in correctional institution in U.S.A.: Tallahassee	Re-empowerment of prison inmates in constructing new self-appraisals	Methods of re-empowerment to reverse socially assigned identities (for prison inmates)

(*Continued*)

Table 0.1 (Continued)

Author	*Arts used*	*Theories and methods*	*Population*	*Setting*	*Emphasis*	*Impact level*
Highland Moon, Catherine	Miscellaneous, music rooms, visual arts materials, sewing	Artworks model to connect people in informal setting, non-contrived activities; role of community art therapy mitigating impact of social inequality	Inhabitants from a gentrifying neighborhood, racially, ethnically, and social economically diverse	Studio Artworks in gentrifying neighborhood where everybody is welcome. Chicago, U.S.A.	Connecting diverse people in informal setting, mitigating impact social inequality	Cultivate community, enhance racial inclusivity, decenter power, foster mutual care
Jansen, Erik and De Bruijn, Paola	Music, Mask making	Neuro cognitive studies, complexity studies, improvisation	Social workers, refugees with an addiction	Care in residential Community in Nijmegen	Why and how arts help to increase improvisational skills	Enhancing improvisational skills through the arts
Kalmano-witz, Debra, et al.	Visual arts using crayons, clay, mandala, waste material (recycling trash)	Art therapy and social action, healing capacity of the arts, creating a potential space	1) People in Palestinian-Jewish neighborhood 2) Underprivileged ultraorthodox Jewish community	Pop up Studio, 1) in public garden during Palestinian Israeli unrest in May 2021 2) underprivileged orthodox neighborhood	Reflection on art therapy concept to work outside clinical settings	Bringing together people to empower and support communities in need

Kelly, Brian	Music-based activities, composition, performance, production	Transitional living program, harnessing structure and support in music-based activities	Emerging adults, being homeless or experiencing other forms of unstable housing	Music studio, residencies for homeless emerging adults in Chicagoland, U.S.A.	Review of studies providing structure and support	Develop talents, strengths, and interests of homeless people through music-based activities
Lopez, Marian et al.	1) Creating an itinerary that enshrines women's memories 2) An interactive map of life stories, (storytelling)	Political artivism, feminism, feminist geography, emotional geography, participative action research, Delphi method	Female citizens of Madrid	Workshops weekly meetings during 3 months, Madrid, Spain	Re-seeing, redefining the geography of Madrid from a female perspective	New narratives on the city to recover "lost geographies" from the female perspective
Patrix, Blaise	Visual arts, murals, painting in circles project, product printed on items: like banners, mugs	Caribbean studies, on colonialism, diversity (Edouard Glissant), construction of self, spontaneous co-creation, equality of participants	Various: Inhabitants of underprivileged neighborhoods, woman victims of violence, communities during an armed conflict	Underprivileged neighborhoods, various places; Burkina Faso, shelter in Brussels, School in West Bank, etc.	Communal painting in various forms	Enhance empowerment of individuals, groups, communities

(Continued)

Table 0.1 (Continued)

Author	*Arts used*	*Theories and methods*	*Population*	*Setting*	*Emphasis*	*Impact level*
Prinsloo, Reineth	Arts and crafts, making finger puppets, felt keyrings, bags	Non deliberative group work in safe environment enabling personal and social growth. Human bonding. Sensitivity to diversity	Older women from a township in Pretoria, homeless men and domestic workers. Social work students of various backgrounds	Township community center, School of Social work Pretoria, South Africa	Method(s) for personal and social growth	Awareness of self, enhancing competencies and skills, cohesion and bonding, earning some income
Schubert, Leanne and Gray, Mel	Visual arts	Complexities "entanglement" of Socially Engaged Art practices (SEAP)and their impact	Practice in 1) hospital 2) underprivileged neighborhood	1) Cancer hospital, project by an artist (not by themselves) U.S.A. 2) Safe at home: neighborhood Australia	Chapter explores concept of SEAP and its complexities, including the issue of (measuring) impact. Adds practice	Generate insight and transform awareness of a pressing community issue and the ethical dilemmas inherent in "entangled" community-based art models
Sale, Gregory et al.	Visual arts, future IDs, narratives	Art as symbolic space, rescripting identity	People returning to society during after incarceration. Anti-Recidivism Coalition	1) Sending out tool Kits 2) Project in Alcatraz, with people who will retry society 3) Visitors exhibition U.S.A.	Approach tool	Enhance empowerment, create a community, engage broader society for possibility to re-script identity

Smirnova, Anna	Creative genogram, photovoice	Effect of Social Arts on identity formation, spheres of recognition	Social work students in St. Petersburg	Classroom sessions	Importance of art on identity formation	Teach social work students to enable individuals and groups who are disrespected to empower themselves
Nachtergaele, Siebren et al.	Miscellaneous, depending on respondents; theater is emphasized. The aim of this contribution is to scrutinize the participatory processes of participatory art practices and reflect on their political or agonistic potential	Political dimension in participatory art practices; power relations; commoning	Various participatory art practices	Communities in Belgium – Ghent	Scrutinization of political dimension of participatory art practices	The political dimension in participatory art practices and its potential to social transformation is linked to a balance of power relations within practices and between practices and the broader society
Sander van Bussel and Maria Kint	Body art	Body as a canvas to share human rights	Various communities, worldwide	Various communities, also connected by the website	Body as political statement	Enhance personal empowerment, create a community of political solidarity

What can we learn about the characteristics of social art from the aforementioned chapters? On a methodological level, we saw that social uses of arts can define arts very broadly, including traditional, cultural, and ethnic community activities, activities in public spaces, place attachment, media networks, and online communities, to name a few. What social aims do social arts encompass? We saw that social aims can span from resilience – where art helps to problem solve and share – to empowerment, in which arts help to subvert dominant discourses through the phenomenology of dominant groups, to conflict resolution, in which art enables humanization and arouses empathy towards the other. What populations and settings use social arts? Again, we see a diverse set of populations and settings.

The chapters in this book span a variety of groups, communities, public spaces, and individuals. Social practitioners utilize the fields of their daily practice such as (community) empowerment, humanization of institutions, professional education, arts in (mental) health, and interethnic conflict, and artists enter these spaces or utilize public spaces.

What can we learn from the summary of the chapters in this book and after reading them? We learn that social arts comprise a diverse field, on the level of theory, method, arts implementation, and aims. Each author utilized the arts as a method to articulate their psychological, social, or aesthetic theory, often combining a few theories: for some, the ability of art to serve as an effective vehicle to carry this theory into social action was the rationale for using the arts. For others, the arts intervention was the central element, and the appropriate theory helped give a rationale for the arts intervention. Thus, vocabularies used can also differ a lot.

Often the aims are grounded in an art activity whose social meanings only become apparent during or/and after the arts activity, or conversely, the focus can be on a specific intended social transformation, and the arts are a (partial) vehicle to reach these. In some of the contributions the emphasis is on a more theoretical approach, while others are more practice oriented.

On the one hand, it may seem as though social arts is such a diverse field that it cannot be defined or that an effort to categorize or list these contributions by definition evades the multiple and rich contributions that often transcend the existing theoretical borders between aesthetic, psychological, and social theories. On the other hand, this multi-literate approach is the power of social arts: maybe we can see it as a rich, fluid repository of arts activities that intend to improve people's lives, communities, and societies. At the same time there is a need to define the field in order to measure its impacts.

This definition will enable us to canonize social arts, reach excellence, and enable appropriate resources and funding. But how should the impact of these interventions be measured? Its impact is connected to the intentions of those who initiate and participate (as active or receptive participants) in these practices. These activities might be initiated by grassroots civic initiatives and/or socials professionals and/or artists (Thompson & Schechner, 2004; Travis et al., 2019). So, the intentions of the initiators and participants guide whether the desired effect is on the individual, group, community, societal, or political level or on a combination of those.

The chapters in this book enable us to reflect on the importance of involving participants. Social arts often are initiated by social professionals, artists, or collaborations between these professionals; some answers arise from the practices described in this book: involvement, participation, and collaboration of clients and citizens is a prerequisite in cases where the arts-based interventions serve to mitigate trauma and enhance empowerment, in cases where the aim is to impact specific individuals. This also holds true for interventions where the aim is to enhance empowerment of groups and communities that are under stress or fragmented. In order for the arts activity to have an impact, some members of these groups need to be involved, though the involvement is less specifically directed at particular individuals. As for social arts more directed at socio-political change, as in politically loaded songs or artworks, involvement of members of the public counts but not necessarily as the collaborators contributing to the creation of an artwork. These cases can be statements made by the artist, and the involvement of the public is not "organized"; rather it is left open how and to what extent the public will participate. The importance of the artistic quality of the art on its impact needs to be explored a bit more; some of the chapters touch on this subject. We know that people and communities do become proud if they themselves or others appreciate their work, and we know that some songs were more helpful for social change than others; still this subject still needs to be studied further.

This book was created in 2020, 2021, while the world was immersed in the COVID-19 pandemic that was felt the hardest by people in precarious circumstances. Given the global realities, it is likely that many of us have and will become increasingly vulnerable due to illness, material insecurity, injustice. As the contributions in this book tell us, the arts can help address urgent social issues that people are experiencing right now. Also, the arts will help us to see that better days will be coming in even periods of crises. We should use the rich opportunities the arts offer us!

Enjoy your reading!

Eltje Bos and Ephrat Huss

References

Altenmüller, E., Kliegel, M., Krüger, T., Van De Ville, D., Worschech, F., Abdili, L., Scholz, D. S., Jünemann, K., Hering, A., Grouiller, F., Sinke, C., & Marie, D. (2020). Train the brain with music (TBM): Brain plasticity and cognitive benefits induced by musical training in elderly people in Germany and Switzerland, a study protocol for an RCT comparing musical instrumental practice to sensitization to music. *BMC Geriatrics*, *20*(1), 418. https://doi.org/10.1186/s12877-020-01761

Antonovsky, A. (1987). *Unraveling the Mystery of health: How people manage stress and stay well.* Jossey-Bass.

Bar-On, D., & Kassem, F. (2004). Storytelling as a way to work through intractable conflicts: The German-Jewish experience and its relevance to the Palestinian-Israeli context. *Journal of Social Issues*, *60*, 289–306. doi:10.1111/j.0022-4537.2004.00112.x

Belfiore, E., & Bennett, O. (2010). *The social impact of the arts.* Palgrave McMillan.

Bell, C. E., & Robbins, S. J. (2007). Effect of art production on negative mood: A randomized, controlled trial. *Art Therapy: Journal of the American Art Therapy Association*, *24*(2), 71–75.

Berridge, K. C., & Kringelbach, M. L. (2015). Pleasure systems in the brain. *Neuron*, *86*(3), 646–664. https://doi.org/10.1016/j.neuron.2015.02.018

Bertinetto, A., & Ruta, M. (2021). *Routledge handbook of philosophy and improvisation in the arts.* Routledge.

Bishop, C. (2006). The social turn: Collaboration and its discontents. *Artforum.* www.artforum.com/html/issues/200602/new

Bishop, C. (2012). *Artificial hells: Participatory art and the politics of spectatorship.* Verso.

Chemero, A. (2011). *Radical embodied cognitive science.* MIT Press. doi:10.1037/a0032923

Cobb, S. B. (2013). *Speaking of violence: The politics and poetics of narrative in conflict resolution.* Oxford University Press.

Csikszentmihalyi, M. (1990). *Flow: The psychology of optimal experience.* Harper and Row.

De Mol, A. (2010). Actor-network theory: Sensitive terms and enduring tensions. *Kölner Zeitschrift für Soziologie und Sozialpsychologie. Sonderheft*, *50*, 253–269.

Dokter, D., Holloway, P., & Seebohm, H. (Eds.). (2011). *Dramatherapy and destructiveness: Creating the evidence base, playing with Thanatos.* Routledge/Taylor & Francis Group.

Eriksson, M. (2017). The sense of coherence in the salutogenic model of health. In M. B. Mittelmark, S. Sagy, M. Eriksson, G. F. Bauer, J. M. Pelikan, B. Lindström, & G. A. Espnes (Eds.), *The handbook of salutogenesis* (pp. 91–96). Springer International. https://doi.org/10.1007/978-3-319-04600-6_11

Fredrickson, B. L. (1998) What good are positive emotions? *Review of General Psychology*, 2, 300–319. https://doi.org/10.1037/1089-2680.2.3.300
Fredrickson, B. L. (2001). The role of positive emotions in positive psychology: The broaden-and-build theory of positive emotions. *American Psychologist*, *56*(3), 218. https://doi.org/10.1037/0003-066X.56.3.218
Frühmann, P., Barel, A., & Dahlsveen, H. (Eds.). (2021). *Common ground, common future: Applying storytelling in conflict and polarisation*. International Theatre & Film Books.
Heiser, S. R. (2020). The art of flourishing: Integrating positive psychology with art therapy to promote growth from trauma. *Master of Applied Positive Psychology (MAPP) Capstone Projects*. 192. https://repository.upenn.edu/mapp_capstone/192
Huizinga, J. (1938, 2010). *Homo ludens*. Amsterdam University Press.
Huss, E. (2012). What we see and what we say: Combining visual and verbal information within social work research. *British Journal of Social Work*, *42*(8), 1440–1459. https://doi.org/10.1093/bjsw/bcr155
Huss, E. (2015). *A theory-based approach to art therapy: Implications for teaching, research and practice*. Routledge. https://doi.org/https://doi.org/10.4324/9781315856810
Huss, E., & Bos, E. (2019). *Art in social work practice*. Routledge.
Huss, E., & Sela-Amit, M. (2018). Art in social work, do we really need it? *Research on Social Work Practice*, *29*(6), 721–726.
Juslin, P. N., & Sloboda, J. A. (Eds.). (2010). *Handbook of music and emotion: Theory, research, applications*. Oxford University Press.
Landy, R., & Montgomery, D. T. (2012). *Theatre for change, education, social action, and therapy*. Bloomsbury Publishing.
Latour, B. (2005). *Reassembling the social: An introduction to actor-network-theory*. Oxford University Press.
Lomas, T. (2016). Positive art: Artistic expression and appreciation as an exemplary vehicle for flourishing. *Review of General Psychology*, *20*, 171–182. https://doi.org/978-0-674-00581-5
Matarasso, F. (1997). Use or ornament: The social impact of participation in the arts. *Comedia*, *4*(2), 1–97.
Matarasso, F. (2019). *A restless art: How participation won, and why it matters*. Calouste Gulbekian Foundation.
Sachs Olsen, C. (2019). *Socially engaged art in the neoliberal city*. Routledge.
Salimpoor, V. N., van den Bosch, I., Kovacevic, N., McIntosh, A. R., Dagher, A., & Zatorre, R. J. (2013). Interactions between the nucleus accumbens and auditory cortices predict music reward value. *Science*, *340*(6129), 216–219. https://doi.org/10.6001/actamedica
Schruers, E. J., & Olson, K. (Eds.). (2020). *Social practice art in turbulent times: The revolution will be live*. Routledge.
Seligman, M. E. P., & Csikszentmihalyi, M. (2000). Positive psychology: An introduction. *American Psychologist*, *55*(1), 5–14. https://doi.org/10.1037/0003-066X.55.1.5

Simon, R. M. (2005). *Self-healing through visual and verbal art therapy*. (S. A. Graham, Ed.). Jessica Kingsley.

Sutton-Smith, B. (1997). *The ambiguity of play*. Harvard University Press.

Thompson, J., & Schechner, R. (2004). Why "social theatre"? *TDR/The Drama Review*, *48*, 11–16. doi:10.1162/105420404166 7767

Travis, R., & Rodwin, A. (2019). Therapeutic applications of hip hop with U.S homeless adults with severe mental illness. In E. Huss & E. Bos (Eds.), *Art in social work practice theory and practice: International perspectives* (pp. 170–181). Routeledge.

Wilkinson, R. A., & Chilton, G. (2013). Positive art therapy: Linking positive psychology to art therapy theory, practice, and research. *Art Therapy*, *30*(1), 4–11. https://doi.org/10.1080/07421656.2013.757513

1 Social action art therapy. An Israel context

Debra Kalmanowitz, Michal Bat Or, and Tami Gavron

Introduction

Increasingly art therapists have begun to understand that there is a need to broaden the definitions of our profession, to work clinically as well as in the community and the society at large (Hocoy, 2007; Kapitan, 2008; Kapitan et al., 2011; Kaplan, 2005; Talwar, 2016). This chapter will look at community-based work that took place in Israel and consider the ideas that inform this work. Viewing art therapy through a social lens has demanded that we, art therapists, expand our theoretical perspectives to include ideas from aesthetics, social criticism, feminist theories, disciplines of community psychology, community arts, social justice, wellness and resilience models, empowerment, and culture. This chapter will look at the *Portable Studio* (Kalmanowitz & Lloyd, 2005) and how this informs our social practices and broadens the boundaries of the art therapy profession. The common denominator of this work is the *art* and the understanding that engagement in the arts and creative process is healing, not only for the individual but also for communities and society.

Art therapy in the community can serve any number of purposes and be used in multiple ways. The work is informed by our training and experience as artists and art therapists and by our intimate understanding of the power of the creative process. Art therapists working in the context of society, social action, and social change can use art as a form of protest, a way of raising awareness, and a way of bringing people together to empower and support communities in need (Kalmanowitz & Potash, 2021). The examples in this chapter fit into the last category. We describe projects that were carried out in response to the most recent political unrest in Israel in May 2021, in an underprivileged ultra-orthodox community, and in response to the COVID-19 pandemic.

DOI: 10.4324/9781003105350-2

Art therapy and social action

Personal suffering is impacted upon by social and cultural events that take place in our environment and is often exacerbated by systemic injustices (Ottemiller & Awais, 2016). As a result, art therapists have called for collective and community engagement (Golub, 2005) and have observed that the art possesses "the potential to mediate between the individual and the collective" (Hocoy, 2005, p. 7). Mediating between the individual and the collective means that we make space to question the structures in which we live and function, how we impact these structures, and the impact they have on us.

Dissanayake (2017) writes that the arts are a prominent feature of group ritual and ceremonies, can help to reduce anxiety and unify participants, and that imagination is an integral part of these. The arts engage creativity and imagination, allowing human beings to bring alternative realities into consciousness and to look at things as if they could be otherwise (Green, 2000). Green's (2000) term *social imagination* relates not only to imagining things as if they could be otherwise but taking initiative to make them so.

As artists and therapists, we hold multiple identities, an understanding and experience of creative process, imagination, art making, and art history as well as a psychotherapeutic and clinical training. This places us in a unique position to work inside and outside of clinical settings. While art therapists have traditionally worked clinically and are aligned to psychotherapy, many also carry out socially engaged work (Golub, 2005). This work has at times led to feelings of discomfort in art therapists, raising the question – "is this art therapy?" It is only in the last decade or so that we have begun to connect this to theory and to an important part of our practice as art therapists.

Israeli art therapists are no exception. If we look at some of the main art therapy training programs in Israel, many now include a course on art therapy and social engagement. University of Haifa, Tel Hai College, Seminar Hakibbutzim (Kibbutzim College of Education), Beit-Berl College, and the College of Society and the Arts and Society in Ono Academic College all include a course on socially engaged art therapy in their training program. Examples in this chapter emerge out of these courses and depict the preoccupations of the students and of the society at this time.

As the dialogue between work on the ground and the social theories has grown it has informed, supported, and expanded our practice as art therapists working as agents of social change. Hocoy (2005) suggests that it is the "versatility and power of the image" (p. 7) that is key. He writes "Social action is ultimately predicated on the relationship between personal and collective suffering, and the image has the unique ability to bring to consciousness the reality of a current collective predicament, as well as the universality and timelessness of an individual's suffering" (p. 7).

When individuals suffer from the events in their society and community, bringing people together aims not only to address each individual but to address the damaged social fabric (Kalmanowitz & Lloyd, 1999). At times this work forms a bridge where a chasm has been created; at other times it serves to build more long-term alliances. Both of these aim to empower the community and the individuals so that they can bounce back to life and day to day functioning, albeit having changed. This preventative measure can make a difference to the mental health of the community as well as to the individual. Defining strengths, emotional and spiritual aspects of communities, and supporting the individual in their social context (Huss, 2015) can contribute to solidifying communities in flux. In this way art-based social activities in communities can affect the social space (Ottemiller & Awais, 2016) and can allow for the articulation of injustice as a silent witness and as an expression of desire for change (Huss, 2015). Art-based social activities can also be a supportive and transformative agent when a community suffers from a collective trauma (Gavron, 2020; Huss et al., 2016; Kalmanowitz & Ho, 2016). Social action art therapy can be a one-off event or a longer-term commitment. Art used during a time of crisis tends to be short term and demands that we take the lead from the community in order to respond to its needs.

Martin-Baro, credited as the founder of liberation psychology and a major force in the field of social psychology, devoted much of his career to adapting psychology to the community as well as to the individual. He claimed that the frameworks we work with in the West that define normality and psychopathology, like the DSM manual, can "mask the relationship between the symptoms that are expressed by individuals and social imbalances" (1994, cited in Kaplan, 2007, p. 25). These definitions "tend to situate the problem within the individual rather than within the broader collective context, and treat 'the pathology of persons' as if it were something removed from history and society, and behavioral disorders as if they played themselves out entirely in the individual plane'" (Martin-Baro, 1994, p. 27 cited in Kaplan, 2007, p. 26). The art therapist as social activist understands this connection and adapts accordingly.

Portable Studio

The move into working in the community and society has prompted much thought and consideration, not only in terms of social theory but also in terms of our art therapy models. Work outside of clinical settings implies more than carrying materials in a backpack. It contains myriad ideas that may be invisible to the onlooker but have an impact on the work that unfolds and differentiates the art therapists from the artists or community worker engaging in art.

Kalmanowitz and Lloyd (1999, 2005) explored these elements at length in their work in the former Yugoslavia during the war (1992–1995) and for years after and called this the *Portable Studio*. They write that an important part of the work in unstable environments was that they carried their internal structures as art therapists with them and that this allowed the work to "physically take place in a wide range of settings" (Kalmanowitz & Lloyd, 2005, p. 108). They described:

> This internal structure comprises a number of key elements which include an attitude both to the art and the individual making it. Central is a belief in the individual as possessing internal resources rooted in experience, resilience and culture rather than being a powerless victim for whom the therapist alone holds the solutions . . . This internal structure can provide an environment which allows for creative expression as well as sustained immersion . . . in the art making.
>
> (Kalmanowitz & Lloyd, 2005, p. 108)

Hyland Moon (2001) writes about the practice of a studio model of art therapy being possible anywhere. Her image of the "mobile therapist" resonates with the notion of the *Portable Studio* and obliges us to identify that which remains consistent. A systematic scoping review on the open art therapy studio carried out by Finkel and Bat Or (2020) found that "The open studio is a flexible therapeutic model that can be implemented among different populations and in different settings" (p. 12).

Following from this, some of the community projects represented in this chapter were named *pop-up studios*. A pop-up shop is the term given to a shop or store that is deliberately temporary. This defines a store that "pops-up" for a limited period of time to achieve a particular goal. Since many social projects are a single art-based action, the idea of pop-up studio immerged spontaneously, a brief project in response to a particular challenge/crisis, one that took into account the needs of the community while embracing the ideas of the *Portable Studio* (Kalmanowitz & Lloyd, 2005).

Social art therapy and the Israel context

Israeli society is diverse and varied, with many cultural and religious groups as well as one of the largest economic gaps between rich and poor in the world (Marlin-Bennett, 2016). Israeli art therapists are often called to work outside the clinical setting within communities who have experienced conflict, trauma, or distress such as in war zones (Segal-Engelchin et al., 2020), groups who have experienced terror and political conflict, as well as issues around identity amongst Jewish and Arab Israeli citizens (Boaz & Bat Or, in press; Podolsky-Krupper & Goldner, 2020; Sarit & Walsh, 2021). During the past two years, similar to the rest of the world, Israeli society has also suffered from the consequences of the COVID-19 pandemic and struggled with the consequences (amongst other things) of the social disconnection among individuals and communities.

The examples in this chapter are drawn from the authors' experience in teaching art therapy master's students in Israel during courses on community-based art therapy. Alongside the theoretical learning, these courses have a practical component – inviting the students to initiate and lead community-based art therapy projects. The students are frequently part of the specific communities in which they carry out their art-based action. The interactions that happen when the art materials are presented in the public space are a combination of much prior thought and consideration alongside a spontaneous response to the situation at the time.

Unrest of May 2021

An outbreak of violence took place within Israel in May 2021. A number of events on both sides (Palestinian and Israeli) triggered the violence that was marked by protests, violence, and police riot control. Without going into further detail, these events became heated and political violence spilled into the streets of Israel, clashes between Jewish and Arab Israeli citizens took place in public spaces, and there was a pulpable threat to the fabric of the society and to the possibility of living together. An art therapy student who lives in a mixed neighborhood used the communicative platform of the neighborhood residents to announce the pop-up open studio that would take place in a public garden in the neighborhood.

She brought art materials in a trolly (usually used for shopping) and arranged them on a carpet in the public park. Passers-by stopped curiously and began to talk about their feelings at this difficult and uncertain time. Some people were led to the pop-up studio by

Figure 1.1 Sign invitation to the mobile art workshop (Arabic, Hebrew, and Russian)

Figure 1.2 Hope and dreams for their city

curious young children, while others came through the notices they saw posted in the neighborhood forums. Held by the art therapy students, this became a meeting place, a first and initial moment for mending – communicating, coming together, sharing fears, shock, and hopes through the art works and conversations. The pop-up art studio allowed the participants, who were overwhelmed by a deep sense of disempowerment, uncertainty, and despair, a safe place, a *potential space* (Winnicot, 1971) in the public arena. Playing, imagining, and creativity all have a place in the pop-up studio. The carpet and art materials created a space in which participants could be active and communicative as well as reclaim and strengthen their relationships (Hocoy, 2007). In addition, participants were invited to visually express their hopes and wishes for their neighborhood. The art product that was created on a shared paper was hung on a building, communicating the creators' messages to and for passersby.

Underprivileged ultra-orthodox Jewish community

The second example is a pop-up studio that was initiated by an art therapy student who lives in an underprivileged neighborhood, where many large ultra-Orthodox Jewish families struggle with lack of economic resources. She was familiar with the reality of these families' children that have rarely a chance to create with art materials due to lack of resources and to the fact that the older children are expected to take care of their younger siblings. With permission of the parents, the art therapy student laid out materials in the public yard including gouache paints, crayons, brushes, white and colorful papers, stickers, glitter, beads, glue, and materials from nature (seashells, rocks, and more).

The materials were organized in baskets on a table and on a carpet on the grass. Many children arrived and were excited by the richness of the art materials, absent in their homes. They worked rapidly, trying to use and explore every art material available. After seeing the children's enthusiasm and creativity and their request to continue, the art therapy student extended the activity for four additional meetings (each one three hours long), and in each meeting, she introduced a new material or technique (charcoal, crayons, clay, and mandalas). For the last meeting, the student brought found objects and ready-made materials she had gathered from waste over the week, modelling that art can be made even in the face of a lack of traditional art materials.

Figure 1.3 Finger paints. Experimenting with materials on the grass

COVID-19

At the beginning of the COVID-19 crisis in March 2020, the medical staff in the Covid departments at a large hospital found themselves overwhelmed and stressed. The combination of unknown hazards of the virus, physical distancing from their clients, their colleagues, as well as from their families and the long, isolated working hours were trying. Two students from the social action art therapy class offered their support and asked the staff what could help them in their fight against the virus. As indicated, the most stressful part was their feeling of isolation from each other and lack of the usual staff mutual support. The students created a visual journal with variety of art materials and suggested that each staff member paint or draw their feelings regarding the stressful situation accompanied by a short piece of writing on their image and then pass it to another staff member. For two months the staff passed the art journal from one to another. The journal contained images in colored pencils, paint, and collage as well as written expression of various themes, such as distress, anger, loneliness, along with hope, positive future images, and a sense of connectedness to the department and its members. This rich and creative art journal served as a tangible yet symbolic shared meeting space and turned into a unique portable mini studio. After a few months the students created a short film that contained all the art works that appeared in the journal. This film was sent to each member of the department. It seemed that the process of sharing and expression did indeed help to support and empower this medical community and allowed them to feel connected and seen by each other. The film was later screened for an additional group of hospital workers, helping them feel less isolated in their work and facilitating coping and resilience to the broader hospital community.

Discussion

These three examples give a sense of the variety of ways in which the arts can be used as a tool for social support and social transformation. Short in duration, the engagement of pop-up art within the community allowed for the individual to find themselves in the group. Whether used in the context of conflict, as in the first example; in a disadvantaged community, in the second example; or in the context of the isolation of health care providers during COVID-19, in the third example, the art was central to the support that was provided.

In the first example, art in the park immediately after the political tension and violent uprising, the environment set up by the student created a space in which imagination and play could take place. People who joined the group shared feelings of fear and anxiety about the events that had transpired and about their own personal safety. The art introduced a *potential space* and opportunity for play, imagination, and experimentation into a tense environment. This may seem counterintuitive, but the facilitation of such an environment is no luxury; it is in fact the foundation of transformation and creative problem solving. McNiff (2011) perceives creativity and spontaneity as "fundamental aspects of wellbeing" (p. 80). The aim of this work in the park was to provide a space that allowed for expression of what was happening but also to remember together the strengths of the community and to begin to enhance resilience and a sense of wellbeing.

Community oriented creative work emphasizes the resources, rather than the deficits, especially after an event like the May 2021 in Israel. Despite this, as art therapists, we understand that the arts can contain multiple aspects of experiences at the same time. While difficult emotions may not always be easy, these community groups acknowledge the importance of allowing them to exist – while not becoming overwhelmed or absorbed by them. McNiff (2011) reminds us that "Just as the process of artistic transformation generates corresponding effects on the individual person, the same applies to social contexts" (p. 90) and later continues "the most fundamental of these features is art's unique ability to compassionately embrace uncertainty and difficulties without preestablished and ready-made plans for change. . . . This antithetical quality of the creative process may indicate expressive arts therapy's most significant impact on social institutions" (p. 91).

Frances Kaplan (2007) speaks about the arts for conflict resolution. "Art can be used to diffuse emotions prior to and after experiencing the consequences of conflict" (p. 98). Referring to the physical engagement in the art making process that sometimes helps to disperse the strength of the emotion, Kaplan adds that making art can "obviate the need to engage in conflict resolution dialogue" (p. 98). Additionally, Kaplan (2007) suggests that "Making art about an experience can help a person come to terms with what was happening" (p. 98) while at the same time being able to take corrective action. The art making of groups in conflict can also help people see the perspective and to undermine stereotypes about the other (Boaz & Bat Or, in press). These aspects formed part of the small but sensitive art group in the park.

Underprivileged community

In the case of this community, we see another strength in the use of arts. One of the tenets of the *Portable Studio* as written earlier is the "belief in the individual as possessing internal resources rooted in experience, resilience and culture rather than being a powerless victim for whom the therapist alone holds the solutions" (Kalmanowitz & Lloyd, 2005, p. 108).

This belief is crucial to work in the community and is evident from the example given on the groups that took place in the underprivileged ultra-Orthodox community. The student planned to introduce materials to encourage creativity and imagination, something that had become dormant. Once she did this, she reminded the parents of their power and gave form to what they did not know was missing. Levine and Levine (2011) explain that:

> Social change and social action require a humble and respectful attitude on the part of the change agent. We need to have an "appreciative curiosity" in Herbert Eberharts' words (2002, p. 126) about the situation in which the community finds itself in order to help the members of the group become aware of their resources and to help them regain an awareness of their capacity for building the world anew.

As a consequence of the pop-up arts workshop, the mothers began to appeal to the local municipality and to demand for their children a place to imagine, create, and play. The deep understanding of this community of the student and her ability to identify what was missing and to try to fill this gap created a snowball effect that – although she hoped for – she did not actually expect.

Working together

During the COVID-19 crisis, hospitals and hospital staff all over the world were overstretched and working under tremendous stress. The visual journal created by the two students and circulated amongst the medical staff helped to combat isolation of the virus and provide a way for the medical staff to communicate their stress to others and see that they were not alone. It was not only the long hours but the isolation that was felt by professionals who were cut off from their natural support systems, no longer meeting formally or informally in the corridors for banter or sharing of experiences. The journal, as a shared creative space, provided this opportunity.

> One of the things that the experience of making art together does is to restore the sense of living community, of being part of a whole that is larger than oneself. It is this sense of solidarity, "the experience of being together with others that is an essential part of being in the world."
>
> (Levine & Levine, 2011, pp. 28–29)

Levine and Levine (2011) also remind us of the importance of "helping people engage in community art practices together" (p. 28) so that they can "regain an awareness of their own poietic capacity" (p. 28) and envision new ways of living.

While of course it is best to come together face to face, here the journal and artistic expression needed to hold the connection, providing a small relief and a sense of cohesion at this time. Knowing that other people were committed to this same mission and getting a sense of their experience as well as sharing one's own enhanced their capacity to cope and allowed them to appreciate their long hours and commitment and to feel that they belonged to a group of people carrying out invaluable work that helped them "regain an awareness of their own poietic capacity" (p. 28).

Conclusion

This chapter illustrates the role of the art therapist and the arts in socially engaged art therapy practice and in bringing people together. Engagement of the arts within the *Portable Studio* and the *pop-up studios* provided a single or brief arts-based action. This single arts-based action cannot be underestimated as it has an important role as a preventative measure as well as for planting a seed or awakening a potentiality. While the meeting may be one-off, the potential can reverberate long after the participation in the art therapy activity. Through *Portable Studio* Kalmanowitz and Lloyd (2005) remind us that while we may only have a single meeting, each of our interactions needs to be in the fullness of the present moment. This is not about a linear process but about inhabiting the current space.

In addition, it is the breadth of our understanding and the multiplicity of the potential of the arts that make it relevant to these contexts. The creation of a creative space that allows for imagination and authentic art expression can allow for the presence of resilience and wellbeing as well as loss, anxiety, and trauma and, in this way, allow for transformation. The ability to create art on whatever is present and neither be possessed by it or deny it is fundamental to this work. The arts are a sophisticated, substantive, innovative, and ancient vehicle for social change and can enrich, embody, and strengthen communities and individuals as well as respond to current social and political realities.

References

Boaz, S., & Bat Or, M. (in press). Jewish and Arab youth create murals in public space: Community-based art therapy exploratory research. *Peace and Conflict: Journal of Peace Psychology*.

Dissanayake, E. (2017). Ethology, interpersonal neurobiology, and play: Insights into the evolutionary origin of the arts. *American Journal of Play*, 9(2), 143–168.

Finkel, D., & Bat Or, M. (2020). The open studio approach to art therapy: A systematic scoping review. *Frontiers in Psychology*, *11*, 1–16. https://doi.org/10.3389/fpsyg.2020.568042

Gavron, T. (2020). The power of art to cope with trauma: Psychosocial intervention after the tsunami in Japan. *Journal of Humanistic Psychology*, 1–19.

Golub, D. (2005). Social action art therapy. *Art Therapy*, *22*(1), 17–23. https://doi.org/10.1080/07421656.2005.10129467

Greene, M. (2000). *Releasing the imagination: Essays on education, the arts, and social change*. John Wiley & Sons.

Hocoy, D. (2005). Art therapy and social action: A transpersonal framework. *Art Therapy*, *22*(1), 7–16. https://doi.org/10.1080/07421656.2005.10129466

Hocoy, D. (2007). Art therapy as a tool for social change: A conceptual model. In F. Kaplan (Ed.), *Art therapy and social action* (pp. 21–39). Jessica Kingsley Publishers.

Huss, E. (2015). *A theory-based approach to art therapy: Implications for teaching, research and practice*. Routledge.

Huss, E., Kaufman, R., Avgar, A., & Shuker, E. (2016). Arts as a vehicle for community building and post-disaster development. *Disasters*, *40*(2), 284–303.

Hyland Moon, C. (2001) *Studio art therapy: Cultivating the artist identity in the art therapist*. London: Jessica Kingsley.

Kalmanowitz, D., & Ho, R. T. H. (2016). Out of our mind: Art therapy and mindfulness with refugees, political violence and trauma. *The Arts in Psychotherapy*, *49*, 57–65.

Kalmanowitz, D., & Lloyd, B. (1999). Fragments of art at work: Art therapy in the former Yugoslavia. *The Arts in Psychotherapy* (special issue), *26*(1), 15–25.

Kalmanowitz, D., & Lloyd, B. (2005). Inside the portable studio. In D. Kalmanowitz & B. Lloyd (Eds.), *Art therapy and political violence: With art, without illusion* (pp. 108–125). Routledge.

Kalmanowitz, D., & Potash, J. (2021, October 23–24). Art therapy, arts and social movements [Conference paper]. Annual Conference of the American Art Therapy Association, Virtual.

Kapitan, L. (2008). Not art therapy: Revisiting the therapeutic studio in the narrative of the profession. *Art Therapy*, *25*(1), 2–3. https://doi.org/10.1080/07421656.2008.10129349

Kapitan, L., Litell, M., & Torres, A. (2011). Creative art therapy in a community's participatory research and social transformation. *Art Therapy*, *28*(2), 64–73. https://doi.org/10.1080/07421656.2011.578238

Kaplan, F. F. (2005). What is social action art therapy? *Art Therapy*, *22*(1), 2–2. https://doi.org/10.1080/07421656.2005.10129463

Kaplan, F. F. (Ed.). (2007). *Art therapy and social action*. Jessica Kingsley Publishers.

Levine, E. G., & Levine, S. K. (Eds.). (2011). *Art in action: Expressive arts therapy and social change*. Jessica Kingsley Publishers.

Marlin-Bennett, R. (2016). Political contestation, Israeli identities, and the arts. *Arts and International Affairs*, *1*(1), 22–30. https://theartsjournal.net/2016/03/13/marlin-bennett/Invited.

McNiff, S. (2011). From the studio to the world. In E. G. Levine & S. K. Levine (Eds.), *Art in action: Expressive arts therapy and social change* (pp. 78–92). Jessica Kingsley Publishers.

Ottemiller, D., & Awais, Y. (2016). A model for art therapists in community-based practice. *Art Therapy*, *33*(3), 144–145. https://doi.org/10.1080/07421656.2016.1199245

Podolsky-Krupper, C., & Goldner, L. (2020). "God is a painter": How Jewish ultra-orthodox art therapists and clients perceive mental health treatment. *Transcultural Psychiatry*, *58*(6), 731–744. https://doi.org/10.1177/1363461520944742

Sarit, B. Z., & Walsh, S. D. (2021). Bridging the cultural gap: Challenges and coping mechanisms employed by Arab art therapists in Israel. *The Arts in Psychotherapy*, *76*. https://doi.org/10.1016/j.aip.2021.101853

Segal-Engelchin, D., Achdut, N., Huss, E., & Sarid, O. (2020). CB-art interventions implemented with mental health professionals working in a shared war reality: Transforming negative images and enhancing coping resources. *International Journal of Environmental Research and Public Health*, *17*(7), 2287. https://doi.org/10.3390/ijerph17072287

Talwar, S. (2016). Creating alternative public spaces: Community-based art practice, critical consciousness and social justice. In D. Gussak & M. Rosal (Eds.), *The Wiley handbook of art therapy* (pp. 840–847). John Wiley & Sons.

Winnicot, D. (1971). *Playing and reality*. Routledge.

2 Applied storytelling and picture talk as a tool for system intervention, behavioural change and diminishing polarization

Arjen Barel, Nesrien Abu Ghazaleh, and Eltje Bos

We seem to live in societies that are becoming more and more polarized. We saw recent examples of polarization during the American elections (2020), the process of Brexit, and the strong divisions within societies during the COVID-19 pandemic. Even families and friends sometimes seem seriously divided and often people stop talking to each other. There are many more examples of these polarizations/divisions, in current day societies and/or in recent history. Most are examples of historically disadvantaged groups that are looking for ways to overcome prolonged oppression and injustice (Hasan-Aslih et al., 2020).

Based on the assumption that it is possible to turn this dynamic around and to connect people instead of dividing them, this project used storytelling and picture talks as intervention tools. The goal of the project (PicS) was to induce a behavioural change in young people in order to establish more respectful, resilient, and peaceful communities.

In this chapter we will address how PicS used storytelling and picture talk for this purpose and how this method can be applied. We will focus on the essential elements that have to be taken into account in designing this type of intervention: empathy as well as the ingredients necessary to share a 'good' story. But before we start, we will elaborate on 'the system' we aim to change.

A system of similarities (and differences)

In almost all urban spaces in Europe, youth from various backgrounds live together. In these most diverse societies, there are not only religious, cultural, and ethnic differences; there also are economic differences, between the *haves* and the *have nots*. These kinds of societies

DOI: 10.4324/9781003105350-3

are referred to as heterogeneous societies. And they are at risk of polarization and even conflict (Vanhanen, 2012).

When looking at polarization, us-versus-them thinking is one of the constructs that occurs in our heads. This is a well-known aspect of how social identities are created and of how these can be governed by perceptions that are subjective (Brandsma, 2017. The us-versus-them thinking may lead to stereotyping.

The construction of social identity depends on "the individual's knowledge that he/she belongs to certain social groups together with some emotional and value significance to him/her of this group membership" (Tajfel, 1972, p. 292). Social identity theory proposes that the focus of people's self-definition is partly caused by their group membership, and this membership contributes to a person's self-concept and self-esteem. People tend to classify themselves and others into categories based on certain features and then identify more with members of their own category (in-group) than with members of other categories (out-group) (Turner et al., 1987). A strong social identity can thus lead to a strong group identity.

Individuals with a high group identity tend to incorporate aspects of that group in their self-concepts. This, in turn, influences their social perceptions or positive feelings about their in-group (Goldman et al., 2006). When interpersonal similarity among in-group members is high, this also tends to increase attraction between individuals (Byrne, 1971). This attraction leads to a similarity bias in favour of similar in-group members and bias against out-group members. The similarity-attraction paradigm posits that the more similar people are, the more the similar people are liked. Considerable research has provided evidence for the similarity attraction paradigm (see Byrne, 1997, for a review).

Based on social identity theory, self-categorization theory, and the similarity-attraction paradigm, we know that people tend to classify themselves and others into categories and in terms of group prototypes that reflect belief sets, attitudes, norms, values, and behaviours. This is the cause of the circular process of strengthening one's perception of one's in-group and the out-group. As people tend to like their in-group members more than the out-group members, bias in favour of similar in-group members and against out-group members is created (Hewstone et al., 2002). We create assumptions and labels to identify the other, and meanwhile we are also reinforcing our own identity. Research has shown that strength of ingroup identification influences processes of identification and reinforcement (Kelly, 1993).

When looking at a potential conflict, we are not necessarily referring to war zones but a conflict that endangers the peace in a society. Not all conflicts endanger peace; they are actually always part of society (Brandsma, 2017). However, when there is asymmetry in a society, conflicts can develop to the point of endangering peace (Shamoa-Nir et al., 2021). Usually, there is an asymmetry between majority and minority groups. They negatively evaluate each other, usually disadvantaging the minority group rather than the majority group (Livingston et al., 2004). The strength of ones' ingroup identification and being part of a majority or minority group influences the potential conflict.

It is interesting to mention a contrasting approach to conflict:

> Conflict arises not through difference but through similarity. In this vision, we suffer conflicts with each other because we all want the same thing; we resemble each other. . . . We strive for the same thing, and exactly because there is a certain degree of scarcity, we clash with each other. We want the same thing, from both the concrete material and abstract immaterial viewpoints. We want economic resources such as income, as well as symbolic resources such as recognition and social status.
>
> (Brandsma p. 63)

This means there are some contrasting views. But, either way, conflict becomes a danger when we do not know how to handle it. Peace is not the absence of conflict; it is the way we deal with a series of conflicts in a constructive way (Brandsma, 2017).

This is exactly where the PicS project came in. This EU Erasmus project, with participants from Lithuania, Estonia, Spain, North Macedonia, and the Netherlands, encouraged young people of communities in the respective countries that do not get in touch easily to overcome their differences and possible conflicts by connecting with each other through storytelling supported by picture talk and by learning how to deal with their differences in a constructive way. These connections are not only for their individual benefit but also – in the long run – for the benefit of their communities. By reducing the risk of conflict, these communities have the chance to become more resilient, more peaceful, and safer environments. As studies point out, people perform better in such environments (Emeodi, 2014).

Before we dive deeper into describing the PicS project, we will take a closer look into what exactly we mean by storytelling in conflict transformation work and consider the role of empathy.

Our vision on applied storytelling

Storytelling is about sharing between two people: the teller and the listener. What is important is that sharing stories is all about 'the other'.

A good storyteller – and every human being with the ability to speak and listen can be one – is always aware of the resonance of his or her story in the mind of the other and is not delivering a monologue. He or she shares his or her values, insights, and emotions and registers the reaction of the listener.

A good story is a journey, taking us along both opposing and supporting forces. Containing personal, emotional, and universal information, it is true and authentic, often expressing the vulnerability of the teller. We focus on oral storytelling as opposed to digital stories, because we are convinced that there is a huge difference between sharing information digitally and face to face. In the latter we can feel, smell, and touch each other. 'Touch' may sound strange when we talk about storytelling, but sometimes a touch means more than a thousand words (de Wachter, 2019).

Empathy

In the end it all comes down to empathy, and this is exactly what a good story can evoke. The teller takes the listener on a journey, and as soon as the two are on this journey together, there is every chance they will find a common ground, something that connects the teller and the listener emotionally. This is the moment we talk about empathic exchange (Brown, 2007).

Without giving and receiving empathy, our survival is in danger (de Waal, 2010), which also emphasizes the importance of living in groups. This is a phenomenon that we seem to be losing quickly in many Western societies but is still the order of the day in many other societies and certainly in the world of primates. The group protects us from dangers from outside, whether these are enemy armies or wild animals. We must continue to like each other – at least within that group – to a certain extent to maintain those groups. In order to survive, empathy is needed. It is the glue between people. Sharing stories plays a very important role with regard to empathy (Harari, 2011). It is perhaps the most important means of empathic exchange.

Storytelling and empathy

It is important to remember that there is only one place for the story to actually take shape: in the listener's head. By pronouncing words, the narrator offers images that are translated into the listener's own images.

Simply put, the resonance causes empathy. The vibration the narrator causes by producing words and images are transmitted through the story, and they also cause a vibration in the receiver. One relates to what one receives through images one knows. When that vibration happens, feelings and emotions are connected to those images. And where the exact memory of the storyteller and you, the listener, are often far apart, those feelings often match. At that moment a sense of connection and understanding is created.

That is what can be called resonance, which is the first step towards empathy.

Personal stories resonate, but so do fictional stories that are well constructed and told in a visual way. The fear the seven goats experience when the wolf knocks on their door is felt just as we enjoy sharing in the successes of the Three Musketeers or feel the pride of Simba in The Lion King when he defeats Scar and takes over leadership to become a good king of the animals.

Small and big emotions take people to a different reality than the one that we base on our own memories, stories, and images. Triggering the imagination is the key concept in this process (Alma, 2020).

The need for personal, emotional, and universal layers

As said, every (good) story contains personal, emotional, and universal information (Barel, 2020), as well as some factual information. It is important to explore these four domains in order to determine their value in the sharing of stories and the need to involve them when storytelling is used as an intervention.

By universal we mean the domain of the so-called big stories, such as well-known fairy tales or folktales. They give direction, teach good and evil and how one's life can be best arranged, at least according to a certain ideology, and teach one the dos and don'ts. These stories can also be described as factual or ideological information.

Factual information has been stripped of all imagination and can be traced back to something that can be established. For example, in a historical story the fact that a certain event has taken place on a certain date and has been witnessed and written down or recorded by people that were present makes it belong to the universal domain (though we are aware of the different perspectives that can colour the facts).

The same counts for stories that certain ideological or religious groups assume to represent a truth. In these stories, the universal domain is the part of the story that is there to teach the listener something: the message. If you look at fairy tales, folktales, and myths, there always is a wise lesson to be learnt – sometimes referred to as the moral of the story.

Often these 'lessons' hardly stick if they are transferred without context. But if these are communicated through a well-told story, they usually resonate and thus will be remembered.

This is because of the other two domains or layers: the personal and the emotional.

The personal domain is touched in a story when personal information is given about a main character and its environment. Not only in autobiographical stories, also in existing fictional stories, it is important to provide the characters (and therefore the situation) with such personal information. Based on the more personal information, the listeners create their own images that enable them to process the information they receive in a logical and meaningful way.

However, this is not sufficient to achieve resonance alone. Therefore, it is necessary to touch the emotional domain. The vibration is only passed on when there is something that can actually be shared. This does not happen on the first narrative level, the level of the anecdote. But if a layer of feelings is added to the story, it changes. After all, emotions are deeply human and enable us to feel and emphasize.

In fact, the emotional domain is the lynchpin in the successful transmission of a story as emotions are understood by most people in most contexts. Without an emotional load, a story loses much of its power. That doesn't mean that the other domains do not matter; the emotional information comes across best when the context is clear and there is a structure based on images in which it can land.

The foundation of a storytelling and picture talk intervention

Creating empathy between different groups that separate themselves based on stories about each other, creating in and out groups, is the objective of designing a system intervention aiming towards establishing more peaceful and resilient communities. Based on the statement that most conflicts arise because of similarities instead of differences but also on the fact that we want the same things in life, finding common ground is critical to reaching this objective. The use of stories is one of the tools for exploring this common ground.

However, we have realized through our work that courage is needed to start sharing stories with the other in a conflict. That is where picture talk comes in. Using pictures as a trigger for the process of finding the common ground has been shown to be effective, especially amongst youth, as they frequently use pictures as a means of communication. When pictures are taken or used, the subjective perception of the way a person sees the world is channelled through that picture. Therefore, they can be used to let participants talk about their everyday experiences as well as express their perspectives and values (Holm, 2008).

Pictures also provide additional value to storytelling interventions because pictures are able to elicit a deeper meaning and understanding of a particular subject. It helps to give people voice in complex subjects; it sharpens their memory and reduces misunderstandings (Collier, 1957). This is because certain parts of the brain that process visual information have been shown to have evolved earlier than the part of the brain that processes verbal information. Thus, the pictures can induce deeper, more unconscious levels of the brain than words can (Harper, 2002). Harper also mentions that pictures can be used as a bridge for cultural diversity. Van der Does et al. (1992) used pictures to highlight the different perceptions of elderly in a neighbourhood and the migrant youth living there. This way people from different cultural backgrounds can look at the same picture but see different things (perception). As the differences in perceptions come to light, they can be defined, compared, and understood by the different groups (Harper, 2002).

One important note: in order to avoid asymmetrical relationships, a necessity in conflict transformation as a part of fighting polarization (Pleumeekers, 2019), pictures with political or cultural biases should not be used in processes of conflict transformation.

In practice

An effective integration of storytelling and picture talk in change processes requires a methodological approach. This may vary depending on the intended purpose, the target group, the duration of the workshop, etc. Nevertheless, we can distinguish some common denominators.

In the PicS methodology, we distinguish five different phases of a workshop. Regardless of the time available, all must be present in the design of your workshop, though you can decide to shorten or extend them.

The five phases are:

1 Team building
2 Triggering creativity
3 Triggering awareness
4 Finding common ground
5 Closing and evaluation

The phases follow each other logically. However, following the structure of the phases is not mandatory. Sometimes switching between them, mainly phase 2 and 3, may be beneficial for the strength of the workshop. For a more detailed explanation of these phases and the exercises that belong to every phase, see the website of the project (www.pictureyourstory.eu).

Creating a safe environment through team building is necessary. A group without trust in each other will not be able to truly share on a deeper and equal level. Mutual trust is imperative. Team building activities should therefore be part of every workshop. Not only at the beginning – but also between activities that may require a great deal of the participants emotionally – team building is critical in order to allow participants to have some fun together and relax a bit. Involving pictures in this process can work magnificently, when common pictures are used. Think of Instagram images that serve to tell something about oneself, just by relating to one of the profiles that are offered. A participant can immediately show and share something personal without revealing him or herself completely. This provides blocks to build the foundation for a strong workshop.

In the next steps, we distinguish two types of activities: Triggering and Creating/Crafting the stories, usually done in this sequence. Triggering is the first step of sharing, leading to common ground. We are not dealing with structured stories yet; we limit ourselves to triggering memories. Often, already in this stage, deep emotions – varying from extreme happiness to extreme sadness and everything in between – are shared and empathy is built up. Sometimes, this step alone is enough to fully connect the members of the group. This is when they dare to cross a threshold and gain the courage to share and experience the wonderful feeling of being heard. They feel that they have really learned something about each other. Consequently, the group dynamics change for the better. Us versus them turns slowly into *we*. The in and out groups are ready to merge. Or better: to vanish.

In one of our PicS workshops we established this by using pictures already on the participants' own phones. We asked them to look for an image that really means a lot to them. Then we invited them to show it to the others in the group and to share the memory it triggered. The effect of this was very significant. Young people started sharing information they would probably not have shared in an ordinary conversation with a relative 'stranger'. However, nobody was judgemental and therefore no one felt judged. After everyone had shared a memory, they couldn't believe what a positive experience had happened to them, which gifts they'd received from their peers. This included all aspects existing in a heterogeneous group of young people: different cultural backgrounds, gender, sexual preferences, and even some handicaps. None of these differences mattered anymore; this one evening they were a group of equals.

It is nice when a workshop, which is limited in time, is this successful. But it is even more satisfying when there is time to deepen this result by creating and crafting the participants' stories; when they have the time to really work on their stories for a couple of hours or even for a couple of days. This requires a little more information about the art of storytelling and imagery, about the narrative structure.

We recommend to first take note of this narrative structure if you want to work with storytelling. In addition it is good to learn how you can use pictures to trigger stories. Preferably in this step, use pictures that are multi-layered as opposed to the more one-dimensional Instagram pictures we recommend using at the beginning of a workshop. Pictures from the media are often very useable in this phase.

Creating and crafting a story leads to much more depth than just sharing memories. The story becomes a friend who walks with you for a while. A friend who is sometimes a mentor but can be a mirror as well.

Working on a story for a longer time leads to self-reflection. The sharing of the final result leads to pride and self-confidence and to the approval of the listeners, who realize the work the storyteller has gone through to craft this story. They will respect the effort and are willing to listen to every word of the story. The journey of the teller easily and truly becomes the journey of the entire group.

The system has been changed and the foundation for behavioural change is built. We, together with – fortunately – many others, are convinced that this foundation can and will lead to a sustainable impact, beneficial to an entire community.

It should be clear that this process needs trained facilitation and some guidance. The tools developed within the framework of the PicS project have been found to be useful in the various contexts

Conclusion

By using creative methods such as sharing stories (through pictures), storytelling can be seen as a humanizing phenomenon that not only reflects reality but also – and maybe more importantly – shapes that reality (Czarniawska, 2004; Spector-Mersel, 2010).

When dealing with contexts of segregation or tension between groups, storytelling can be seen as a basis of virtually all human knowledge development. We know that storytelling has a strong connection to empowerment aspects on individual, group, and community levels (Rappaport, 1995) and therefore, as seen in this project, it can diminish polarization. When various personal stories and community narratives are shared and valued open-mindedly, the process is empowering (de Kreek, 2014; Rappaport, 1995).

When involved in storytelling, connections between selves and others are created and a mutual understanding of self and others is developed (Rossing & Glowacki-Dudka, 2001). However, it requires precise strategies, grounded in the theories about socio-psychological behaviour and about how stories can be used. One should always be aware that stories are also used as tools by the forces that benefit from polarization, and they can also easily be crafted as a reinforcement for further separation.

However, when applied properly, storytelling can be the perfect combination for initiating, setting up, and executing interventions aiming at connecting between groups of people, developing mutual empathy, and contributing to more peaceful and resilient communities.

References

Alma, H. (2020). *Het verlangen naar zin: de zoektocht naar resonantie in de wereld* [Longing for meaning, the search for resonance in the world]. Utrecht: Ten Have.

Barel, A. (2020). *Storytelling en de wereld* [Storytelling and the world]. Amsterdam: IT&FB Publishers.

Brandsma, B. (2017). *Inside polarisation: Understanding the dynamics of us versus them*. Alphen a/s Rijn: BB in Media.

Brown, B. (2007). *I thought it was just me (but it isn't): Telling the truth about perfectionism*. Minnesota: Hazeldon Publishing.

Byrne, D. (1971). *The attraction paradigm*. Orlando USA, FL: Academic Press.

Byrne, D. (1997). An overview (and underview) of research and theory within the attraction paradigm. *Journal of Social and Personal Relationships, 14*(3), 417–431. https://doi.org/10.1177/0265407597143008

Collier, J. (1957). Photography in anthropology: A report on two experiments. *American Anthropologist, 59*(5), 843–859. www.jstor.org/stable/665849

Czarniawska, B. (2004). *Narratives in social science research*. London: Sage Publications.

de Kreek, M. (2014). Empowerment from a narrative perspective: Learning from local memory websites. In 2014 Digital Methods Mini-Conference: My Sentiments Exactly: On Methods of Early Warning, Detection and Monitoring through Online and Social Media. Amsterdam: Digital Methods Initiative – University of Amsterdam.

de Waal, F. (2010). *The age of empathy: Nature's lessons for a kinder society*. New York: Broadway Books.

de Wachter, D. (2019). *De kunst van het ongelukkig zijn* [The art of being unhappy]. Tielt (Belgium): Lannoo Meulenhoff-Belgium.

Emeodi, C. L. (2014). *Understanding learning difficulty in adult education among immigrants in Oslo, Norway: A teacher's perspective*. (Masteroppgave). Oslo: Universitetet i Oslo. Hentet fra http://urn.nb.no/URN:NBN:no-44931

Goldman, B. M., Gutek, B. A., Stein, J. H., & Lewis, K. (2006). Employment discrimination in organizations: Antecedents and consequences. *Journal of Management*, *32*, 786–830.

Harari, Y. N. (2011). *Sapiens: A brief history of humankind.* London, UK: Vintage.

Harper, D. (2002). Talking about pictures: A case for photo elicitation. *Visual Studies*, *17*(1), 13–26.

Hasan-Aslih, S., Shuman, E., Goldenberg, A., Pliskin, R., van Zomeren, M., & Halperin, E. (2020). The quest for hope: Disadvantaged group members can fulfill their desire to feel hope, but only when they believe in their power. *Social Psychological and Personality Science*, *11*(7), 879–888.

Hewstone, M., Rubin, M., & Willis, H. (2002). Intergroup bias. *Annual Review of Psychology*, *53*(1), 575–604.

Holm, G. (2008). Photography as a performance. *Forum: Qualitative Social Research*, *9*(2), http://nbnresolving.de/urn:nbn:de:0114-fqs0802380

Kelly, C. (1993). Group identification, intergroup perceptions and collective action. *European Review of Social Psychology*, *4*(1), 59–83.

Livingston, R. W., Brewer, M. B., & Alexander, M. G. (2004). Images, emotions, and prejudice: Qualitative differences in the nature of Black and White racial attitudes. Annual Meeting of the Society for Personality and Social Psychology, Austin, TX.

Note the PicS Project website with pictures & methods. https://pictureyourstory.eu›homepage-nl https://pictureyourstory.eu/

Pleumeekers, S. (2019). *Creating connections in a structure of asymmetry: The potentials and limitations of storytelling as a tool for conflict resolution in asymmetrical conflict.* Amsterdam.

Rappaport, J. (1995). Empowerment meets narrative: Listening to stories and creating settings. *American Journal of Community Psychology*, *23*(5), 795–807. https://doi.org/10.1007/BF02506992

Rossing, B., & Glowacki-Dudka, M. (2001). Inclusive community in a diverse world: Pursuing an elusive goal through narrative-based dialogue. Journal of Community Psychology, 29(6), 729–743. https://doi.org/10.1002/jcop.1045

Shamoa-Nir, L., Razpurker-Apfeld, I., Dautel, J. B., & Taylor, L. K. (2021). Out-group prosocial giving during childhood: The role of in-group preference and out-group attitudes in a divided society. *International Journal of Behavioral Development*, *45*(4), 337–344.

Spector-Mersel, G. (2010). Narrative research: Time for a paradigm. *Narrative Inquiry*, *20*(1), 204–224. https://doi.org/10.1075/ni.20.1.10spe

Tajfel, H. (1972). Some developments in European social psychology. *European Journal of Social Psychology*, *2*(3), 307–321

Turner, J., Hogg, M., Oakes, P., Reicher, S., & Wetherell, M. (1987). *Rediscovering the social group: A self-categorization theory*. Oxford, UK: Blackwell.

van der Does, P., Edelaar, S., Gooskens, I., Liefting, M., & van Mierlo, M. (1992). Reading images: A study of a Dutch neighborhood. *Visual Sociology*, *7*(1): 4–67. https://doi.org/10.1080/14725869208583694

Vanhanen, T. (2012). Ethnic conflict and violence in heterogeneous societies. *The Journal of Social, Political, and Economic Studies*, *37*(1), 38–66.

3 Using arts as a contact method in group work with latency age Arab and Jewish youth in Israel

Noa Barkai-Kra

Introduction

One of the strategies of coping with the Arab-Israeli conflict on the educational and social level has involved attempts to bring together Jewish and Arab youth, citizens of Israel. Beginning in the 1980s, many encounters have taken place in Israel with the aim to influence mutual perceptions and improve relations between Jews and Arabs. While some places – regions, nations, towns, and villages – manage to remain peaceful despite ethnic diversity, others experience enduring patterns of violence. Research about conflicts around the globe has found that the missing link, which causes this difference, is closely related to inter-communal civic engagement. Civic engagement may lead to building more peaceful relations between communities and ethnic groups (Harel-Shalev, 2010). However, most of these groups are based on dialogue around self-identity and around the political problem and so target older adolescents and young adults such as students, who can take part in dialogue using more abstract concepts and narrative self-disclosure as a reflective method. However, latency-aged children are less suited for this type of dialogue due to their more cognitive rather than emotional focus and less abstract thinking. This also makes them difficult candidates for group work that is not action focused. Additionally, the tension between individual and group is complex since at this age much effort is put into fitting into the group. This makes shifts in group norms toward accepting the other, in a country in a direct conflict between groups, especially complicated at this age.

Additionally, difficulty in regulating behavior, in general, makes social responses of adolescents to complex social situations such as meeting the other more complex. However, in the Arab-Israeli conflict, likely one has already experienced political violence by the age of thirteen, and desperate violent acts of stabbing have been conducted by children at even younger ages. The extreme violence and racism are

DOI: 10.4324/9781003105350-4

typical of the rest of the world as well. It seems that we have to find ways to utilize group work to address hate of the other, lower negative stereotypes, and enhance complex understanding and empathy at an earlier age (Bar-Tal & Teichman, 2005).

Based on the experience of group work with latency-aged students, Contact Theory (Allport, 1954), which relates to meeting members of the other group, would seem most suitable for work with young adolescents who do not yet have the abstract skills to discuss conflicts on a higher level. An action-based approach aiming at gaining familiarity, having good times together, and creating joint projects seems more developmentally appropriate than intense dialogues as a method to create cooperation, friendship, and good neighbor relationships.

In the following case study, we turned to the arts to create positive interaction based on joint activity between two groups of youth from communities in conflict, in this case from the Bedouin-Arab and Jewish youth of the Negev/Naqab area in southern Israel (Huss et al., 2016). We envisioned that the project would enable broad and long-term intercommunal interaction based on the groups' common physical living area and that getting to know youth from the other group personally would help participants reduce or eliminate prevailing stereotypes as well as create a sense of joint ownership of the geographic region through group contact and activity.

In this study we ask: what are the advantages and pitfalls of bringing together youth for action-based group work in conflict situations? We discuss the complexity of creating these meetings and both their benefits as well as the challenges in order to illuminate the methodological and theoretical dilemmas of creating such encounter groups with young adolescents.

The qualitative findings produced a complex picture – including both enhanced contact and fun on the immediate group level and contact on the personal level, but also a continuation of stereotypes and continued discomfort with the other group as a group, even when individual friendships were created. Thus, the results did not find that the personal "fun" and connection generalized to the political or ethnic level. This raises interesting questions about how to address racism, othering, and political contact in group work.

Theories of encounters between youth in conflict groups

There is a wide range of research on encounter groups between Jews and Arabs youth in Israel (Maoz, 2011). Over the past decade, several qualitative assessments of the encounter groups have been published, relating to description and analysis of the interaction processes that occur within the encounter, as well as to group dynamics, interpersonal connections formed in the groups, and emotions and reflections that the participants bring up as a result of the encounter. However, most of these have been undertaken with older youth (Berger et al., 2015; Binder et al., 2009).

Biton and Salomon (2006) examined a variety of peace education programs in the world – among them encounter groups – and noted that only the minority conducted assessments. Maoz (2011) comprehensively investigated Jewish-Arab encounter programs based on the confrontation model and attempted to define several assessment criteria: the establishment of the encounter experience over time; the quality of relations created between the group participants; the capacity to reduce the inherent asymmetry; and the capability to define goals and fulfill them. Katz and Kahanov (1990) claimed that, in light of the conflict's complexity and the multiple dilemmas that arise in designing and conducting the encounter groups, a process of clarification of the goals for the individual participant should replace the delineation of unambiguous and universal objectives.

Researchers have suggested that an understanding of the dilemmas resting on the foundation of the encounter can be an objective in itself and that the role of the encounter is not to instantaneously solve dilemmas in the external reality but rather to assist in participants' overall comprehension and to offer possible tools for coping (Maoz et al., 2004).

The research literature presents three primary models of encounters between groups in conflict. The encounter model, developed at the Wahat al-Salam/Neve Shalom School for Peace in response to criticism of the Contact Hypothesis (Pettigrew & Tropp, 2011), focuses on collective identity and the asymmetrical power relations between the parties, at the expense of the opportunity to create personal connections among the participants (Halabi, 2000). The purpose of this strategy is to empower the minority group and help the dominant group cope with ambivalence and conflicts surrounding control and domination. This model demands the reflective skills that are absent at the time of late latency and adolescence and so we did not choose this model for our group.

The second model is the life-storytelling model, a relatively new methodology. Participants from both sides share their family stories with the group, which they have collected by interviewing family members from two generations. The mutual storytelling allows and encourages a personal connection, as well as a discussion of the collective components of the stories (for example, the Holocaust for the Jews and the 1948 Al-Naqba catastrophe for the Arabs). Through the stories, in-depth personal and group work on the topics tied to the conflict is made possible. This method could be attempted with our age group, but it is not clear that the youth can compose and address the family narrative from an emotional standpoint, as it is often very overwhelming.

The third model, based primarily on the Contact Hypothesis by Pettigrew and Tropp (2011), holds as a central objective the creation of personal relationships between the participants, under the understanding that through personal acquaintanceship it is possible to prevent and change stereotypic perceptions, attitudes, and behavior. In these encounters, there is very little discussion of the historical background and the current political realities of the groups. Research has shown that this approach has short-term advantages but fewer long-term advantages, as in most cases the hostile political and/or historical reality eradicates the beneficial effect of the interpersonal connection (Maoz, 2000). This model was felt to be most relevant for late latency and early adolescence, based on the literature on this developmental stage mentioned earlier.

The foundation of this project is based on Contact Theory (Allport, 1954), which emphasizes the sense of social equality that has to exist for acquaintance programs to be successful. Four prerequisite features are important for contact to be successful at reducing intergroup conflict and achieving intergroup harmony. First, equal status within the contact situation; second, intergroup cooperation; third, shared common goals; and finally, the support of authorities, law, or custom (Pettigrew & Tropp, 2011). All of these elements have been incorporated into the project design of meetings between Jewish and Bedouin youth in southern Israel.

An important factor for the development of intergroup friendships is the opportunity for personal acquaintance between the members. During encounters and meetings if members of two groups were able to form a team to face an outside factor together, it was good, and if they chose each other as partners on an assignment that was the greatest success. It should be noted that when personalization occurs with those whose characteristics do not support stereotypic expectations it enhances positive contact and reduces stigmatization (Bar-Tal & Rosen, 2009).

As a result of creating positive intergroup interaction within the contact encounter, new norms of intergroup acceptance develop that can be generalized to new situations, and attitudes toward the out-group can be facilitated. Moreover, a favorable intergroup contact leads to psychological processes that reduce dissonance and produce more favorable attitudes toward individuals from the other group or/and toward the group as a whole. Dissonance reduction can also serve as justification for the interaction with members of the other group and, as a result, positive behavioral interactions may induce greater intergroup acceptance. Furthermore, not only can attitudes be changed by intergroup contact, but the interaction can also enhance empathy toward members of the other group (Brown & Hewstone, 2005).

Latency-age and early adolescents in groups

Adolescence is a period of growth and development between childhood and adulthood. This developmental period involves new demands on the individual. A major task of this period is moving from dependency on the family toward independence, as peers become a crucial socialization circle for the adolescent (Erikson, 1982). Adolescents have difficulty with social cues during challenging situations, due to their difficulty in regulating behavior in general. This makes adolescents' social responses to complex social situations such as meeting the other in a conflict more complicated, based on emotion rather than a rational response. At the same time, this age is a particularly important developmental stage, since social, emotional, and cognitive processes are involved in the attempts to navigate these increasingly complex relationships. Indeed, it is during these years that abstract thinking and cognitive processing develop along with enhanced moral reasoning and judgment. These positive processes enable the adolescent to explore the world, gain competence, and contribute to the world around him/her (Binder et al., 2009).

Arts as action methods in group work

The arts are a deep and universal psycho-neurological construct through which people process their experiences. Arts are central to human functioning, contributing to the individual's sense of self, to the ability to remain oriented in the world, and to the effective pursuit of goals in light of memories of their experience and future problem solving (Hickson & Barker, 2002; Huss, 2012).

The use of arts in conflict as a form of contact and as an indirect transitional space within which to structure interactions is discussed in the art therapy literature (Liebman, 1990). A multi-model arts theory claims that art processes enable joint interaction and "doing" within a safe and symbolic space that enables structured interaction and the creation of a joint product that can demonstrate the joint interaction. These processes also create a tangible product as evidence of the possibility of working together and creating new items within a group context. The resulting artworks are experienced as a jointly created image that becomes a jointly owned resource that connects all of the viewers, creators, and participants (Ben-Ezer, 2002; Benson, 1987; Dokter, 1998).

The arts are also utilized for members of groups in conflict as a way to learn the central symbols and cultural beliefs of the other in a safe non-confrontational context such as decoration or cooking, which encourage empathy and offer a way to meet on a basic, universal level. Cooking, crafts, and music are often used to enhance empathy and identification within groups facing situations of conflict and forgiveness. In reconciliation activities, learning about and creating traditional craft activities together is also cited as a way of distancing the conflict, exploring differences in a non-threatening context (Kalmanowitz & Lloyd, 2005).

In latency-age, art tends to be action-oriented toward a tangible result, rather than used as a trigger for a personal narrative and self-reflection (Huss, 2012). This was incorporated into the use of arts; additionally, latency-aged youth are especially culturally invested in the technology of visual images. This enabled them to define their joint youth-culture symbols as organizing metaphors for identity.

Research methods

This chapter describes a multiple case-study of three encounter-based mixed groups of Bedouin-Arab and Jewish youth in southern Israel, in which each group participated in ten meetings together over the course of a year. The encounters took place in alternating locations, in the Bedouin or Jewish communities as well as in neutral places – such as at the university. All of the encounters included a variety of action-based activities and structured interaction games based on the aforementioned literature. These included learning about each other's community, learning about and making traditional foods and holiday items, outdoor challenge activities, arts activities such as crafts, skills, and creating a joint Facebook page. The encounters took place in the framework of an extra-curricular after school activity in neighboring communities. Recruitment of participants took place in schools for the Bedouin-Arab adolescents and via youth workers in the Jewish community. Master's students from the conflict management and resolution program at the university led the encounters as Arab and Jewish co-leaders for each group and the groups aspired to include half Jewish and half Bedouin participants.

These students received ongoing supervision from the author while leading the groups.

Research strategy

The qualitative components of this research strategy will be described in this chapter. Methods included observation and transcribing as well as summarizing discussions with the participants. Observation is important because it enables the leaders to show how the youth interacted on non-verbal as well as verbal levels (Denzin & Lincoln, 2000). The data sources included transcription of 30 meetings and photography of all artwork and activities for each program.

Analytical strategy

Qualitative data were analyzed on two levels. First, the transcripts were analyzed narratively as a process, looking at each group over their full ten meetings. This enabled the author to make observations of developments and progressions over time within each specific group.

Reliability and validity

Reliability and validity were created through peer analyses between research colleagues and triangulation of the various qualitative methods including observation and interviews (Miles & Huberman, 2002).

Ethical issues

Because of the political climate in Israel, taking part in a mixed group can be stigmatizing and can meet with disapproval from peers and adults: This was overcome by maintaining anonymity in all materials published. Any images of participants received permission from the specific participant before use. Additionally, the author received clearance from the university's Ethics Committee for this research. For each participant, the parents signed a consent form to approve the documentation for his/her child (Miles & Huberman, 2002).

Presentation of the data and discussion

The data has been divided into two central themes. The first theme shows how the arts-based contact theory worked to create unity in these groups. The second theme shows the limitations of that unity.

Contact theory: themes connecting to "doing" together

Using games and activities that mix the groups: According to contact theory, this program was constructed around joint assignments using mixed groups of Jews and Arabs and competition between these mixed groups. The rules of the interactions were used as a model for cooperation as in the following example:

> A stick game that demands balance – you have to balance yourself, and then you have to check what is happening with everyone else, and help them reach balance- so that you will all stay in balance and each child can walk on the sticks, you have to notice what is happening to each child, and to hold the sticks together in a way that he won't fall.

Focusing on shared global youth-culture: Focusing on shared global youth-culture such as favorite singers. The children interacted about this easily. They exchanged Facebook addresses and showed each other videos of their favorite singers. This created lively discussions and inter-group cooperation.

Re-mixing of sub-groups: Remixing of sub-groups to create as much contact between Jewish and Arab participants as possible was the third way of creating contact. The program used constant mixing of the groups and structured the time so that children did not go back to their Jewish or Arab group of origin but rather were in constant interaction with both Arab and Jewish participants.

These three methods produced a lot of observed contact and interaction between the Arab and Jewish participants as described here (all names are pseudonyms):

- Five children (two Jewish and three Arab) were discussing what to put on their collage-poster. They sat around it, talking, cutting, and sticking things on. They then planned a strategy that some would stay sitting and stick on the new pictures, while others would go to find more pictures. The sticking and finding groups were mixed Arab-Jewish.
- Yosef, Ofer, Muhamad, and Hassam were sticking pictures that they gathered together inside the areas that they colored with paint. The boys were very active around Ofer (a girl). Muhamad stuck a picture of Ofer in the center and covered elements around her picture in white paint. He wrote her name next to the picture in blue on white.

In the end, all the groups observed all the posters they had made, and each (mixed) group boasted that their poster was best.

Maintenance of contact beyond the limits of the group: The question arose whether this interaction would be maintained over time, outside of the shared activities. We saw that the youth learned each other's names and exchanged Instagram and Facebook details. We saw a reduction in the number of stigmas that were verbalized compared to the beginning, as in the following examples.

- One Jewish child started the meetings with a fear that the Arab children would smell bad and fear of going on an Arab bus, but by the end of the year of meetings she had a good Arab friend and was not scared of the bus. She also initiated cooperation with the Arab girls in a joint game.
- One Arab boy, who only stood on the side in the first meetings, became very active and interactive with the Jewish boys in making a joint Facebook page in one of the meetings.

Cultural differences: Although the participating in the group is voluntary and so by definition the participants on both sides come from families with a peace-oriented outlook and from relatively similar educated and middle-class families, there were still many cultural differences. The Arab children were shocked by the lack of respect of the Jewish children toward the adults, and the Jewish children were shocked during a visit to one participant's home, when an Arab child shouted at his dog.

Similarly, the addressing of the differences in their villages, through alternating meetings held in the Jewish and then Arab village (as compared to meeting in the neutral ground such as the university), raised issues of asymmetry between the social realities of the two groups. The Jewish children were from the middle-class settlement, with many more financial resources, while the Bedouin children were from the poorer settlement, visually apparent in terms of size of houses, lack of green areas, and more. The Jewish children had many extracurricular activities and found it hard to find time to fit in the meetings, whereas the Arab children had fewer activities after school.

Cultural difference was manifested in gender roles, with the Arab girls keeping away from all boys while the Jewish girls seemed to feel free to interact with both Jewish and Arab boys. These differences were also apparent in their behavior; for example, in non-formally organized time, when they were not placed together, the children separated into Arab and Jewish groups and did not mix.

Limitations of the language

We witnessed many times how Arabic, the language of the minority group, disappeared from the discourse, not only during the conversation. The dominance of Hebrew over Arabic was maintained even in the artwork:

- Salam made another part of the poster and wrote that Rahim and Rabat (two of the boys) are best friends forever. He stuck pictures of the group as a whole on it and signed his name with a red star in English and Hebrew. No one wrote in Arabic on the poster.

Summary and discussion

We see in the themes mentioned earlier that while having fun and interacting together worked on the immediate and interpersonal level, it seems that the core differences – including the differences in culture, class, and social power – between Arab and Jewish youth as part of their collective group were not influenced toward the social transformation as we expected to see.

It seems that the collective elements were disconnected from the personal elements in this encounter. This is true also in adult society, where one can personally like someone from a different ethnic group but still maintain negative stereotypes and conflict attitudes toward the group as a whole. Similarly, the action methods in this program created "fun" and cooperation on an embodied level, but it seems that this must be taken further in order to address conflicts on the verbal level and to make a social transformation in perception for the long term in the lives of these youth.

This is a challenge in itself. It could be that holding separate meetings to discuss experiences of the "other" might have helped to process these differences. However, the difficulty of finding youth that even agreed to come to these meetings was so intense because of the challenge of putting Arab and Jewish youth together at this age, such that the youth leaders were invested in keeping the groups together, through implementing action methods and through making them "fun" enough to attract the youth. That emphasis did not enable us to address the issues of conflict or move the group into the working stages. This orientation can be understood as part of the focus on "fun" in the way youth are educated in this era. Together with the difficulty in bringing participants together in a period of escalation of the conflict in the south, these factors made it difficult to challenge the youth enough to address conflicts.

On this level, we can say that the method of joint activity is at risk of becoming a way to remain stuck in the honeymoon stages of group work (Benson, 2018). At the same time, as in all group work, we cannot know the long-term impact of this program or know whether "having fun together" will generate a social transformation and influence these youth in the future.

Our overall conclusion from this study is that while action methods did create personal contact and long-term connections and as such is useful in meetings with latency-aged youth living in a society in conflict who are not old enough to engage in deep reflective discussion, the action-based encounters are not enough in of themselves, and we need to find methods that are suitable for this age group. This resonates with other findings (Rosen & Salomon, 2011). One solution could be to hold unilateral group meetings between every few several bi-lateral group meetings, in which participants can work through impressions and difficulties with the other. Inclusion of difficult subjects such as the political conflict in a mediated discussion may be another solution, and using the arts not just for mixing and positive experiences, but as a space to explore and contain the reality of living in a conflict, may yet be another possibility (Steele et al., 2002). We hope these findings will be of interest to those working with multicultural or multi-ethnic groups with latency-aged children in the context of a conflict as well as for workers leading other diverse groups.

References

Allport, G. W. (1954). *The nature of prejudice*. Cambridge, MA: Addison-Wesley.

Bar-Tal, D., & Rosen, Y. (2009). Peace education in societies involved in intractable conflicts: Direct and indirect models. *Review of Educational Research*, 79(2), 557–575. https://doi.org/10.3102%2F0034654308330969

Bar-Tal, D., & Teichman, Y. (2005). *Stereotypes and prejudice in conflict: Representations of Arabs in Israeli Jewish society*. Cambridge University Press. https://doi.org/10.1017/CBO9780511499814

Ben-Ezer, G. (2002). Merchav h'yitzeera ha'meshutefet klaley avoda bein-tarbutit: Avoda kvutzatit eem oley Ethiopia [The collective creative space as a tool with inter-cultural work: Group work with Ethiopian immigrants]. In L. Kacen & R. Lev-Wiesel (Eds.), *Avodah Kvutzatit b'chevrah rav-tarbutit* [Group work in a multicultural society] (pp. 149–163). Cherikover Publications.

Benson, J. (1987). *Working more creatively with groups*. Tavistock Publications.

Benson, J. (2018). Working More Creatively with Groups (4th ed.). Routledge. https://doi.org/10.4324/9780429452369

Berger, R., Abu-Raiya, H., & Gelkopf, M. (2015). The art of living together: Reducing stereotyping and prejudicial attitudes through the Arab-Jewish class exchange program (CEP). *Journal of Educational Psychology*, *107*(3), 678–688. http://dx.doi.org/10.1037/edu0000015

Binder, J., Zagefka, H., Brown, R., Funke, F., Kessler, T., Mummendey, A., Maquil, A., Demoulin, S., & Leyens, J.-P. (2009). Does contact reduce prejudice or does prejudice reduce contact? Longitudinal test of the contact hypothesis amongst majority and minority groups in three European countries. *Personality and Social Psychology Bulletin*, *96*(4), 843–856.

Biton, Y., & Salomon, G. (2006). Peace in the eyes of Israeli and Palestinian youths: Effects of collective narratives and peace education program. *Journal of Peace Research*, *43*(2), 167–180. http://dx.doi.org/10.1177/0022343306061888

Brown, R., & Hewstone, M. (2005). An integrative theory of intergroup contact. In M. P. Zanna (Ed.), *Advances in experimental social psychology* (Vol. 37, pp. 255–343). Elsevier Academic Press.

Denzin, N., & Lincoln, Y. (2000). *Handbook of qualitative research*. Sage Publications.

Dokter, D. (Ed.). (1998). *Arts therapists, refugees and migrants: Reaching across borders*. Jessica Kingsley.

Erikson, E. H. (1982). *The life cycle completed*. W. W. Norton.

Halabi, R. (2000). Yehudim v'Aravim nifgashim [Jews and Arabs meeting with the other]. In R. Halabi (Ed.), *Dialogue bein zehooyot: Mifgashey Aravim v'Yehudim b'Neve Shalom* [Dialogue between Identities: Meetings of Jews and Arabs in Neve Shalom] (pp. 16–9). United Kibbutz.

Harel-Shalev, A. (2010). *The challenge of sustaining democracy in deeply divided societies: Citizenship, rights, and ethnic conflicts in India and Israel*. Lexington Press.

Hickson, A., & Barker, C. (2002). *Creative Activities in work with groups*. Routledge.

Huss, E. (2012). *What we see and what we say: Using images in research, therapy, empowerment, and social change*. Routledge.

Huss, E., Kaufman, R., Avgar, A., & Shuker, E. (2016). Arts as a vehicle for community building and post-disaster development. *Disasters*, *40*(2), 284–303.

Kalmanowitz, D., & Lloyd, B. (Eds.). (2005). *Art therapy and political violence: With art, without illusion*. Psychology Press.

Katz, I., & Kahanov, M. (1990). Skeera dilemmot b'hanchayah shel kvutzot mifgash bein Yehudim l'Aravim b'Yisrael [Some dilemmas in the analysis of Arab-Jewish encounters]. *Megamot, Lamed Gimel*, (1), 29–47.

Liebman, M. (1990). *Terapiyah b'omanoot l'kvutzot* [Group art therapy]. Ach Publishing.

Maoz, I. (2000). Power relations in intergroup encounters: A case study of Jewish-Arab encounters in Israel. *International Journal of Intercultural Relations*, *24*(2), 259–277. https://doi.org/10.1016/S0147-1767(99)00035-8

Maoz, I. (2011). Does contact work in protracted asymmetrical conflict? Apprasing 20 years of reconciliation-aimed encounters between Israeli Jews and Palestinians. *Journal of Peace Research*, *48*(1), 115–125. http://dx.doi.org/10.1177/0022343310389506

Maoz, I., Bar-On, D., Bekerman, Z., & Jaber-Massarwa, S. (2004). Learning about "good enough" through "bad enough": A story of a planned dialogue between Israeli Jews and Palestinians. *Human Relations*, *57*(9), 1075–1101. https://doi.org/10.1177/0018726704047139

Miles, M. B., & Huberman, A. M. (2002). Reflections and advice. In A. M. Huberman & M. B. Miles (Eds.), *The qualitative researcher's companion* (pp. 393–399). Sage Publications.

Pettigrew, T. F., & Tropp, L. R. (2011). *When groups meet: The dynamics of intergroup contact*. Psychology Press.

Rosen, Y., & Salomon, G. (2011). Durability of peace education effects in the shadow of conflict. *Social Psychology of Education*, *14*(1), 135–147. http://dx.doi.org/10.1007/s11218-010-9134-y

Steele, C. M., Spencer, S. J., & Aronson, J. (2002). Contending with group image: The psychology of stereotype and social identity threat. *Advances in Experimental Social Psychology*, *34*, 379–440. http://dx.doi.org/10.1016/S0065-2601(02)80009-0

4 Art in society at a time of political and cultural transformation

The Polish case

Beata Bigaj-Zwonek and Jolanta Gisman-Stoch

This chapter focuses on the dynamic relationship between social and artistic values that have come to realization within selected practices. The relationship is viewed in the context of the historical perspective of change that Polish culture has seen since the 1980s. Social value is understood to be something society desires and chooses from within a specific cultural place and at a given historical moment and something a community desires and needs in order to be a community. But it is also seen in the personal need of belonging and the personal need for transcendence.

In this chapter, historical reflections are illustrated by examples of past and present projects, where a "project" means a one-off or long-term activity that implements a group's, institution's, or person's individual mission with an awareness of the artistic and social values being pursued. The authors are associated with different outlooks on the arts and their social dimension: on the one hand, an elitist approach and academic, "professional" art that, regardless of its social objectives, is subject to institutional aesthetic evaluation – and on the other hand an egalitarian approach and art defined as a unique language immanent in every person, which embodies personal and community values in aesthetic forms. Analyses of various artistic practices show the social value of art as both essential (inherent) and complementary (added).

Artistic practice and change

Art that is understood as a form of human creativity is closely related to change. Polish philosopher Władysław Stróżewski (1983) argued that the work of art is a dynamic whole – the unique result of the "dynamic complementarity of opposites". He saw the process of art making and its novelty as subjected to complex dialectical forces, as

DOI: 10.4324/9781003105350-5

a result of a complex dialogue – dialogue between what is and what is not yet, between the creator and his/her work, between the creator and the recipient, between the author and other authors, and between the creator and the reality experienced by him/her. Among many other dialectical opposites of vital importance in the creative process, Stróżewski distinguished: the new and the old; acceptance and rejection; submission and domination.

Such a holistic character of artwork makes any separation of social and personal meanings and values risky. We are convinced that this is because of the dynamic combination embodied into one aesthetic tissue that makes the essence of art to provoke both personal and social change. However, we also see that some artistic practices can be described by the unique selection of (what Stróżewski calls) the "dialectical moments" that makes them more socially engaged.

As Malcolm Ross (2011) convinced us in his complex and holistic theory of creative process in arts, artworks, no matter how subjectively determined and enjoyed, are created in a context: they draw from the past, modify the present, and invest in the future. No artwork exists in isolation, as the creators of art practices live and work in a unique political, social, and cultural reality. Art practices are conceived and delivered within a living tradition, both drawing fruitfully upon it and daring to resist and amend it. Sometimes these practices provoke social change.

The locus

Art practices are situated – they speak to the values represented by a cultural community and serve as a community binder by delivering experiences that allow it to celebrate what it cherishes. A sociological study (Nowak, 1979) of the values espoused by Polish society at the dawn of the "Solidarity" movement showed that the nation, understood as a moral community of Poles, was of a great value and, importantly, did not equal the Polish state. Loyalty to the state, its law, and the institutions representing it was demonstrably seen as an anti-value. The conflict between the people and the institution of the State produced a clear-cut division between "Us" (members of the national community unified by history, religion, and tradition) and "Them" (nameless representatives of the current regime). As research showed, in 1979 the values held by all social groups in Poland were undeniably freedom of speech and civic involvement in state management. The Solidarity movement in the 1980s fought for these values.

The Polish nation can be characterized as one with exceptional historical sensitivity. Deprived of their state from 1795 through to 1918,

Poles strove to keep up the national spirit by cultivating their traditions, language, and cultural heritage during their fight for political freedom. This doubtless also shaped Polish culture after World War II, as well as social activity during the systemic political crisis of 1980 and thereafter.

In the second half of the 20th century, Polish history was marked initially by falling into the Soviet sphere of political influence and then by rejecting communism in the 1980s. The collapse of the system in Poland was an outcome of a long-lasting process of opposition. Although demonstrations against the communist party dictates had started already in the late 1960s, only the strikes in the 1980s truly uprooted the regime. The resistance movement in Poland stemmed largely from patriotic attitudes forged in homes and churches, with strong impetus coming from the words of John Paul II in 1979.

The rise of independent culture

Until the turn of the 1980s and 1990s, the popularization of art was supported by the communist government through a network of amateur art initiatives (at workplaces and cultural centres) and an educational programme for making elite art more accessible. The Polish professional arts looked back to history or focused on formal issues. The subject matter in the independent movement of engaged art ranged from World War II to criticism of the current reality, the latter often encrypted in titles and symbols in order to be acceptable for State censors. Artists today still remember the time of politically prescribed forms and artistic themes (socialist realism) restricting the freedom of their expression.

Although already in the 1960s individual artists and artistic circles had taken up the issue of political sovereignty, the wider and more direct criticism of the system and stronger involvement in current social issues did not come until the unprecedented *Carnival of Solidarity* (1980–1981) and as part of the independent culture movement (a concept associated in Poland also with manifestations of independent culture before 1989). Audience engagement is now viewed as culture's key contribution to the system change of the 1980s.

Formats varied from artistic and patriotic meetings, to different manifestations of cults of the communist system's victims, to popular comedian shows rich in political allusions, as well as highly popular problem-based exhibitions about cultural heritage or national identity (e.g., "Self-portrait of the Poles", 1979). Additionally, audiences were attracted by independent shows at artists' homes and studios. Art was looking for a space that could offer the relative freedom of expression, a feeling of hope, and cultural identity; this was offered by the Polish Catholic church. Churches staged exhibitions and underground meetings – often patriotic or existential in nature – and organized money collections for the Solidarity movement. Religious iconography was used as a universally legible communication. The Catholic liturgical phrase: *Let us offer each other the sign of peace* sounded (for many people) like a Solidarity clarion call, not necessarily one for reconciliation with God (Grzywacz, 2001).

The yoke of this period is assessed ambiguously today. Some artists notice that restrictions imposed at the time made for radical, personal axiological choices. Since the 1990s, independent culture has not only moved away from the Catholic Church, which is a clear cultural change in Poland, but it has also made the very institution of the church the subject of radical criticism.

Cultural change can be traced in the history of art milieus and art communities. Art groups had to take into account the censorship of the authorities, which is why some of them had an informal character. Those that did not follow the aesthetic canons of socialist-realist art struggled with a lack of trust and official support. Art groups established in the 1980s, like "Łódź Kaliska", "Gruppa", and "LuXus", became important actors during the transformation of the political system. As the new democracy was taking shape, groups formed less frequently, and were mostly of a temporary nature, focused around exhibitions. In the 1990s, they were replaced by projects centred around specific studios or artists associated in collaboration with a single gallery. At present, social objectives are promoted by informal associations and artistic initiatives in order to achieve the right to independent existence and higher subsidies for cultural activity.

The unique example of a large, grassroots social and art movement was "Orange Alternative" started in the 1980s by Wroclaw students. Founded and headed by Waldemar "Major" Fydrych (Fydrych, 2010), it turned into a large-scale project (60 happenings spanning 1985–1990). The method worked out by the Orange Alternative positioned it halfway between the two powers that dominated social life: the Solidarity trade union and the communist government. Graffiti and the zany happenings that engaged people in large Polish cities poked fun at the social and political absurdities of the communist system. The Orange Alternative applied the same media and techniques as Surrealism or Dada, drawing ironically on themes and terminology known to Polish society from political propaganda, thus making it look absolutely ludicrous. The open formula of happenings helped

Figure 4.1 Orange Alternative happening "UPAŁY" Wrocław, 1987. Erasing of one person or letter changes the neutral and funny slogan into an anti-totalitarian one

Source: Lewiński, P. Courtesy of the Orange Alternative Foundation, www.orangealternativemuseum.pl

not only to activate bystanders (10,000 residents of Wrocław took part in the *Dwarf Revolution* event on 1 June 1981) but also to intelligently provoke and to anticipate reactions of the militia and security services so as to make them unintentional co-performers in events. In *The Manifesto of Social Surrealism* (Students' leaflet 1980), Fydrych stated, "The whole world is a work of art so a single militiaman standing in a street is a work of art, too". The movement vitally contributed to peaceful protests in *carnival resistance* staged against regimes in Poland and beyond. The artistic media it proposed gave an impulse to other social art actions in the years following.

Transformation

The artist's social role in Poland has been cemented historically. Already in the 19th century, an artist was expected to demonstrate social sensitivity, which was understood to mean protecting national unity in the face of threats. Since the 1960s, many artists and groups have raised issues that triggered social responses, and the audience saw them as champions of political change and protectors of human dignity. Yet system changes and open borders called for a revision of values, while the intensity of the labor market and chaos in cultural policy cut back interest in culture.

The early 21st century saw a discussion initiated by Artur Żmijewski. In this chapter we would like to draw attention to the progressing institutionalization of art, which makes "the ideological fermentation" of the arts dwindle down: "This is a new limit for revolt, the more so that the art market is eager to commodify even contestation" (Żmijewski, 2007, p. 17). Redefining art was suggested in order to increase its social impact by reducing the weight of purely aesthetic issues, and questions were raised about the place of art and about who assigns specific meanings to a performance and for what purpose. The artist's or curator's difficulty with causing social change was well illustrated by the Polish pavilion at the 7th Berlin Biennial in 2012 (coordinated by Żmijewski), which pivoted around issues of how to link art and politics, yet it remained a niche event. The fact that the subject of the social functions of art was raised nevertheless unveiled a need to consider methods for better communication between artists and society and the role of social ideas in art.

Systemic transformation in Poland helped many artists join international movements. Critical art initiatives made their presence felt, exemplified by artists such as Artur Żmijewski, Katarzyna Kozyra, and Zbigniew Libera. Studies of art emphasize that in critical art the artist's ethical responsibility is pivotal. A good example is provided by Kozyra's work, *The Pyramid of Animals* (1993), which started widespread social discussions on animal death and the limits of art.

Of particular interest are projects initiated by grassroots initiatives and already nested in the local or wider environment, where art has a meaningful role as a form of communication and is a bountiful source of benefits for its participants/recipients. These projects include art movements, societies and foundations that collaborate with cultural institutions or work independently and use the boons of the virtual world. One such initiative is the Imago Mundi Foundation (since 2005). Its founder, Łukasz Trzciński, stressed that it is aimed at institutional criticism in practice, in the broadest possible sense of institutionalism. Built on the residence model, its project *Metropolis* initiated international discussion between artists and theoreticians who treat visual arts as a tool of cognition and social change. The project put emphasis on working with local communities and the promotion of contemporary art where no institutions of art existed previously. In the project *A Place Called Space* the main sections problematized the conditions for and environment of creative work, as well as the concept of limits (political, social, and artistic), and updated and contemporized elements of local cultural heritage, which they put into a global framework. Trzciński said, "*I'd find it hard to say with and for whom we do not work*", emphasizing a wide range of recipients. He also admitted that in terms of thinking about art, the foundation is now far more interested in art's future than in the past. Asked about the social viability of art, he noted, "*Art is effective when it is but a nucleus of a process, when it initiates, is gentle and provokes*".

As for the good practices and social benefits of institutions of culture, note should be made of the currently evolving new role of museums. From the places where selected cultural heritage used to be protected, they have become open educational institutions with a social mission that can be understood as building communities and social environment, provoking reflection on community roots and the role of tradition in community life. They have begun to offer a new interpretation of community history (sometimes politically involved) and to show the shape of its present culture. Museums become the places of important local meetings and the source of local initiatives addressed to purposefully selected groups of visitors. Among the noteworthy many are The Night of Museums, art initiatives carried out in urban spaces or different socially inclusive art projects such as *Touch Art* (2011 [the Silesian Museum collection adapted for the visually impaired]), exhibitions directed at elderly visitors and children and accompanied by practical workshops preparing them to be good recipients of art. It seems the museums have stopped believing that very presence of artwork is enough. The context of the reception must be included.

As an interesting grassroots initiative, launched not by an institution but by artists themselves, clubs and coffee shops opened that hark back to the traditions of artistic bohemia. It seems that the activity of Krakow's Otwarta Pracownia (= Open Studio) hovers in the free zone between a social initiatives-oriented institution of culture and an art club. The Open Studio was founded in 1995, and its ambit covers visual arts, theatre, poetry, and education. It has its informal seat in a privately owned space in a building in Krakow. According to a Studio member, their audience is very mixed, from artists and art theoreticians, to art buffs and accidental viewers. Respecting the social dimension of their activity, the artists said, "Every exhibition is a social project. The key value is meeting and experiencing in the context of the featured exhibition or artwork. The key mission is art: to develop it and to convince people that this is the most natural social type of practice".

Figure 4.2 Exhibition of paintings by Bigaj. B.: *The Stab*, Open Studio, 2016

Source: Szanduła, A

Figure 4.3 From the workshop designer and led by Gisman-Stoch, J.: *I-You-We from this Earth* – street workshop for youth in Ustroń. Natural material: soil, sand chalk, 2015; *Banners of The Two. The Talented* from Pomerania Project, CIE: Zakopane 2016

Source: From the archive of Gisman-Stoch, J

Figure 4.4 "Independence Day", CIE – Making the Eagle Fly. Happening, Karuzy town square, 2010

Source: From the archive of Deren, A

Activating society through culture and for culture in Poland is a professional field of socio-cultural animation. This activation is meant for both personal growth and community development without separating them, neither in practice nor in theory. The idea came to Poland from France as an echo of concepts from the 1960s, along with the concept of egalitarian and integrated culture, and it met the Polish practice and theory of cultural and social education connected with creativity (Korniłowicz, 1976; Radlińska, 1961). Cultural animation involves animating/reviving the cultural and social participation of local communities by creating environmental factors that will support an individual's and a group's passion and creativity. Socio-cultural animators in Poland are enthusiasts, artists, art therapists, or educators frequently connected with the informal education sector. Their practice is assisted by local, public cultural centers, as well as civic initiatives and is implemented directly in the space of social life. They reach for art – seeing in it potential that supports individual and social identity, dialogue, and development processes.

A good example of this is a socio-artistic civic organization called The Centre for Educational Initiatives (CIE) in Kartuzy (2001–2019), founded and headed by Anna Dereń as a community-activity project. The mission of the CIE is: *Integration of the Kartuzy community around social values like freedom, responsibility, patriotism but also community engagement and respect for other cultures*. In the public space of the town's marketplace, the CIE has organized youth culture festivals, and social and artistic happenings celebrating big historical events and interactive artistic and literary exhibitions. On the role of arts, Dereń said, "*The art happenings helped us show what is fleeting so as to exert powerful emotional impact*". That power, according to CIE, stemmed from metaphor, allegory, and symbol as a socially resonant means of expression. The CIE set up socio-artistic situations that helped to relive intimate common cultural material.

Similarly, the "Teatr Grodzki" Bielsko Art Association (since 1999) with Maria Szejbal, the founder and a person professionally associated with a puppet theatre, builds its practice around a mission statement: *We are here to offer our beating hearts and open hands to everyone who needs help*. The association runs educational, artistic, and social programs in cooperation with different organizations, among them theater activities for the disabled and for underprivileged people. Shejbal is the author and leader of workshops dedicated to the use of elements of puppet animation in social integration and personal development:

> I show how art and creativity can be useful in promoting dialogue between religions and cultures, in addiction therapies, or to engage a person with a disability in the life of the local community, how art can help encourage social participation among various groups, and support someone in self-development, overcoming barriers, acquiring new abilities and taking up challenges.

A unique example of transformation for co-creative practices is a cultural institution with a distinctive socio-artistic program: The Cultural Centre "Borderland of Arts, Cultures, Nations" in Sejny, founded by local authorities and inspired by artists (since 1991). The project mission focuses on transcultural dialogue built via the personal experience of a culture where artistic practices are viewed as the best form of meeting in transcultural space. As Czyżewski said in a radio interview, "Insight is an opportunity for culture. I understand it as coming closer to people, creating together and participating together in the creative process of local communities and neighbourhoods" (Siwek, 2020). The location of the Centre at a historical junction point of cultures is symbolic. Tellingly, its example long-term projects include: *The Borderlander*, *Open Regions of the Central and Eastern Europe*, and *A Gypsy Art Village*. The old (and forgotten since World War II) Polish tradition of intercultural society has been seen as an occasion for co-creative practices and has been recalled in the Centre's projects. The transformation can be provoked by rediscovering old, forgotten values and framing them as promising during the present time.

Challenges of the present

Several conclusions can be drawn from reviewing the events that contributed to the transformations of the 1980s and subsequent art activities. The idea of social unification is on the rise in crisis situations, also in art. If elites who proclaim a need for political transformation invoke high culture, the ambitions of the society joining the cultural cycle increases. At such time, references to legible signs and tradition become more socially desirable. In societies undergoing change, where governments do not take proper care of the nations, socio-cultural practices are often initiated by informal groups, and a growing role of art being born outside the artistic milieu is observed.

In Zygmunt Bauman's opinion, today "the arts have lost (or at any rate are fast losing) their function as a handmaiden of a social hierarchy struggling to self-reproduce – just as some time earlier culture as a whole lost its original function as a handmaiden of emergent nations, states and class hierarchies" (Bauman, 2010, p. 111). Following the transformation of the political system, Poland saw a growing number of art projects devoted to the global challenges or the problems of individuals excluded for a variety of reasons.

Although today digitization seems to be conducive for communication, a variety of traditional and innovative art methods are used to roll out a social mission, and the wealth of socio-art practices still awaits a deeper field research project to examine their different motivations. To evaluate the arts in terms of social effectiveness requires in-depth studies on the nature of art activity itself.

The Polish case indicates that, for art to stay vivid, no matter its social or institutional context, resistance as much as the space of freedom is required. At the same time, the Polish experience shows that using art as a tool for any political indoctrination results in diminishing its artistic, consequently its inherent, social value. Culture and its social context are now standing up to new threats. Political tensions and an endangered democracy are sparking a shift toward an art that will contest the existing order, and even highly elitist art activities are gaining popularity on the wave of building communities of protest. Art in its new forms appear to be rising in prominence as a language of communication and a practice satisfying a variety of individual needs.

Living art has found a new place in local initiatives and civic movements where frequently division into elitist and egalitarian art makes no sense and is no longer a criterion of the value of art. What can be, however, a source of concern (and both authors agree with this) is how not to lose the very essence of art in that transformation. The authors agree with Malcolm Ross (2011) that, "The singular reward that art making offers is the possibility of individual and collective spiritual renewal: anima mundi". Even if the artist touches on pressing social problems or his/her work is recognized as valuable because of its social or political engagement, it is worth remembering that "The sovereignty of the work issues from its dialectical provenance (the dynamic connections between social and personal meanings and values): its autonomy and freedom are therefore sacrosanct" (Ross, 2011).

References

Bauman, Z. (2010). *44 letters from the Liquid Modern World*. Polity Press.

Boruta, T. (2012). *Pokolenie. Niezależna twórczość młodych w latach 1980–89*. IPN.

Fydrych, W. (2010). *Żywoty Mężów Pomarańczowych*. Fundacja Pomarańczowa Alternatywa.

Grzywacz, Z. (2001). Interview with A. Gralińska-Toborek. *Wycieczka do obozu wroga. Rozmowa ze Zbylutem Grzywaczem*, Tygiel Kultury, 10–12.

Korniłowicz, K. (1976). Pomoc w tworzeniu jako zadanie pracy kulturalnej. In O. Czerniawska (Ed.), *Pomoc społeczno-kulturalna dla młodzieży pracującej i dorosłych. Wybór pism* (pp. 128–140). Ossolineum.

Nowak, S. (1979). System wartości społeczeństwa polskiego. *Studia Socjologiczne*, 4(75), 155–173.

Radlińska, H. (1961). *Pedagogika Społeczna*. Ossolineum.

Ross, M. (2011). *Cultivating the arts in education and therapy*. Routledge.

Siwek, P. (2020, December 16). Interview with K. Czyżewski. [Radio Broadcast] Polish Radio 2 *Poranek Dwójki*.

Stróżewski, Wł. (1983). *Dialektyka twórczości*. PWM.

Żmijewski, A. (2007). Stosowane sztuki społeczne [Applied Social Arts]. *Krytyka Polityczna* [Political Criticism]. 11–12.

5 Future IDs at Alcatraz

Transforming lives in immediate and necessary ways

Gregory Sale, Rebecca Jackson, Luis Garcia, and Jacquelyn McCroskey

When the California senator voted for juvenile justice reform bill SB-260, he credited his encounter with Dominique Bell, *Future IDs* project collaborator, as the moment he made up his mind. Dom described it thus, "I said, 'Listen, you don't have a lot of time. I just want to show you something.' And I reached into my pocket and pulled out my old prison ID. The Senator looked at it, and then I went in my other pocket and showed him this college ID. And I said to him, 'This is the different side. That is the difference.' And he responded,

Figure 5.1 Zoom video meeting with Gregory Sale, Rebecca Jackson, Jacquelyn McCroskey, and Luis Garciz

Source: Screenshot Gregory Sale

DOI: 10.4324/9781003105350-6

'Enough said.'" Dom's story of personal transformation demonstrated the powerful and immediate potential of visual representation. Dom was a member of a committed group of arts and justice advocates led by artist Gregory Sale, who worked in various contexts over five years to translate criminal justice reform efforts into an artistic language capable of evolving public opinion about reentry into society after incarceration.

Their collective work came to fruition as *Future IDs at Alcatraz*, a year-long, socially engaged art project, exhibition, and community program series about justice reform and second chances. Gregory, together with core project collaborators Dr. Luis Garcia, Kirn Kim, Sabrina Reid, Jessica Tully, and others, presented *Future IDs at Alcatraz* in partnership with National Park Service (NPS) and the Golden Gate National Parks Conservancy at the iconic prison-turned-national park in San Francisco Bay from fall 2018 to fall 2019.

The socially engaged art project comprised two interrelated artistic gestures: an art exhibition and a community program series. The exhibition featured artworks made by individuals with conviction histories as they conceived and developed a vision for a future self. In stark contrast to prison-issued IDs, these self-portraits represented individual stories of transformation and, importantly, self-determination. The exhibition also acted as a conceptual frame and container for the series of community programs, co-created with 20+ partner organizations and institutions. Acknowledging the layered history of Alcatraz, these performances, workshops, and roundtable discussions were co-designed to engage specific needs of those most impacted by the justice system. Together, the exhibition and the programmatic series created an evolving civic space for open dialogue, mutual learning, and stories of trauma, transformation, and resilience.

Having completed this project on Alcatraz, three members of the *Future IDs* creative team – Gregory, Luis, and Rebecca Jackson – talked via Zoom with Dr. Jacquelyn McCroskey, social work professor. They reflected on how *Future IDs at Alcatraz* centered the reentry community, engaging practices integral to both socially engaged art and social work. They explored how this transdisciplinary work might lead to social transformation. The conversation has been edited for clarity.

Figure 5.2 Future IDs project collaborator Kirn Kim traveling on the ferry to Alcatraz Island

Source: Photo Gregory Sale

Welcome

GREGORY: Thank you all for joining me in this virtual conversation that will become a book chapter. Working in this open-ended way and considering *Future IDs at Alcatraz* together honors the kind of socially engaged art practice I believe in. It's a dialogical, deliberative practice based on a belief in co-creation. We are all in this together. No one person has a magic-bullet solution.

Integral to the growing field of socially engaged art practice in which artists collaborate with citizens on aesthetic responses to social problems, *Future IDs at Alcatraz* is deeply engaged with the consequences of mass incarceration in the US while illuminating the complexities of how we care for each other.

Future IDs emerged from a fluid collaborative process I initiated with men and women who were or had been incarcerated. It has grown over five years into a multifaceted initiative involving more than 20 community organizations, social service programs, cultural and educational institutions, funders, and prisons.

I see us addressing a series of interrelated inquiries: the development of *Future IDs*, the interface of art and social work in a project like this, and the intersectionality of art making, personal and social transformation, and the construction of space, systems, and practices to make it happen.

Beginning a socially engaged artistic process

LUIS: I remember in 2016 when Gregory led that early *Art and Future Planning Workshop* at the Anti-Recidivism Coalition in Los Angeles. That was my first connection to *Future IDs*. He asked questions about childhood likes and dislikes, family background, parents, hobbies. Viewed through social work, the worksheet was like a self-created psychosocial assessment. It really sparked my imagination.

GREGORY: Together we explored some early passions and modeling as we worked to identify personal content for the identity-card-inspired artworks. The questions helped ground the participants in their lived experiences. We worked together to provide a structured and safe environment for participants to conceive and develop a vision for their future.

LUIS: Going through the process, as someone who has been incarcerated and also has a certain skill set from earning a master's degree in social work and a doctorate in educational leadership for social justice, I observed the other participants – my peers in reentry (to society) – who were going through their own reintegration processes. Having the co-facilitators (artist, writers, therapists) and support systems in place, like you did, was really important. In those exercises, memories come up for people. Asking them to trust you and put that stuff on paper can be triggering.

Some were like, "Why are we doing this? Why does it matter what this past means? I'm just focusing on *now*." I saw that it was uncomfortable for some of them to have to deal with deep inquiry and reflection.

In the artistic phase, where we began to translate our answers into images and symbols, an artist facilitator encouraged me to consider stuff that I used to enjoy doing but was just too constrained to embrace. The work allowed me to untangle all that shame and stigma. I left there feeling like, well, there's really something here worth exploring. I signed on to be part of the project long-term and joined the other project collaborators, offering workshops around California.

When the creative team started to run workshops inside prisons, having individuals with conviction histories involved, like me, helped build trust and allowed the curriculum to unfold organically and set a solid foundation for the project as a whole. The *Future IDs* project respected and promoted participants' self-determination, another parallel to social work.

GREGORY: Let me say more about the inception of the workshops. In 2015, I met Luis and the other early collaborators when I became an ally and an embedded artist for the Anti-Recidivism Coalition (ARC), a support and advocacy network for current and formerly incarcerated individuals. A self-selected group of ARC members and I started meeting regularly. We'd reflect on community needs, make and think about art together, and go to museums. We studied everyday images of incarceration. We discussed taking ownership of those images and investigated how to harness their power to positively shift the narrative of reentry.

Then ARC member Dominique Bell told that great story about activating the transformative power of juxtaposing his two IDs. So we started working with that inspirational foundation. An ID as a

Figure 5.3 Dr. Luis Garcia's future ID created for the Future IDs at Alcatraz project

Source: Courtesy of the artist

form has all kinds of potential. You can dream. You can set goals. You can decide how you're authorized and who authorizes you.

But how you identify yourself – and how others identify you – is difficult for anyone to negotiate. As a white, middle-class man who has never been to prison, I didn't feel comfortable leading an assignment-based project. Think about notions of white saviors and how fraught it can be when someone steps in to fix a problem without lived experience or deep understanding. Someone in the group said "Gregory, we are on this journey with you. We're always talking about leaning into our discomfort. This time, you'll have to lean into yours."

Luis, talking about moving outside comfort zones makes me think of your journey creating an ID.

Authorizing your own future

LUIS: Yes. I joke about this now, but when I went to prison at 23, I was wearing shorts, Birkenstocks, and a USC sweatshirt. That was my middle class, Mexican-American family background. In prison, I had to put on a facade and identify as southern Mexican just to survive.

Questioning my heritage was the beginning of my future ID. I wanted to use a photo of the Chicano Moratorium in 1970. My dad took me to that protest as a small child. I realized my ongoing identity work and protesting with my father gave me hope when there was no hope for me.

In summer 2017, we were working on our future IDs. I was in a transition professionally and didn't know my next career step. Initially, I was uncomfortable claiming the title "Director of Higher Education in Carceral Settings." I asked myself, "Why are you afraid to just put that on paper?"

Remember, I first had "the University of Southern California" on the top of the card? And then one day I thought, "Why do I have USC up there? I just graduated with my doctorate from Loyola Marymount. What's my real story?" That's when the name *University of Resilience* popped into my head. And it all came together – the image that I had, my background story, the job title, and my resilience throughout these different life journeys.

REBECCA Listening to Luis talk, I remember my really good friend Sabrina Reid calling me during her process. She would say, "What is wrong with me? I redid this thing like nine times. I can't see myself." And she's an *artist*! She's also a returned citizen and advocates for lifers coming out of prison.

She ended up making her ID about serving on the Advisory Board of Formerly Incarcerated Individuals for the San Francisco District Attorney's office. Even though it wasn't as solid of a look into her future as she'd hoped, she chose that role because she had accomplished something profound that could be a springboard to future success.

GREGORY: Some people like Sabrina mostly made their IDs on their own. By then we were mailing out kits that included materials and instructions, so people who could not participate in a workshop could still be part of the project independently. Even people who went through a workshop series reported beginning with one idea or no idea and struggling until they figured something out.

REBECCA: Exactly. I think people struggle to see the things that they could be, even when others can see it in them.

The project and exhibition on Alcatraz

GREGORY: As participants completed their future IDs, we began to see the collective power of rescripting identity and dreamed about expanding the work as a social impact campaign. And so, we proposed the project to NPS and Parks Conservancy and secured their commitment for the year on Alcatraz.

We began in November 2018 as an artist studio that the public could visit and officially launched in February 2019 with a *Day of Public Programs* and concluded late September with an *Art and Justice Summit on Alcatraz*. It was so great that we got to use the New Industries Building. That cavernous space was perfect with its large exhibition and programming room, the flexible space for workshops and meals, the video viewing room, and, importantly, the separate, quiet *Space for Processing and Reflection*.

REBECCA: Walking into the exhibition full of almost 50 bright, colorful, mural-sized *Future IDs* surrounding you, you couldn't help but be inspired. I think there's something super powerful in Sabrina, Luis, and all these people having the courage to put their ambitions and dreams out there. That opens this door for others. I saw that happen with the clients from Cameo House, the residential facility I run for justice-impacted women with children as an alternative to prison or jail.

When we brought them to see the exhibit, we explained what the artwork was really about, and then they got to go to these tables with art supplies. Bringing art to people who are in the middle of reentry and giving them this space to be creative, even if it's just for the afternoon, was so powerful. They talked about it for months. We still have the pictures they painted up at the facility.

Prior to taking them to Alcatraz, they couldn't see past their next probation visit. They couldn't see past making it through our year-long program, let alone dream of a future for themselves that doesn't have to be dictated by their past.

The women all want to graduate from the *University of Resilience*. They all want to be *Mom Too*. They want to be these things that they could physically see. There was a deep psychology to looking at those huge self-portraits.

Figure 5.4 Gregory Sale taking a picture of Rebecca Jackson and women from Cameo House in front of Cirese LaBerge-Bader's "Mom Too" ID (The women's faces have been blurred to protect their privacy and anonymity.)

Source: Photo Ben Leon

Reflecting on the relationship between social work and the arts

JACQUELYN: Both my brothers were in and out of prison. My first job out of college was as a Deputy Probation Officer, which led me to social work, because I thought "this system is so broken." Social work has been my lifelong passion. As a USC professor, advocate, and researcher working with LA County government around child welfare and juvenile justice, I appreciate what social work has to offer. I also see what it doesn't have to offer, particularly around art.

Creating a *Future ID* and then showing the artworks all together really gets at the core of trauma and personal development, at missed opportunities and at opportunities that still lie ahead. That's why the visual parts of this project, both the *Future IDs* artworks and the videos that were screened on site, are really important.

How many conversations do we have where people are coming from parallel fields and professional formations that don't really intersect well? The interface between art, social work, and bureaucratic systems is difficult because we don't share a common vocabulary or understanding. In clinical social work, we're more likely to see art as a tool for engagement and improved mental health; in organizing and policy work, it may be a tool for communication.

This professional interface is important to acknowledge. Otherwise, art is seen as ancillary in that setting and not central to a shared purpose. It's easy to say, "Goodness, now we're funding a lot of arts organizations to work with people in residential settings." As a probation officer, I thought my role was to sit there until the outside people were done working with the girls and then go, "Okay, line up. Dinner time." I couldn't see what I had to do with community programming.

Future IDs gets to the core of the issues differently, involving institutions, putting art in the lead and nurturing communities around the art. In this case, the people you're trying to help are deeply engaged in creating the pathway. Then it's possible for artists, social workers, and everyone else to join together and take the same trajectory. *Future IDs* is a great example of how to do that, activating what each contributor has to offer and what's really possible in a particular place and time.

This takes me back to Luis comparing *Future IDs* and social work at the beginning of our conversation. Really, the things that social art practice focuses on, and Gregory's ideas and other artists who work like him, are a physical embodiment of person-in-environment, of "start where the client is," of relationship-based practice, of working simultaneously at micro, mezzo, and macro levels, and of other things that social workers hold dear. It's an embodiment of all of that.

The opportunity is there. We're aiming for the same goal.

GREGORY: Differently than social work and importantly, art allows for the work to step into a symbolic space. And then our artistic gestures and forms can operate in the cultural sphere, the realms of art and culture where they begin to do this different civic and cultural work.

Alcatraz, as a site, holds significance in our culture because of the propaganda of imprisoning "the worst of the worst," its glorification in Hollywood movies, then the demand for sovereignty from the Native American Occupation of Alcatraz (1969 to 1971) and the birth of the Red Power movement there.

Creating this project on Alcatraz and engaging the island's layered history were symbolically crucial for our community programs. We invited ecosystems of individuals and groups doing work around incarceration, justice reform, and abolition to come in and co-design programs with us. We said, "we have this charged site with a specific message around shifting narratives of reentry. Would you like to use it? Can it somehow expand work you're doing?"

Our partners, NPS and Parks Conservancy, are committed to the island serving as an equitable civic forum for communities to consider incarceration, justice, and our common humanity. This intention is linked to Alcatraz's designation as an International Site of Conscience (2014), providing a safe space to preserve traumatic memories while connecting the past to today's social justice concerns.

Because of how Alcatraz operates, this work required complex negotiations. For example, as a federal agency, NPS can't host direct political advocacy, but they can host first-person storytelling.

As an art project operating quasi-independently on Alcatraz, *Future IDs* could model new systems of engagement that NPS could use in the future. We navigated the parameters set forth by NPS and the desires of various community partners to co-produce meaningful community programming.

Figure 5.5 Future IDs artists Candice Price and Emiliano Lopez in discussion with Roberto Bedoya (arts administrator/thought leader) during the Art and Justice Summit on Alcatraz

Source: Photo Peter Merts

Hosting civic space for community programs

REBECCA: Having that space on Alcatraz where the programs and conversations could take place, where you could see it affecting people, where it's a living thing, and a beautiful thing because you look around the room and it was so . . . *diverse*. People were open emotionally, and their brains were open. Round table discussions, big circles and small circles, plays and prayers – these programs made space for people to have those experiences.

The *Art and Justice Summit on Alcatraz* was amazing. I mean, wow, directly involving the reentry community and hearing the voices of justice-impacted people engaging with powerbrokers. And how civic engagement and arts meet and marry in that space was extremely powerful.

It was differently powerful when my daughter and I were part of "*The family's in prison too*" program. I can't begin to tell you how important that was for our relationship. Our journey to healing the wounds my absence caused is still in its toddler stage, and having an audience to share some of that withheld so much positive energy and support that she needed in that moment. It could not have made as much of an impact if we said the same things to each other alone in a room. We were both sobbing and coming to this revelation with the entire audience, and I looked up and people were crying too. . . . Sorry. I just got choked up thinking about that.

GREGORY: Thank you, Rebecca. I felt that our group really came together to understand how to foster fluid, civic space for discussion and deliberation, where questions are asked and where resistance and resolution can happen.

REBECCA: And where it can be messy, if that's what's needed.

GREGORY: Yes, where it can be messy. This work requires that those who are leading learn to nurture and negotiate complex relationships across disparate constituencies and through fraught politics and policies. We kept refining the project space as a mechanism, as a tool, so that whatever was unfolding could flow from safe space to engaged space for the participants, the public, and our partners.

If programs became uncertain for whatever reason, trust was essential. Some of our work with system-affected individuals and organizations needed to be private or semi-private. Sharing those moments with the public would have been premature.

Early on, we recognized programs that were cathartic for some could be triggering for others. Just being on Alcatraz, for people who have been incarcerated or who have incarcerated loved ones, can bring up deep emotions.

So we created that separate *Space for Processing and Reflection* within the exhibition. You could have coffee or tea, make some art, or chat with somebody compassionate. Before every program, we invited people to lean into their discomfort and also asked them to be our partners in making certain that they were safe. If they needed to step out, we offered that separate space.

JACQUELYN: From a social work point of view, you want people who are really good at what they do organizing all those activities, who are familiar with the range of complexities that can come into play.

There's not a handbook like "first you do this, and then you do that. You're new to the field, come on down, and we'll help you facilitate." It's so important to be working together, to have others around so you feel safe, where you can be comfortable exploring and moving outside yourself, where you can learn from each other. I think it's important and edgy to try to transmit this message.

LUIS: On Alcatraz, things arose organically. We talked about relationships being one of the materials of the arts practice. We cultivated a culture of mutual respect and a willingness to say things that are uncomfortable or critical. And that's where different people's experiences came into play, and certain voices that are not heard as commonly as other voices came forward.

GREGORY: Our collaboration required flexibility and acceptance all around. Sharing control among collaborators was crucial to the project. As the lead artist, I invited project participants to help conceptualize social-aesthetic structures, to produce and co-produce artistic components, and to direct the advocacy intention of the work.

I have come to think about our work more like the way political and cultural movements advance. A bunch of people contribute to it, and the kind of culture that we champion values each person's expertise.

We knew we had to hit some pretty high levels in ethical engagement all around – in community organizing, in artistic production, and in justice advocacy – or we wouldn't accomplish the project's objectives.

Serving multiple audiences

JACQUELYN: You've pointed out many pieces of the *Future IDs* project, but we haven't talked about engagement with the tourists on Alcatraz. You introduced material that's so real, so vibrant, and so immediate into a major tourist attraction, where people weren't expecting that. But because it was subject-matter-related, the tourists were open to the project, so not like, "What are you doing here?" but more like, "What is this?" in a good way.

LUIS: Yes, many days we had over 1,000 people visit the space, maybe 250,000 visitors in total. Events, like the *Higher Education and Reintegration Roundtable* were open to everybody, to the public and to the stakeholders who were participating. Maybe tourists were exposed to these ideas for the first time. Everything else on Alcatraz looked to the past. But our project grapples with the present and looks to the future. We knew it mattered a lot to them because of how long they stayed and the great questions they asked.

GREGORY: Alcatraz really afforded us the opportunity to reach a broad and diverse audience in varying degrees of engagement. Casual tourists who stumbled upon *Future IDs* ideally understood justice in expanded ways. Those participating in community programs seemed to embrace deep civic engagement. The men and women sharing their future visions reported feeling validated and seen. *Future IDs at Alcatraz* fostered those communal moments. It played a critical role in helping Alcatraz expand its work as a valuable civic forum, changing underlying cultural biases, and transforming lives in immediate and necessary ways.

Summary: the method, a role for art in individual and social transformation

Emphasizing pedagogical modes, the method fostered in *Future IDs at Alcatraz* activates creativity as a tool of social transformation and encompasses multidisciplinary strategies borrowed from social, cultural, and political inquiry. By co-creating with individuals with conviction histories in inception, development, and presentation, the socially engaged art project promoted self-determination and modeled strategies for centering those most negatively impacted by social systems.

Focused on aesthetic inquiries into identity, the project opened up safe symbolic space, creatively positioning individuals and groups to move toward civic engagement. Viewed through social work, it physically embodied person-in-environment, starting where the individual is – relationship-based practice – and working simultaneously at micro, mezzo, and macro levels.

Importantly, unlike social work, art allows for project efforts to step into a symbolic space, with artistic gestures and forms operating in the social/culture sphere, leading to meaningful social change. As a symbolic gesture, *Future IDs at Alcatraz* engaged the layered, iconic history of Alcatraz to host critical, civic deliberations and allowed a wide audience to participate in various ways. *Future IDs* required its leaders to nurture and negotiate complex relationships across disparate constituencies and through fraught politics and policies. This interface among individual positionalities, fields of practice, bureaucratic systems, government, and institutions is especially difficult because they do not share a common understanding. *Future IDs* softened conventional boundaries and resistance, allowing for open dialogue and the development of mutual learning that could undo the social othering and cultural biases that stigmatize individuals and communities.

6 Group bonding through cutting, gluing, and sewing together

Using arts and crafts in social work with groups: "when members see what they have done with their own hands, this is a feeling no one can take away"

Reineth Prinsloo

Introduction

It is human nature to interact socially, and groups offer a context for social interaction (Shenaar-Golan & Walter, 2018; Toseland & Rivas, 2017). Groups, natural or formed, provide foundations on which society is built. Groups provide opportunities for growth, support, socialisation, education, and different viewpoints and resources, and mutual aid benefits group members. Huss and colleagues (2012) have recommended the use of group work to provide support and opportunities for sharing in a safe environment that enables social change.

Group leaders have used exercises: activities that the group does for an explicit purpose such as reducing a group member's anxiety, revealing important information, and generating conversation, directing discussion and experiential learning in a relaxed atmosphere (Jacobs et al., 2016). Lang (2016) referred to deliberative group work as focused talking and discussion while non-deliberative group work used spontaneous engagement in experiential exercises in an artful way.

In this chapter, the focus will be on social work with groups. The concepts of social work and art are not usually used in the same context. A general perception of social work is that it relies on talk and text (River et al., 2017). Where does art fit in social work? To contextualise arts-based exercises in social work, it became clear that there is no single definition for art. Wong (2019) referred to art as human behaviour and River et al. (2017, p. 768) mentioned that creativity is intrinsic to "our 'human being-ness'". All arts are different, be it painting, dancing, writing, and more, yet they are all art.

DOI: 10.4324/9781003105350-7

This chapter will discuss arts and craft exercises used in groups to improve group work practice in two South African case studies. The first case study will discuss groups in which the making of the craft products brought members together to improve their skills and to develop a small social enterprise for both social and economic development. The second case study will discuss a project where university level social work students made finger puppets depicting the diverse families in the country for early childhood development centres and their experiences of bonding, sharing, and growing personally and professionally through the group work process.

Social work with groups and arts and crafts exercises

Group work is a goal-directed activity to support and educate group members, to help members with socialisation and to achieve personal growth or render treatment services for problems (Toseland & Rivas, 2017). We have used arts and crafts in groups in social work to address socio-emotional needs because art as a form of human expression has intersecting purposes and is a tool that can be used for social change (Flynn, 2019; Wehbi et al., 2016). Wong (2019) asserted that art affects the human mental state in that it can relieve stress and improve psychological wellbeing. The evolving process of producing the art and the art as a product facilitate social bonding.

Art contributes to knowledge. Capous-Desyllas and Bromfield (2018) referred to Eisner (2008) who distinguished among four contributions. First, the arts direct attention to subtle differences of contexts that would not be obvious and might not be noticed otherwise. In the arts-based exercises discussed in this chapter, all the products, namely the symposium bags, animal key rings, and the finger puppets, directed the attention of the group members to the differences among their situations. Second, the arts create empathic awareness. Empathy opens the avenue for action (Sinding et al., 2014). In both case studies, group members referred to increased empathy for each other and challenging issues faced in society. The third contribution – artistically created objects – gives a new and fresh perspective on situations (Sinding et al., 2014). One student in the finger puppet project responded that she never realised the challenges of mixed-race families until they made such a finger puppet family and discussed the family type. The fourth contribution of arts is that it evokes emotion, affects the way humans feel, and helps people to discover their humanity. Arts-based exercises can assist group members to express their experiences verbally and through non-verbal mediums (Lang, 2016). Huss and Sela-Amit

(2019) found that the use of arts, especially in social work, can extend to verbal communication.

The use of arts and crafts exercises facilitates the expression of emotions and thoughts, often in a way that is easier than verbalising (Capous-Desyllas & Bromfield, 2018; Huss & Sela-Amit, 2019; Wehbi et al., 2016). In a group context, arts and craft exercises can create energy and enable the group to find an entry point for discussion. Exercises such as arts and crafts can be the means to an end, namely, to facilitate bonding, sharing, and discussion (Lang, 2016). Huss and colleagues (2012) referred to the interactions among group members while being involved in art processes. Art can be used in groups to do first and then to think (Lang, 2016). Through doing and creatively making an item, arts-based exercises can increase socialisation, improve self-worth and self-esteem, and contribute to improved wellbeing in general (River et al., 2017).

Case study one: sewing as an arts-based exercise in group work to facilitate bonding and growth

Poverty is a major issue of concern worldwide and rife in South Africa. Minority groups such as women suffer the most and often have little or no access to opportunities for employment. Social work must contribute to social change for social justice. Small business ventures can address poverty and overcome unemployment (Flynn, 2019). In this case study, the author facilitated a project where groups were formed to sew and create objects, thus establishing a small social enterprise.

The author submitted a proposal to an international association to allow these groups to provide conference bags for their annual symposium. The association accepted the proposal and ordered 300 conference bags, along with animal-shaped key rings, which allowed an opportunity to involve three groups of people: a group of older women in a township in Pretoria who made the conference bags and a group of female domestic workers and a group of homeless men who made padded felt animal key rings.

The project's goal was to create income for people facing economic challenges. In this case study, one of the groups (women) had been gathering every Monday to Friday to sew various products, encouraging, supporting, and learning from each other. However, their market had been limited until the opportunity for the conference bags came along.

The group work process and outcomes are discussed in this section, looking at the groups involved in the project.

The conference bags

The older women's group was an existing group that met regularly at a centre for older people that serves as a haven for old and frail people in a township in Pretoria. The author arranged a meeting where a contract was drawn up, and the women were excited about the prospect that people in another country would be introduced to their work.

The women formally drew up a division of roles where each one received a task: to measure, cut, sew, make the handles for the bags, sew on a South African flag tag, fold the final products, and count the completed bags. This task-oriented group became one with elements of mutual aid, support, growth, and socialisation. Discussions focused on the members' families and raising children, especially their grandchildren. While working together their challenges with young people and societal changes and how to budget in their economically challenged situations received attention. Very importantly, they had opportunities to reminisce about the "good old days", allowing the women to socialise and experience support and growth.

The participants feedback revealed a sense of humility and gratitude for how the project unfolded, but also one of extreme pride in what was accomplished. Wong (2019, p. 212) states, "every human can and should make their own art". Engaging in making something special can contribute to identifying their specialness and influencing self-actualisation and wellbeing (River et al., 2017). The groups provided the context to both identify and share the specialness and, in the process, this led to group cohesion (Cramer et al., 2018).

One member of the sewing group, showing pride both in her own and in the group's accomplishments said:

> I never believed I could make such beautiful work. I am so happy my work is going to the other countries. The people from the America must come visit me. My people are very, very poor. The sewing is good to teach to the children. I will show them how to do this.

The group continued as a self-help group where leadership was rotated among members and the focus remained on social change (Jacobs et al., 2016; Toseland & Rivas, 2017). This group shared elements of education in respect of the new skills they had learned, support because they shared numerous factors, and socialisation while sewing and talking.

The felt animal key rings

The accepted proposal provided an opportunity to set up two new groups: one for homeless men and one for domestic workers in which participants would learn a new skill and be able to gain income. Being involved in creating the objects opened new ways of communication and allowed participants to verbalise their emotions (Lang, 2019; Shenaar-Golan & Walter, 2018; Sinding et al., 2014). Group members discussed their daily challenges with each other with new cohesion evident in the groups (Corey, 2012; Pooler et al., 2014). The group experience was of value as is evident in the response of one of the homeless men, "you guys [facilitators] are different, you are not like them [other professionals in the organisation] who come and give you the work to do it while they are the boss, you work with us". Through the arts-based exercise, their awareness of each other and their daily context was enhanced; they supported each other both in and outside the group (Shenaar-Golan & Walter, 2018). The members mastered the art of producing key rings and created quality products. These groups were then examples of skills development for social transformation, as captured in the following comment:

> I am proud to do the animals. Even my eyes were not good, but I manage to finish. I like to talk to the ladies. We talk about our children in Zim. I miss my child every single day. The other lady, her children are also in Zim. It was nice to make friends. I enjoy. Thank you.

Case study two: finger puppets and teaching group work theory

The second case study describes a project in a module called: Social Work with Groups in the Bachelor of Social Work programme. The 64 third-year students in the module were divided into 9 groups with diverse membership in terms of gender, race, and culture. The task was to make finger puppets for early childhood development centres of the diverse families in South Africa. The project had multiple aims. First, students were expected to reach the learning outcomes for advanced group work through the in-depth and practical experience of being a group member and alternating group leadership. Second, the aim was to integrate knowledge about the diversity of families in South Africa in preparing the social work students to work with families and children in practice. Cramer and colleagues (2018) and Leonard and colleagues (2018) emphasised the use of arts-based approaches in social work education to integrate knowledge. Third, the author aimed to explore the use of an arts-based exercise in social work with groups to encourage creativity and innovation (Moxley et al., 2012). The group work project emphasised growth, socialization, education, and support. A number of research teams have underscored the use of arts-based approaches in social work education to integrate knowledge and deepen cognitive understanding (Cramer et al., 2018; Leonard et al., 2018; Moxley et al., 2012; Wehbi et al., 2016).

The author introduced the project by asking students to make finger puppets that represent the diverse types of families in South Africa related to module content that they received in their first year of the BSW programme. Every group received glue, scissors, needles and thread, and different colours of wool and felt material. The groups had weekly sessions for six weeks. The content included the role of social work in addressing diversity in families and even personalizing family of origin issues on the premise that group trust and cohesion allowed it. Group members rotated the leadership of the group to integrate group leadership skills. All the members contributed to the process of social transformation that transpired through the groups as emphasised in the methods described by Huss and colleagues (2012). Sharing the power and rotating the leadership in the case under discussion empowered each participant to feel full ownership of the group process as well as increased knowledge (Cramer et al., 2018).

Students' initial reactions varied. One male student said: "At first the student saw the idea of making these puppets as very childish and inappropriate, after all the student is in his third year". Another student responded as follows: "when the lecturer announced that we will be making puppets I was a bit anxious since I had never done such before. I was also excited that I would for the first time be part of such a group".

The students' experiences of doing the arts-based exercise and the subsequent personal and professional growth are discussed in the themes section in this chapter.

Creating awareness

As in the case presented by Huss and colleagues (2012), this art-based activity of making finger puppets helped group members to talk about their family contexts but also to understand their personal experiences in their different family types. Being involved through an art exercise creates *awareness* (Capous-Desyllas & Bromfield, 2018; Jacobs et al., 2016; Shenaar-Golan & Walter, 2018; Wong, 2019).

The comment of one group member illustrates the safe environment that the group provided: "This exercise demonstrated the trust and comfort level in the group because all the group members shared personal information about their families to another group member, without feeling uncomfortable or afraid that they will be judged". An insightful comment about *awareness* of the self was made by a female group member: "By focusing on our ideas and beliefs, we were able to gain insights into the inner family person and their dreams about how a family should be like".

Sensitivity to diversity: "the elephant in the room"

Clements (2017) and Sinding and colleagues (2014) alluded to how an arts-based activity in a group opens the issues of racism and judgement, something that would otherwise not have been discussed. It is not always easy for people to talk about their family types, especially if the specific family type is different from the socially accepted nuclear family. Making the finger puppets together created a space for sharing. The group dynamics enabled a safe context to openly reveal information about the constellation of their own families and learn about and from each other. The cohesion in the groups led members to talk about issues that they would not normally have spoken about (Corey, 2012; Lang, 2016; Pooler et al., 2014). One of the group members mentioned the following:

> Topics allowed us to think deeper about the different family structures, roles, and cultures and we were able to dig deeper into the different families across cultures as our group members were all racially and culturally different. Most of these topics were invisible as we often were reluctant to share about it due to racial and cultural perceptions and stigmas, but during this group series, we were able to deal with the elephant in the room and realized how important it is to know and learn about different cultures and races to bring about a difference in our lives.

The activity made group members sensitive to the *diversity* amongst their fellow group members and in the larger society. A group member said: "with diverse members, shared insights and some opinions made members conscious about things such as the Gay/Lesbian communities and mixed-race marriages".

Not only did the arts-based exercise make the students more aware of diversity, but it also enabled a deeper integration of social work values and ethics (Flynn, 2019; Toseland & Rivas, 2017). One group member demonstrates the integration:

> Through the sharing of life experiences with the group members, the student began to have a more holistic understanding of families and how family dynamics are deeply rooted in culture and religion. The social work values of congruence and unconditional regard were experienced personally, especially when controversial statements were made by the group members.

Competencies and skills

Kelly and Doherty (2016) referred to creative *competencies* that surface through using arts-based activities in group work. These competencies can be of value in members' lives outside the group (Wong, 2019). Being engaged in pleasant and meaningful creative exercises makes people feel special (Wong, 2019). Making the finger puppets made group members aware of *competencies* that they were not aware of. The art-based activity not only made members aware of creative *competencies* but also contributed to several other professional and personal *skills* that inevitably set a process of transformation in motion (Cramer et al., 2018; Leonard et al., 2018; River et al., 2017). Group members mentioned an improvement in group leadership skills, in communication skills, and in gaining self-confidence. Kelly and Doherty (2016), in their review of non-deliberative group work practice, emphasise the acquisition of *skills* on different levels as an outcome of arts-based activities.

Arts-based exercises can deepen the focus of group discussions (Jacobs et al., 2016). Group members gained insight into diversity in families while being creative as reflected in this response: "It was an exciting and insightful experience to make different family types out of finger puppets. I thoroughly enjoyed being creative, but I also enjoyed talking about different family types".

As a lecturer experimenting with combining theory lectures with experiential work, it was satisfying to identify the various *skills* that the students as group members acquired.

Cohesion and bonding

Arts-based exercises contributed to a process of identifying with fellow group members and providing a sense of solidarity (Shenaar-Golan & Walter, 2018; Wong, 2019). The *cohesion* united the group members and gave them the courage to discuss their family contexts (Corey et al., 2018) as affirmed by one participant who said:

> The group leader came up with an exercise where each member had to talk about their own families. . . . After this exercise that is when group members started feeling free and comfortable to talk because they did not feel like strangers anymore.

While making the finger puppets, group members' attraction to each other and their *cohesion* strengthened. The finger puppets provided the medium for deeper communication (Moxley et al., 2012) as evident in the response:

> Group four initially set out to make a child-headed family household but as the series went on, they realized they had made a diverse family system which the student personally feels was just a reflection of the *cohesion* of the group and the acceptance within the group, the group then expressed their acceptance of each other onto the family puppets.

Summary

Human bonding is crucial for "being" and existing (Wong, 2019). Group work in social work provides a platform for belonging, sharing, bonding, growth, socialisation, and education through learning new skills and receiving information. Social work is often associated with talking and verbal interventions to affect social change on micro, mezzo, and macro levels. However, the use of arts and crafts exercises contributes significantly to the outcomes of a group process. From the two case studies discussed, multiple beneficial outcomes were identified. Being involved in the making of arts and crafts objects opened avenues for communications. Not only did the activities allow for non-verbal expression of the self, but they facilitated deeper and more in-depth verbal communication about issues that would perhaps not have been discussed otherwise. In the case of the finger puppet project in teaching a social work module, a prominent theme was enhanced awareness that resulted in empathy and sensitivity to diversity.

In both case studies, group members bonded through the activities. Even with initial reactions of fear of not being able to make the specific object, the encouragement of fellow members helped participants to believe in their abilities. The cohesion was a result of being involved in the process of making the objects and ultimately in the feelings of pride in the completed objects. The arts-based activities in the two projects led to social change. Group members reported increased confidence, improved self-esteem, better communication, creative and innovative thinking, viewing themselves and their fellow group members differently, and having the need to contribute to societal transformation. The activities developed skills that several group members could take further, either by teaching others how to make the objects or by creating an opportunity for earning and income.

Many of the students in the finger puppet project mentioned increased knowledge about social work and the scope of practice. Group work theory and group leadership skills were integrated. Several students undertook use of finger puppets in their work with families and their children.

From the themes identified in these two case studies, it can be concluded that arts-based activities in social work with groups are beneficial and serve as a pathway to address socio-emotional needs and affect social change. Although it is not possible to generalise qualitative findings, it is recommended that social workers explore the use of arts-based activities in group work to strengthen their practice.

References

Capous-Desyllas, M., & Bromfield, N. F. (2018). Using an arts-informed eclectic approach to photovoice data analysis. *International Journal of Qualitative Methods*, *17*, 1–14. https://doi.org/10.1177%2F1609406917752189

Clements, J. A. (2017). Invisible people don't need masks. *Social Work with Groups*, *40*(1–2), 17–20. https://doi.org/10.1080/01609513.2015.1069540

Corey, G. (2012). *Theory and practice of group counselling* (8th ed.). Brooks/Cole.

Corey, M. S., Corey, G., & Corey, C. (2018). *Groups: Process and practice* (10th ed.). Cengage Learning.

Cramer, E. P., McLeod, D. A., Craft, M., & Agnelli, K. (2018). Using arts-based materials to explore the complexities of clinical decision-making in a social work methods course. *Social Work Education*, *37*(3), 342–360. https://doi.org/10.1080/02615479.2017.1401061

Eisner E. (2008). Art and knowledge. In Knowles G. J., Cole A. L. (Eds.), *Handbook of the arts in qualitative research: Perspectives, methodologies, examples and issues* (pp. 3–12). Los Angeles, CA: Sage.

Flynn, M. L. (2019). Art and the social work profession: Shall ever the twain meet? *Research on Social Work Practice*, *29*(6), 687–692. https://doi.org/10.1177/1049731519863109

Huss, E., Elhozayel, E., & Marcus, E. (2012). Art in group work as an anchor for integrating the micro and macro levels of intervention with incest survivors. *Clinical Social Work Journal*, *40*(4), 401–411. https://doi.org/10.1007/s10615-012-0393-2

Huss, E., & Sela-Amit, M. (2019). Art in social work: Do we really need it? *Research on Social Work Practice*, *29*(6), 721–726.

Jacobs, E. E., Schimmel, C. J., Masson, R. L., & Harvill, R. L. (2016). *Group counselling: Strategies and skills* (8th ed.). Cengage.

Kelly, B. L., & Doherty, L. (2016). Exploring nondeliberative practice through recreational, art, and music-based activities in social work with groups. *Social Work with Groups*, *39*(2–3), 221–233. http://dx.doi.org/10.1080/01609513.2015.1057681

Lang, N. C. (2016). Nondeliberative forms of practice in social work: Artful, actional, analogic. *Social Work with Groups*, *39*(2/3), 97–117. https://doi.org/10.1080/01609513.2015.1047701

Leonard, K., Hafford-Letchfield, T., & Couchman, W. (2018). The impact of the arts in social work education: A systematic review. *Qualitative Social Work*, *17*(2), 286–304. https://doi.org/10.1177/1473325016662905

Moxley, D. P., Feen-Calligan, H., & Washington, O. G. M. (2012). Lessons learned from three projects: Linking social work, the arts, and humanities. *Social Work Education*, *31*(6), 703–723. https://doi.org/10.1080/02615479.2012.695160

Pooler, D. K., Qualls, N., Rogers, R., & Johnston, D. (2014). An exploration of cohesion and recovery outcomes in addiction treatment groups. *Social Work with Groups*, *37*(4), 314–330. https://doi.org/10.1080/01609513.2014.905217

River, D. H. M., Thakoordin, J. M., & Billing, L. (2017). Creativity in social work education and practice: Reflections on a survivor arts project. *Social Work Education*, *36*(7), 758–774. https://doi.org/10.1080/02615479.2016.1266320

Shennar-Golan, V., & Walter, O. (2018). Physical activity intensity among adolescents and association with parent–adolescent relationship and well-being. *American Journal of Men's Health*, 12(5), 1530–1540. https://doi.org/10.1177/1557988318768600

Sinding, C., Warren, R., & Paton, C. (2014). Social work and the arts: Images at the intersection. *Qualitative Social Work*, *13*(2), 187–202. https://doi.org/10.1177/1473325012464384

Toseland, R. W., & Rivas, R. F. (2017). *An introduction to group work practice* (8th ed.). Allyn & Bacon.

Wehbi, S., McCormick, K., & Angelucci, S. (2016). Socially engaged art and social work: Reflecting on an interdisciplinary course development journey. *Journal of Progressive Human Services*, *27*(1), 49–64. https://doi.org/10.1080/10428232.2016.1108167

Wong, S. K. S. (2019). Applying an ethological perspective of art to the community arts and socially engaged arts. *Journal of Visual Art Practice*, *18*(3), 205–220. https://doi.org/10.1080/14702029.2019.1613614

7 Interacting through art to re-empower prison inmates in constructing new self-appraisals

Dave Gussak, Elizabeth Odom, and Evie Soape

Interacting through art to re-empower prison inmates in constructing new self-appraisals

Outcast, offender, deviant, and criminal – these words conjure feelings of fear and animosity that are often assigned as societal and institutional labels to the prison inmate. As a result, negative perceptions of such individuals and how they are expected to behave are established. From these perceptions and labels self-appraisals emerge, influencing their current identities.

Through art making, art therapists can help those in prison explore their identity and instil internal/external validation despite the power of assigned labels. Through a review of the sociological perspectives of social/symbolic interactionism and labelling theory and supporting case narratives, this chapter will demonstrate how art therapy can provide opportunities to create new and healthy labels, thus contributing to personal, ultimately social, transformation.

Dehumanizing identities

One factor that contributes to a person's imprisonment is how they are perceived by society, not just because of their crime, but also where they live, the colour of their skin, and the god to whom they pray (Aguilar, 2014). For some, oppression begins early; many are judged even before their details are entered in the forensic system and are "unable to escape from a repressive environment" (Gussak, 2019, p. 51). Adverse childhood experiences and environments, along with discrimination, stem from and contribute to this ongoing oppression and control. Such experiences and societal categorization lead to predetermined biases. Some live up to such expectations by committing crimes, perpetuating the cycle.

DOI: 10.4324/9781003105350-8

Once inside, dehumanization and marginalization are carefully cultivated. Security is perceived to be successful only if the institution maintains objectification of the inmates. Their identity is stripped and they are assigned numbers and a uniform, instilling and perpetuating a process of dehumanization (Fox, 1997). This further reinforces the schism between prisoners and society, making it almost impossible to reintegrate successfully upon parole or release – or to create a sustaining experience inside.

Thus, those identified as inmates are faced with the challenge of reversing these ingrained labels, making re-acceptance into society seem impossible. Providing inmates with tools to reverse these detrimental identities is required for their adaptation and success. Art is just such a tool.

Creating a scaffolding: social/symbolic interactionism

To best explain how this oppression is instituted and how art can reverse this, we rely on labelling theory, a perspective that emerged from social/symbolic interactionism. The social self emerges from the interactions of the individuals within their social groups (James, 1890/1918). How people define themselves begins with how they are perceived by others, creating interdependence between individuals and their social environment (Cooley, 1964). People interpret what others see in them and through this "the self emerges. . . . [They] respond to and internalize aspects of ways others have of acting toward [them]" (Hall, 1981, p. 50). People interpret the reactions of those with whom they interact and will conduct themselves based on how they translate these actions (Blumer, 1969). As the self develops within its experiences, interactions further alter and define social situations (Mead, 1964), ultimately facilitating personal and social identity and transformation.

Interactions are not just with other people – they also occur between a person and an object. Meaning is "not intrinsic to the object but arises from how the person is initially prepared to act toward it" (Blumer, 1969, pp. 68–69); its meaning emerges by how it is perceived. Furthermore, when these perceptions are accepted by more than one person, more interaction emerges. The sharing of these objects – and the interpretations thereof, – define action and interaction. Meanings of such objects become reinforced through ongoing interactions. Through such interpretations and shared meanings, a societal context and the roles of its people are defined. From this, an identity is formed or re-formed.

Of course, logically, the rejection of the shared meaning may also create an identity that runs counter to the group – thus a negative self-appraisal emerges (Bartusch & Matsueda, 1996). Such identities and labels are also reinforced.

The detrimental label

Labelling theory posits that designations are established and solidified by those dominant within a society – the "majority labels the minority" (Gussak, 2019, p. 53). The people who are labelled *deviant* are those whose behaviour provokes hostile reactions or runs counter to the established norms (Becker, 1991; Sagarin, 1975). Rules and sanctions that result from breaking societal norms emerge through a cooperative, social act (Lauer & Handel, 1977). Those designated as "normal" are positioned to agree upon the prescribed standards of who is acceptable and who is a deviant (Cloward & Ohlin, 2001). "[B]ehaviours are not recognized as deviant, or criminal, unless others . . . react to them as such" (Hagan, 2001, p. 6).

Once someone receives such a label, a new identity is formed; the person accepts this identity, and the real or perceived deviance is reinforced (Becker, 1991). Emerging negative behaviour that ensues from the provided categorization perpetuates and amplifies this identity. Retribution is often the result. This includes imprisonment, which may create further deviant self-appraisals, solidifying the individual's criminal identity (Becker, 1991).

However, what is considered deviant outside of prison becomes the norm inside. Newer inhabitants learn the cultural expectations by witnessing the anti-social tendencies of those institutionalized. These become the "normative behavioural systems of groups that support, encourage, and condone" the inmate identity (Vigil, 2003). Such behaviours are not only accepted within that subculture but are expected. Thus, simply "locking someone up" likely reinforces this negative identity and their own deviant self-appraisal (Rubington & Weinberg, 2002).

This identity is further maintained through the interactions between those who break the rules and those who enforce them (Zimbardo, 2007). The punishment does not deter the behaviour; rather, it confirms what the perpetrator has come to realize; "how others respond is crucial to the process of acquiring a deviant identity" (Brownfield & Thompson, 2005, p. 23). Their designated labels continue even after they achieve parole, likely contributing to recidivism.

Re-creating new labels through art-making

It is through re-labelling, validating new behaviours and identities that such tendencies can be halted and perhaps reversed that, ultimately, a full transformation may emerge. Interactions occur with objects and with other people through the objects. By sharing these objects and the interpretation thereof, relationships develop from which new meanings emerge, and social change becomes possible. Such objects include art (Becker, 1982; Gilmore, 1990; Gussak, 2019).

Within the prison walls those who make art are esteemed (Kornfeld, 1997) by both the inmates and the correctional staff. This is valuable in bringing art therapy into the correctional milieu, even for those who have never created art before.

Applying theory to institutional practice

In 2020, the Art Therapy in Prisons Program was created in partnership between a state university and the state's Department of Corrections. It focused on youth offenders who experienced significant challenges that impacted their academic progress. Yet, while several enjoyed making art, none of the participants had formal art training.

Initially, the participants were hesitant, uncertain about their creative abilities. To mitigate this, emphasis was on the art-making process, not the finished product.

The participants quickly became engaged. While some of them saw the experience as a way to break from their routinized boredom ("there ain't much to do here"), some participated to mitigate their troubles and improve how they saw themselves ("it helps to put my feelings on paper, and [this could be] something to keep me mellowed").

A new experience yields a new identity

Within the art therapy group, the young inmates were empowered toward self-expression, thereby highlighting their human-ness. The focus was not on their crimes, gang affiliation, or inmate status but rather on engaging in the process. From this, new identities emerged.

Introducing art materials to those who had previously been determined as unworthy created an opportunity for new interactional patterns and a dawning sense of self-worth. As they began to make art, new social interactions developed, and a shared art world between artist and viewer developed (Becker, 1982; Gilmore, 1990). As art making continued, the participants recognized that these objects – and by extension, they – were accepted.

Not just limited to the artists and their audience, interactions occur between the artists and their creative process, between and with the media used, between the artists and their products, and even between artworks within the creators' series (Wix, 1995). From these interactions, new self-appraisals solidify.

Through interactions, creation, exploration, and identification between therapist and client, client and art, and therapist and art, new inter-subjective meanings, realities, insights, and transformations emerge (Gerlitz et al., 2020). Once the creator feels validated, images may evolve into more complex and thought-inducing products. Simultaneously, as re-definitions and new self-labels become internalized, they can be concretized through interactions with others and eventually re-externalized.

Art making can help the creator begin to understand themselves and how they may become part of societal groups outside the prison walls. This becomes even more pronounced and significant if the materials available are scarce. Mastery over few materials demonstrates mastery over limitations.

Derek was a 21-year-old Black man, referred to the program for academic challenges due to an intellectual disability. He had been incarcerated for five years and was scheduled for release early the following year. Unfortunately, shortly after he began, the COVID-19 pandemic intervened, sharply curtailing art therapy. In response, the art therapy team developed a remote program by creating workbooks for inmates that could be completed in their respective dorms. While Derek had never made art prior to the program, he embraced the process. He even surprised himself: "Thanks for the help; I never thought it would work."

Derek remained engaged throughout the eight months that in-person interactions were suspended. He eventually began processing difficult emotions related to incarceration and the increased isolation due to COVID-19. His drawings became more detailed and his correspondence with the art therapist more introspective.

Early in the program's genesis, Derek was prompted to draw his perfect day, which reflected anticipation of his release ten months away. [Figure 7.1]. He drew a watchtower and himself outside a gate next to an Audi automobile. He labelled the hastily sketched features

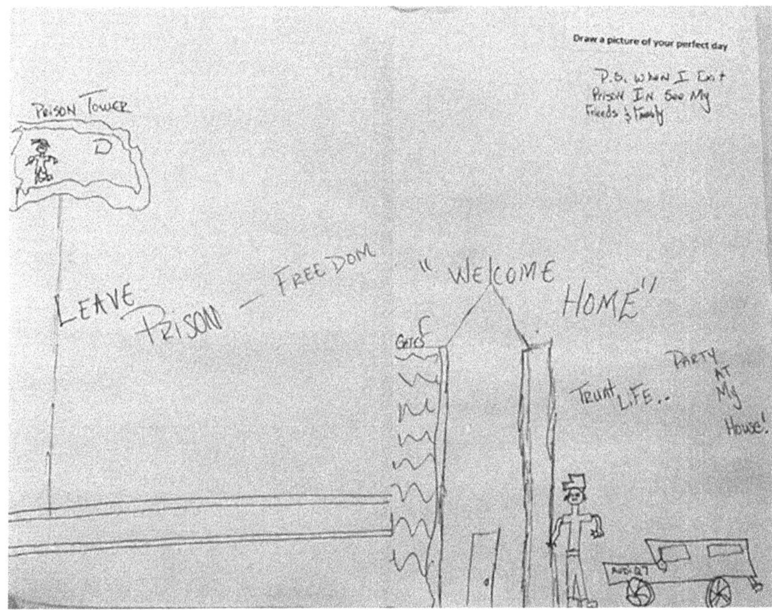

Figure 7.1 "Welcome Home"
Source: Derek

and wrote, "Welcome Home." It clearly and superficially represented wishful thinking.

Created eight months later, Figure 7.2 stands in stark contrast. Derek was prompted to create a road representing the direction he was going in life, including his options and obstacles. Although he somewhat deviated from the suggested instructions, this detailed image included a single road and a sign indicating an accompanying statement that reflected his feelings. His written response was a great deal more introspective than in his previous works:

> I had to change a lot of things, like ways of thinking, [and] people I choose to hang around." [I will leave prison with] "a clean sober mind". I hope to start a family with "a lot of property to raise animals [and] dogs . . . the biggest thing I got up my sleeve is don't let family down after what they done for me. . . . I'm ready to show the family what I learn . . . [and] becom[ing] a man after these 5 years.

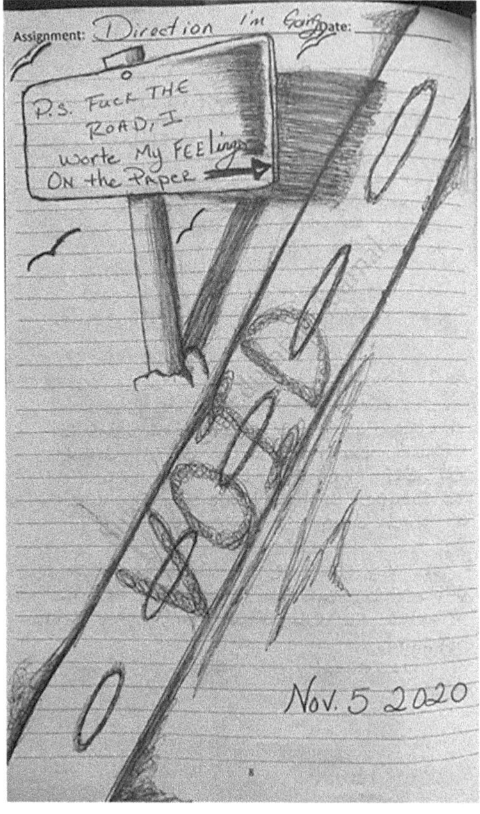

Figure 7.2 "Road Forward"

Source: Derek

His drawings moved beyond hasty sketches, reflecting more adept value change, shading, and complex composition. The new pictorial imagery revealed a transition from a defensive cognitive position to one that was more expressive and personal, surpassing the material's limitations. This change demonstrates success despite the lack of direct social interaction; a connection was created through the shared art products and Derek was seen and heard. As a result, his focus and investment improved significantly, and he considered potential opportunities more realistically. Over eight months, he had shifted from creating self-imposed, superficial fantasies to acknowledging his own responsibility in shaping a new identity without fear of judgment.

An art piece is an extension of the artist; if a piece of artwork is accepted by a gallery, by an audience, or for publication, by extension the creator is accepted. This has the power to reverse oppressive practices and may facilitate personal and social transformations.

Interactions between self and art can lead to personal re-labelling and a new identity, which then becomes externally accepted. In some cases, externalization and internalization happen simultaneously and in parallel.

The prisons in which the art therapy program was offered provided 12–16 hours of regimented programming for their youth offenders aimed at reducing institutional empty time. Undoubtedly, some students were hindered by this structure; those with more advanced skills grew bored, while others with cognitive, emotional, or behavioural challenges had difficulty engaging.

Despite such structure, there was still constant flux, contributing to ongoing frustration and confusion. This was compounded by inconsistency in programming due to the COVID-19 pandemic and related regulations. As a result, trust within the program was compromised.

It is common for those with poor self-appraisals to have issues with trust. This is magnified in prison where individuals remain hypervigilant and fearful, reinforced by a system that distrusts the inmates, solidifying poor self-concept (Gussak, 2019). This dynamic creates a challenge for art therapy.

At the time of this writing, the art-therapy-in-prisons program was re-establishing in-person group art therapy services after months of limited contact. The groups focused on re-building rapport and a sense of safety while practicing self-expression. Still, some negative self-appraisals remained.

Confronting hard-earned, negative self-appraisals

The participants often sought approval from the art therapist or each other. As the participants created, the art therapists were available to support those having difficulty. They were often met with self-deflating and rigid defences: "I can't draw," "It's no good."

One mindfulness exercise addressed self-awareness by asking the participants to notice, without judgement, sensations in their bodies. They were provided outlines of the human figure to draw where these sensations resided. Tommy, a 17-year-old man with a 2-year prison sentence, reported that he did not feel anything; his drawing reinforced this as he simply drew clothing on the figure. When asked if there was anything else he would like to add, he responded, "No, he doesn't deserve shoes," underscoring how often maladaptive self-perceptions were firmly ensconced. Still, the drawing provided valuable insight, allowing the team to provide a clearer plan.

Developing internal validation

The participants' internal and external interactions with the art materials, their products, and others around them strengthened. Nevertheless, their boundaries remained rigid. While participants seemed to relax in sessions, they often made light of topics or superficially focused on food or music.

However, they eventually engaged with the materials, explored their abilities and expressed their vulnerabilities. Trust was developing.

Carl was a 16-year-old boy sentenced to 2 years in prison for armed burglary. He drew Figure 7.3 quietly while the other group members

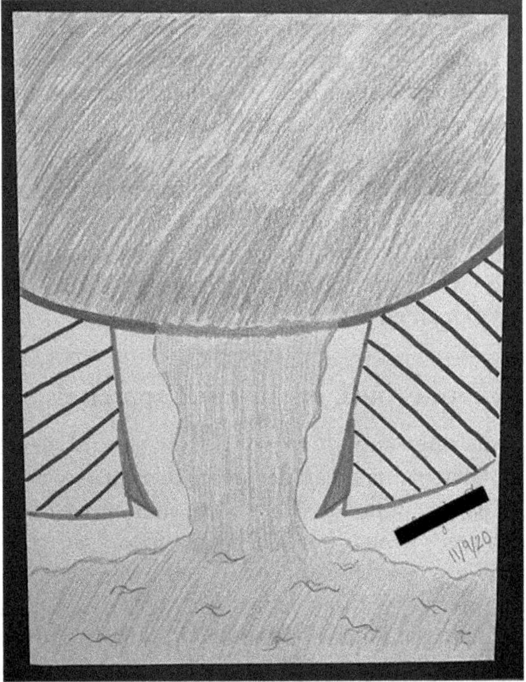

Figure 7.3 "The Dam Wall"

Source: Carl

talked amongst themselves. A curved barrier appears to open in the centre, allowing water to flow over the top. Above the wall is a starry night sky. While the flowing water and sky may reflect openness, his boundaries remained firm. Carl was beginning to open up but required patience. Trusting him to know when and how to do so would facilitate a stronger rapport, eventually leading to positive identity development. Paradoxically, limited verbal communication yet greater visual communication instigated positive interaction and a burgeoning affirming self-label. He was shifting from external validation to internal fortitude.

Externalizing internal states

Through art making, emotions originally suppressed emerge and are externalized (Bateman & Fonagy, 2004; Haeyen et al., 2015). This allows the maker to see and reflect on what they have said (Eisner, 2002). As the art process continues and the products evolve, so does the creator's self-conceptualization and perceived labels.

One particular art process helped the youth offenders identify the benefit of feelings and become aware of emotional states. It also focused on the fundamental elements of creative expression – colour, line, shape, and form – as a guide to visual communication.

Participants were provided coloured markers, white paper folded into quarters, and an emotion wheel delineating positive, negative, high-energy, and low-energy states of feeling. They were asked to choose a state that they identified with most often. Ronny's chosen state was *burnt-out* (Figure 7.4). When asked to choose a colour that represented this state, Ronny chose brown and, following instructions, coloured the first square. The second square contained a line, and the third a simple shape that reflected this chosen emotion. Ronny drew a trapezoid in the third square, and labelled it, "trap." He combined the first three elements to create an abstract composition in the fourth square.

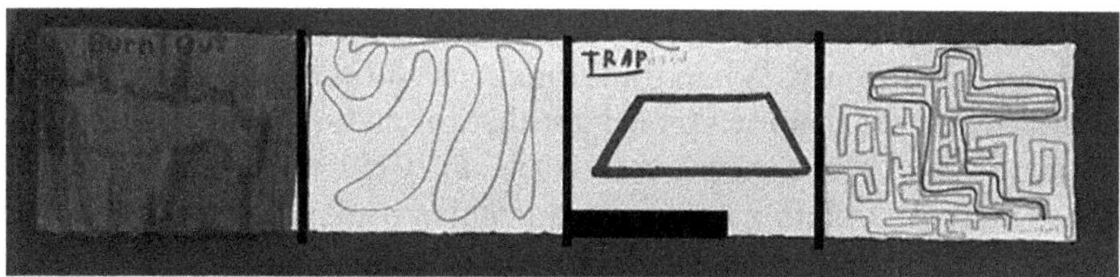

Figure 7.4 "Burnt-out"

Source: Ronny

Although a simple process, it provided him the opportunity to externalize his state for reflection and eventual acceptance. Providing such a mechanism that reinforced a sense of identity and positive self-appraisal eventually led to new labels.

Acceptance within an interactive web

Art making allows for the emergence of aesthetic forms of knowing, leading the creator to recognize symbolic expressions. In this way, art making can lead to constructing knowledge of self that emerges from reflection of the self and others. The resultant creations become part of an interactive web among person, environment, and thoughts that informs the emergence of a social identity (Dewey, 1930) and eventually promotes social change.

Private to public – being seen and accepted

In the same way that identity shifts depending on societal context (James, 1898/1918), so does one's art, depending on who interacts with the piece and under which circumstances. In other words, considering the context of the piece – whether it's part of a series, part of a temporal process, or stands alone – changes its meaning. Furthermore, as an extension of the self, when and how an art piece emerges is just as instrumental in helping establish a definable interaction. An art piece constructed in an art therapy session informs one kind of identity; once introduced to a gallery, that art – and by extension the artist – may be relabelled – oftentimes outside the control of the creator. Furthermore, similar to how an art piece changes as it's being completed – its middle passage differs from its preparatory state and from its final formation (Beittel, 1972) – a person's identity evolves depending on temporal and environmental influences.

Again, while an identity can be re-created through engagement with the art material *and* the self, it becomes important for others to engage with, receive, and value the products created. Art exhibitions allow for such an opportunity. While traditionally the idea of exhibiting works completed in art therapy seemed antithetical and, in some cases, detrimental to the therapeutic process (Garlock, 2019), the program considers an annual exhibition to be instrumental in recreating new, successful identities. Through such exhibitions, participants can present themselves and communicate through alternate means, speaking a language that is understood intrinsically by others on a human level. This platform not only allows the larger society to see the unseen but also allows an inmate to connect with individuals with whom they interact daily and who otherwise know them by their deviant/criminal identities.

Exposure to such artefacts alters negative perceptions about their value; presenting the tangible results of an arts program often demonstrates success. The art has the added benefit of increasing one's opportunity to reverse detrimental perspectives and oppressive labels. Eventually the positive perceptions become internalized and those inside begin to alter their self-appraisals.

Art products can be a significant catalyst for individuals to accept themselves, externalize feelings, experience validation, and create social connections. Art therapy can challenge existing societal labels and elicit openness, allowing the individual to consider new self-appraisals when reflecting on art products and themselves. In essence, it can rehumanize the dehumanized. As these new labels are adopted and evolve, lasting personal transformations are potentially created. Through ongoing social interactions, systemic acceptances of these new identities are solidified. As enough of these changes occur and new interactions within the systems expand, social transformation is inevitable.

References

Aguilar, D. N. (2014). Oppression, domination, prison: The mass incarceration of Latino and African American men. *The Vermont Connection*, *35*(2), 13–20.

Bartusch, D. J., & Matsueda, R. L. (1996). Gender, reflected appraisals, and labelling: A cross-group test of an interactionist theory of delinquency. *Social Forces*, *75*(1), 145–176.

Bateman, A., & Fonagy, P. (2004). *Psychotherapy for borderline personality disorder: Mentalization-based treatment*. Oxford University Press.

Becker, H. S. (1982). *Art worlds*. University of California Press.

Becker, H. S. (1991). *Outsiders: Studies in the sociology of deviance*. The Free Press.

Beittel, K. R. (1972). *Mind and context in the art of drawing: An empirical and speculative account of the drawing process and the drawing series and of the contexts in which they occur*. Holt, Reinhart and Winston.

Blumer, H. (1969). *Symbolic interactionism: Perspective and method*. University of California Press.

Brownfield, D., & Thompson, K. (2005). Self-concept and delinquency: The effects of reflected appraisals by parents and peers. *Western Criminology Review*, *6*(1), 22–29.

Cloward, R. A., & Ohlin, L. E. (2001). Illegitimate means and delinquent subcultures. In B. R. E. Wright & R. B. McNeal, Jr. (Eds.), *Boundaries: Readings in deviance, crime and criminal justice* (pp. 359–380). Pearson Custom.

Cooley, C. H. (1964). *Human nature and the social order*. Schocken.

Dewey, J. (1930). *Human nature and conduct: An introduction to social psychology*. The Modern Library.

Eisner, E. W. (2002). *The arts and the creation of mind*. Yale University Press.

Elkins, E., & Deaver, S. (2018). *Preliminary findings from 2016 AATA membership survey*. American Art Therapy Association. https://arttherapy.org/news-preliminary-findings-2016-aata-membership-survey/

Fox, W. M. (1997). The hidden weapon: Psychodynamics of forensic institutions. In D. Gussak & E. Virshup (Eds.), *Drawing time: Art therapy in prisons and other correctional settings* (pp. 43–55). Magnolia Street.

Garlock, L. R. (2019). Art for sale? In A. E. Di Maria (Ed.), *Exploring ethical dilemmas in art therapy:50 clinicians from 20 countries share their stories* (pp. 140–146). Routledge.

Gerlitz, Y., Regev, D., & Snir, S. (2020). A relational approach to art therapy. *The Arts in Psychotherapy*, 68. https://doi-org.proxy.lib.fsu.edu/10.1016/j.aip.2020.101644

Gilmore, S. (1990). Art worlds: Developing the interactionist approach to social organization. In H. S. Becker & M. M. McCall (Eds.), *Symbolic interaction and cultural studies* (pp. 148–178). The University of Chicago.

Gussak, D. E. (2019). *Art and art therapy with the imprisoned: Re-creating identity*. Routledge.

Haeyen, S., van Hooren, S., & Hutschemaekers, G. (2015). Perceived effects of art therapy in the treatment of personality disorders, cluster B/C: A qualitative study. *The Arts in Psychotherapy*, *45*, 1–10. https://doi-org.proxy.lib.fsu.edu/10.1016/j.aip.2015.04.005

Hagan, J. (2001). Seven approaches to the definition of crime and deviance. In B. R. E. Wright & R. B. McNeal, Jr. (Eds.), *Boundaries: Readings in deviance, crime and criminal justice* (pp. 1–12). Pearson Custom.

Hall, P. (1981). Structuring symbolic interaction: Communication and power. *Communication Yearbook*, *4*, 49-60.

James, W. (1890/1918). *The principles of psychology* (Vols. 1–2). Henry Holt and Company.

Kornfeld, P. (1997). *Cellblock visions: Prison art in America*. Princeton University Press.

Lauer, R. H., & Handel, W. H. (1977). *The theory and application of symbolic interactionism*. Houghton Mifflin.

Mead, G. H. (1964). *On social psychology*. University of Chicago Press.

Rubington, E., & Weinberg, M. (2002). *Deviance: The interactionist perspective*. Allyn and Bacon.

Sagarin, E. (1975). *Deviants and deviance: An introduction to the study of disvalued people and behavior*. Praeger.

Vigil, J. D. (2003). Urban violence and street gangs. *Annual Review of Anthropology*, *32*, 225–242.

Wix, L. (1995). The intern studio: A pilot study. *Art Therapy: Journal of the American Art Therapy Association*, *12*(3), 175–178.

Zimbardo, P. (2007). *The Lucifer effect: Understanding how good people turn evil*. Random House.

8 Socia(B)le art

Towards culture for all

Blaise Patrix (translation from French by Els Luberti)

Introduction

Opening up to the unforeseen by encounter in order to develop the creolisation of the world are words by the Martinican born poet and philosopher, Edouard Glissant (Torres, 2010). Among the thousand and one ways of changing the world by art, I choose to develop practices combining artistic creation and creativity to improve social ties.

In my view 'creation' describes the profession of the artist while 'creativity' is a state of any living being. Born in a family of artists, I became a painter. Numerous travels as a teenager and in particular my choice to live in the Sahel for twenty years led me to explore the social usefulness of art.

"A village without a stranger is a dead village". This Burkinabe proverb shows the importance of openness to others in order to optimise living together. Through this symbiotic way of considering the world I was in particular brought to put the diversity of points of view in perspective. The culture that received me also taught me as how to express and feel gratitude, which enabled me to develop a 'sociable view' on my work. This view is based on what I understand as the phenomenon of recognition, a theme that will be developed later.

Thus in parallel with the production in my studio, partnerships, formed on a case-by-case basis for thirty years, with education-, social work-, corporate- and/or urban development professionals, allowed me to involve diverse audiences while developing spontaneous co-creation methods called Art Socia(B)le. For seven years I have also been giving, as an external actor, theoretical and practical training to social work students, as well as to coaches, teachers, mediators, psychologists, and others. (See short video "Formation en Haute Ecole" in playlist: Socia(B)le Art-YouTube.)

As a result, anyone among a broad audience (participant, viewer, user) can easily engage in and become part of productions that carry

DOI: 10.4324/9781003105350-9

a strong message of solidarity, while recognising their own creative touch and that of others.

Principles of art socia(B)le – phenomena of recognition

"Changing by exchanging with each other, while remaining ourselves" (words of Edouard Glissant; Torres, 2010). Exploring and discovering oneself, the other, the common future, identifying and gratifying each other's particularities is what an exchange can bring us. I am convinced that the symbolic space, which the arts provide, helps us to feel and formulate signs of recognition. Therefore, it is a unique approach to encourage respect and development within a society.

In 1983, my attention was drawn to the importance of artistic signs of recognition and their effects on relationships by a proud farmer in a village in northern Burkina Faso. "That's us", one of the farmers said while pointing at the procession of masks at the funeral of a traditional high dignitary. The scarifications on his face were identical to the signs on the masks. Braided, pyrographed, dyed, these symbols still are used to decorate utensils, clothes – every detail of his daily life.

In France it was also said, not very long ago, that every village was proud of its bell tower. But in fact, the work of the architect, the sculptor, and the painter allow the villagers to recognise their distinctive characteristics. Signs gathered or replicated in the work of artist craftsmen in places of worship are then copied in daily life in the form of embroideries on traditional regional clothes, the furniture, the mantelpiece, the cornerstone at the threshold of the house. These signs mark with dignity the particularities of an ethnical, village, professional, and (or) family identity. They signify belonging: Here's what I am, I see who you are, what differentiates us, what brings us closer.

While specialisation tends to devaluate the creativity of artistic amateurs and while mass management is making individuals anonymous, soliciting individual and collective creativity as part of an art creation is a way of giving to all the right to exist and to contribute fully to the future of the world: A future in which each one can recognise himself and feel recognised.

In both elitist and popular art recognition is beneficial as it can be shared. Artist and viewer recognise themselves in the same work and yet they don't see the same thing. I even happened to see artists of opposing camps being mutually appreciative of each other's work during an armed conflict. Recognition is shared and allows, as we can see later, different points of view to be shared, including those that if raised in a discussion would lead to conflict.

From "I" to "we"

In order to ensure that 'being together' is regenerating for participants, being oneself is necessary. But who am I? Even before affiliating myself to archetypes, how should I approach the intimate and inexplicable particularity of my being? How to simultaneously explore my intuition, my impulses, my desires, my hopes, my will, my choices, my ideas, my sensitivity?

In painting, specifying details, using one colour rather than another, deciding where to place it, each choice relates to the intimate through which my personality is affirming itself, helps me to express it, and opens it to the other. Creativity is useful, in terms of exploration and identification. Who am I? Who are you? It helps to take one's responsibility in exchange with the others and to get an answer to the question: Who in fact are we and what kind of beautiful things can we make together?

Spontaneous co-creation

Nothing is set in stone. Everything is constantly changing; life is in perpetual movement. My body is the seat of my being. I was born in this body. My body is perceiving, feeling, analysing, breathing, and inspiring my presence. Being myself within a relationship means being fully in my body here and now. This factual immanence motivated my choice for soliciting spontaneity.

My experience confirms the importance of this choice. Spontaneous co-creation automatically frees those who have never painted before from their inhibition and generates meaning and **enthusiasm**: "at the beginning, I was afraid, I ended up singing. Step by step we found the **meaning**" a participant said after a workshop. Spontaneous co-creation also generates **pride** in its result, "I learned that nothing is ever lost, we always manage to make something good together", said another participant. Spontaneous co-creation generates **optimism**, helps us to recognise particularities, enables participants to compare themselves with one another, and ideas and emotions come together and are mixed. Also, these might interfere with and even contradict each other, nonetheless allowing a surprising image in which each person can recognise her/himself to emerge. This is illustrated in an example of the painting of a heart containing three religious symbols on a rainbow background that appears in a fresco that was carried out by 760 pupils and teachers from a school from which a former pupil, a fanatic, was one of the attackers of the Bataclan in Paris in 2015.

Figure 8.1 Interfaith painting

The practices of collective improvisation give a prominent place to amateur creativity, which is central to the creative process of Art socia(B)le and at whose service the (professional) artist puts his profession.

The methods of art socia(B)le

The methods of art socia(B)le aim to value personal and collective creativity of a given public in its daily surrounding. Better than the word 'individual', appropriate to what is indivisible, the word 'person' evokes an active being connected to the others. Calling 'person' and 'personality' 'individual' and 'individuality' strikes me as symbolically violent. As if a being's presence is denied to reduce him to a numerical quantity. Instead it's by the recognition of one's personal contribution that someone's sense of existing develops in a responsible way.[1] The approach is simple and easily adaptable to any kind of context. The most important features are addressed in the following paragraphs

The artist uses the products of spontaneous co-creation painting workshops, which are open to various audiences, to create works of urban art or design from paintings that are made around a circular base. More specifically, the artist's role is to unify the collective artwork. Also, in consultation with his partners, the artist studies the context, which includes identification of the public, actors, and spectators involved, definition of objectives and expected results, the eventual adoption of a theme, and the implementation of appropriate communication. In the case of a mural, the study includes the symbolic importance of the walls receiving the fresco and in the case of design creation, the type of postproduction that has been chosen and its mode of dissemination.

Partnerships are critical for the success of a project. Through partnerships, in my practice, developed on a case-by-case basis with urban development with education and social work professionals, a variety of outcomes have been realised. Partnerships have helped to encourage not only intercultural and interreligious dialogue but also mediation, social inclusion, and conflict management. Moreover, team spirit has been built while everyone was given the opportunity to express themselves freely within a shared process.

During workshops, any oral or visual information by any of the participants may help develop understanding of the situation in all of its complexity. It is important to emphasise that during the projects **all participants are equal**: relationships should be horizontal. As for the artistic direction, the artist interacts on an equal level with all the participants in order to connect their interventions. S/he will have to let go of his/her ego, look beyond personal convictions in order to accept without judgement the situation as it is. S/he thus smoothly integrates the unexpected in all its forms while paying close attention to identify and involve those with frustrated aspirations. In my workshops it is agreed that the participants in return allow the artist to use and reproduce their contributions.

The results are murals, frescoes, or prints in the form of, for example, communication tools, merchandise such as t-shirts, mugs, or earrings. To this day, creative workshops including thousands of participants have been involved in producing creations that have been seen by hundreds of thousands of spectators or users.

Figure 8.2 Installations in the public space of printed canvases: Brussels.

In Belgium for example, the exhibition of a printed banner resulting from the project called Soleils on the pediment of the Fédération Wallonie Bruxelles, which is located at a busy road in Brussels, for ten months, valued and shared the creative talents of women who had been victims of violence. This project raised awareness via visibility to the many motorists passing by about three specialised agencies that offer help to such victims.

Examples from Practice

Frescos and mural painting

(Please see videos "La Paix" and "Fresque participative" in playlist: Socia(B)le Art-YouTube.)

Depending on the case, co-creation of frescos on banners or mural painting involved between a few dozen to over 700 participants on 40 to 600m2 surfaces.

A delicate operation in times of armed conflict

In the summer of 2004, during the second intifada at a summer camp for the children of a small town in the occupied Palestinian territories on the West Bank, it was necessary, for example, to feign a provocative naivety.

Sheikh Yassin, leader of Hamas, had just been killed. Right here two months ago, civilians who entered the city in a civilian car publicly executed three youngsters in front of the terrace where they were drinking tea. Every afternoon, masked armed groups, fist raised, were marching through the main street. Their powerlessness against the occupation army was creating high tension between two clandestine rebel units whose graffiti of belligerent slogans were competing in overlapping each other on the city walls. Approaching their members directly was not possible because of their fear of being identified.

The mayor allowed me to use any of the walls of the school. "The authors of the graffiti should have the courage to write on their own houses instead of putting our children at risk", he said. Incursions of the occupation army, who could charge the pupils with subversion, are frequent.

Two nineteen-year-old high school students served as interpreters. Prior to my invention in the city, a three day workshop at the headquarter of a school allowed me to choose about twenty of the most extroverted children among a group of sixty, aged seven to fourteen. I took care to earn their trust so that they would follow my order to get away if a military convoy entered the city. Those who would throw stones risk going to prison.

I pretended to paint on the wall of the martyrs. This wall is twenty meters long and frames the main entrance of a large school. Photos of Sheikh Yassin and the three local victims are stuck above two monumental calligraphies. The largest one, in green, is clearly the one of Hamas. Next to it is the red mark of the Fattah, which is smaller. Our little group was putting paint cans and cases with brushes on the pavement. We started singing and forming a chain in order to remove some bricks that are stored against the wall. Our intention to paint on this highly symbolic wall became clear now. Two young men ran up to us and cried out:

"We're not from Hamas!"

"Aaahh! OoooK!"

"But not over there, NO!"

"I'm surprised, I called the municipality, who gave me free choice."

A municipal officer, looking very worried, arrived. A crowd gathered. The discussion became animated.

"Our intention is to honour this place. Of course, we're not going to cover the photos, we're not going to cover the green logo either."

"NO WAY!" our interlocutors were asking us then to intervene only on the part of the wall with the red logo.

The municipal agent then proposed that we choose the adjacent wall: three hundred fifty square meters over eighty meters long (my untold dream).

Accepted! The workshop could start. 170 children were participating.

On the morning of the third day of the workshop "Qassam, free Palestine" appeared inscribed vertically so as to preserve the existing paintings. At the other end of the fresco "Al Aqsa" features a depiction of the emblematic mosque. Both parties were respecting each other's intervention.

With the exception of a photo of a new victim that was stuck the following year on a depiction of the separation wall, at the corner of the street, the fact that the work remained intact for eight years until it faded in the sunlight shows acceptance by the people. The organisers of the summer camp then asked for a new intervention of Art socia(B)le to celebrate its tenth anniversary. For this time a theme was chosen entitled "advancement of women and freedom of speech" (please see video "Strong together" in playlist: Socia(B)le Art).

Share the rainbow

The project "Share the rainbow" carried out in 2009, showed that maintaining such a sense of gratitude in a rather more individualistic cultural background requires more constant monitoring.

Bullet holes in a corridor leading to the Brussels subway show the aggression of about twenty young people who meet here every day. The objective of the program aimed to promote the reappropriation by all the local residents of the passage while making a fresco on the theme of sustainable development issues.

A poster and flyer campaign were launched. Meetings with the community network, local schools, and awareness-oriented organisations made it possible to get in touch with the young people. With their consent and their participation, 650 persons of all generations helped to realise a mural fresco of about 120 m^2 in ten days. "We didn't know we were able to paint such a beautiful thing" we heard at the inauguration.

After ten months degradations reappeared in the corridor, in the area where the young people get together. "We have little chance finding a job, we're bored, we get drunk, we mess around", "We need you", "Come more often", they told me. Together with the most motivated ones a second phase of the project was designed. One day a month for fourteen months, seven young people were trained and paid to engage passers-by of all generations in painting. Their self-esteem improved, and three of them got jobs in the city. Unfortunately the action has not been followed up. Over time, confidence between generations, being insufficiently supported in this way, has faded away, and degradations of the corridor have reappeared.

Suns (soleils): painting-in-circle-workshops

During the 'painting-in-circle' workshops, participants are invited to paint together around a circular base. Between 3 and 20 people arrange themselves around the same table or on the floor. The diameter depends on the number of participants. Various collective works, sort-of suns, all radiant from traces of the spontaneous encounters that have produced it, are thus created.

Circle formation changes the game. Collective energy encourages the participants to surpass themselves. No matter if a participant's artwork overlaps with another's – these tangled outcomes will always produce something meaningful. This type of workshop is sometimes followed by a discussion reviewing the experience through viewing

Figure 8.3 Project "Dear Neighbor", Brussels

together photos projected on a screen for viewing of the produced works. The artist creates colourful items (banners, mugs, or other items) with this material to publicise that carry a strong message of solidarity. These can reach many spectators: from the community or passing through.

Another example: the exhibition at popular events of the flags from the itinerant installation "Bonjour Voisin, Beste Buurman" decks the streets of Brussels in the colours of the participation at "painting-in-circle workshops" in which over 7,000 Brussels residents participated since 2007 in various contexts.

A workshop that was held in a shelter for female victims of violence

The workshop took place on the ground floor of a typical Brussels house with two rooms in a row opening out onto a small garden on one side and onto a street on the other. A poster next to the window facing the street warned: "Ladies, don't come too close – you might be seen from the outside". The address is kept secret. Twelve women are accommodated in this house for a three-month period during which they receive psychological and legal support. A circular table with a canvas to be painted on was set up in each room. Participants could move freely between the two tables. A third table with materials has been set up between the tables.

From the first brushstrokes silence reigned and not a single word was said; the participants were fully concentrated on what they were doing. "The painter is depicting himself when he's painting and his hand is delivering his soul", as the artist Jacques Lagrange wrote (Patrix, 2019).

For these women as well, the act of painting releases the expression of their innermost self: a woman created a heart pierced by a knife, “I’ve seen my husband stab my son”, she confided later. Another woman painted herself on her knees with her arms in the air and an embryo in the womb. Over there appeared a house without a door, two windows were placed, each as far away as possible from the other, in the upper corners of the rectangular façade. Above this rectangle the roof planes formed a triangle with a question mark in its centre. While objectivising their cases – which were taking shape from their brushes– the sense of unease was moving away from them.

Others reported their pride to feel comforted by their stay in the shelter. A self-portrait highlights opulent wavy blond hair. “For years I haven’t been to a hairdresser”, said the creator. A smile was drawn upon an image of a broken mirror: “I’m happy, by breaking the mirror, to be rid of the image that it was sending to me”.

Energy decreased after an hour; one by one the women stopped painting to go to the adjoining hallway where some chairs and a couch, tea, and coffee awaited them. However, their activity was not finished yet. We heard them whispering while we were putting away the materials.

Though obviously no interaction occurred between the participants during the time of painting, the decision made after consultation is optimistic. It seems that looking at each other, which was enabled by the setup in a circle, had encouraged them to share information that would normally be shared only in private discussions. Seeing each other in an identical situation they felt solidarity, and this stimulated their optimism.

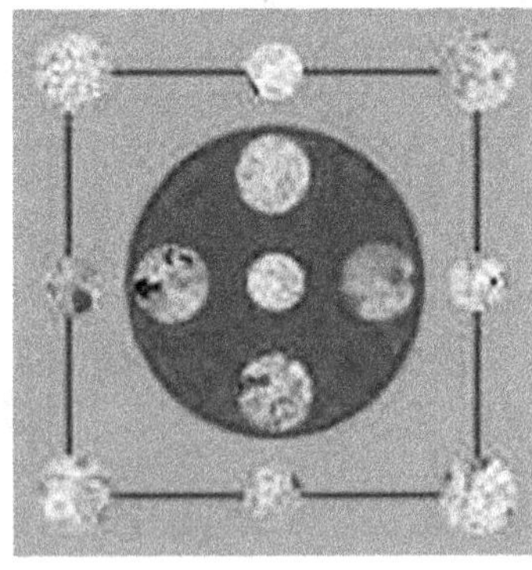

Figure 8.4 Support for female victims of violence. Addis Abbebba (Ethiopia)

Suddenly, before we could take care of the second table, eleven of them came back to it and started painting a pink background on which they wrote, using all the colours that were available, the positive words: love, family, education, wellbeing, respect. . . . When they put down their brushes again and went back to sit down, the twelfth woman, who was more reserved, got up and added, in very small writing, the word *hope*.

Therapeutic virtues of "painting-in-circle-workshops"

In addition to facilitation, the artist provided training and assistance, which allowed non-artists (teachers, social workers, coaches) to initiate their own additional creative workshops and to give the results to the artist. This practise provides a playful and attractive tool to offer professional support of persons in distress.

Hence over several years, the project "SOLEILS" assisted the activity of three Belgian organisations that work to support female victims of violence. One of the reception centres sought to familiarise current shelter residents with former shelter residents. Since the women met for a workshop, a printed banner has adorned the entrance of the centre. A second organisation had been working to restore mother-child relationships and distributed "Soleil" key rings with the emergency number. The third one created a screen for theatrical animation sessions. In addition, fifteen of the sixty beneficiaries were occasionally

Figure 8.5 Welcoming migrants in Frankfurt am Oder (Germany): murals

employed and paid to lead creative workshops for visitors of popular events in the centre.

At the end of the project, as mentioned earlier, a large, printed banner hung for six months on the pediment of the Fédération Wallonie Bruxelles facing a very busy thoroughfare. This allowed the organisations to communicate their message to the general public in a way that was highly visible to many motorists.

An art that gives hope

Anchorage, milestone, astonishment, inclusion, coexistence, dignity, intuition, common future – the methods of socia(B)le art explore and analyse on multiple levels the complexity of the world. Through the artworks they allow participants to familiarise themselves with the other. The workshops arouse curiosity, deconstruct preconceptions, bring out unexpected and astonishing signs of recognition. With freedoms acquired since the late nineteenth century, socia(B)le art takes creation out of individualism to make it an optimistic way of learning how to live together. A hope for a savoir vivre that is respectful for everyone is born from the project and uplifts the path of culture for and by all.

Note

1 Better than the word 'individual' appropriate to what is indivisible, the word "person" evokes an active being connected to the others. Calling "person" and "personality" "individual" and "individuality" strikes me as symbolically violent. As if a being's presence is denied to reduce him to a numerical quantity. Instead it's by the recognition of one's personal contribution that someone's sense of existing develops in a responsible way.

References

Patrix, B. (2019, Décembre). *Précisions d'un de ses fils Blaise Patrix au sujet de Michel Patrix*. www.le-musee-prive.com/207-biographies-artistes-contemporains/2274-precisions-d-un-de-ses-fils-blaise-patrix-au-sujet-de-michel-patrix-decembre-2019.html

Torres, F. J. S. (2010). Edouard Glissant (1928–2011). *Caribbean Studies*, *38*(2), 149+. https://link.gale.com/apps/doc/A270895739/AONE?u=anon~35037b68&sid=googleScholar&xid=c8e811f6

9 Jamming through life

Social complexity and the arts

Erik Jansen and Paola de Bruijn

Being a citizen in contemporary societies can be daunting. The crises and changes that one has to deal with are rapid and spawn insecurity and existential threats to the lives we aspire to live. Social workers often are the first professionals to meet people facing such crises. In this chapter, we focus on dealing with social complexity as a central, existential matter of concern to social work.

Several authors have emphasised that social complexity in contemporary Western European societies is increasing and have noted that coping with it is a difficult and often daunting task for individuals, requiring special abilities and opportunities (Bauman, 2007; van Ewijk, 2014). However, these abilities and opportunities are not equally distributed among people, thus leading to new and increasing social injustices, often with an existential overtone. It has been proposed that improvisation is an adequate behavioural strategy in dealing with complex societal issues in particular (e.g., Boutellier, 2013) and postmodern epistemological and ontological complexity in general (Kroese & Jansen, 2016).

In this chapter, we explore the question: how can artistic practices form opportunities for vulnerable people to experience ways to handle complexity at large and transformative individual or collective questions in particular?

Rationale

What is the nature of this complexity? What exactly is complex about the lives we live? We have discerned three existential crises. First, it is possible to speak of a *social crisis*, which materialises in the ever-increasing and involuntary separation and inequality among groups of people, notably the haves versus the have-nots, abled versus disabled,

DOI: 10.4324/9781003105350-10

privileged versus marginalised, elites versus commoners (Bauman, 2007; Latour, 2018; van Ewijk, 2014). Second, as a result of postmodernist cultural developments we seem to have entered an *epistemic crisis*, in which predefined categories are insufficient for grappling with reality (e.g., Deleuze & Guattari, 2005) and in which (scientific) knowledge and science are no longer valued institutions – a situation which has become reality in the post-truth era in politics (Neiman, 2017). Third, existing values relating to how we live our lives economically, as well as socially, are increasingly being questioned or exposed as unsustainable as they are based on mechanisms of extraction and instrumentalization (Latour, 2018), leading to an ethical crisis. Particularly the latter forces us to ideologically reorient towards new sets of values to anchor the lives we aspire to lead.

Whereas these existential crises may not overtly appear in everyday life, they do lead to symptoms that affect it and yield it as increasingly *liquid* (Bauman, 2007). Accordingly, the lives we used to live are becoming less stable and dependable in many ways, often based on circumstances and events beyond individual control, such as economic crises, global conflicts, or pandemics. Thus, we are left in a dependent state, bereft of a sense of control over our own fates. This leads to questions such as: Who do I want to be? What group do I belong to? What is my identity? How secure are my basic conditions for quality of life? What can I influence with my decisions, and what are my dependencies? What are my aspirations and how, if at all, can I realise them? Moreover, whether these existential questions can be answered adequately depends on one's individual capacities and the opportunities one is offered, and it is a well-established fact that both capacities and opportunities are distributed unequally across populations. This leads to a new type of unjust inequality: inequality between being capable of handling social complexity and existential insecurity versus not being able (van Ewijk, 2014).

Dealing with the consequences of the loss of existential ground as a result of social, epistemic, and ethical crises requires the practical wisdom to find new foundations; it requires one to acquire or apply new skills in dealing with one's practical reality. Thus, on a personal level, individuals in today's societies need to transform their practical reasoning to adapt to the complex and liquid world, but groups and collectives also need to develop similar skills in collectively transforming to withstand the global threats of collective life on our planet such as increasing health inequalities and climatic unsustainability. In what follows we argue that artistic activities can yield special opportunities to learn how to transform individually or collectively by learning to improvise (see also Muijen & Brohm, 2018). In other words: how can we jam our way through life on earth as it reveals itself in the here and now? Before we arrive at the arts as a potential avenue, we explore the issue of social complexity further.

Theoretical approach

Social complexity

Based on the previous points, we acknowledge that complex societal crises confront human beings with fundamental and existential questions about what it means to be a human being at this time and on this earth. These questions are not easily answered and may impose existential fears. In all, the mere sense that what one is capable of today might prove insufficient tomorrow is a social and psychological stress factor. How should one deal with such complexity in our social environments?

In the field of governance studies, Boutellier (2013) argues that in the face of increasingly networked and globalising societies, governments and public institutions fail to adequately respond to complexifying circumstances in a top-down and planned fashion. Improvisation, which is defined in detail later, is an appropriate way to deal with such complexity, because it allows individual actors in a system to respond within their own fields of influence, thereby designing and adapting their collective behaviour in a bottom-up, responsive fashion (Boutellier & Trommel, 2018). Moreover, improvisational approaches in art therapy apply a similar rationale to enhance individual transformation using methods in which art-based process development sparks psychological transformation by analogy and experiential insight (Smeijsters, 2005). Thus, acquiring new skills by improvising within a certain field may be a promising way forward for both individual and collective transformation. This resonates with the concept of practical reason as an essential human capability as Nussbaum (2012) proposed. Therefore, being capable of improvisation puts one at a considerable advantage in a challenging and changing world – even more so, if we consider the state of contemporary society in which, as discussed earlier, uncertainty and insecurity is paramount. How can vulnerable individuals enhance such skills?

Art and epistemic resources

Art-based methods have a long-standing but not so well-documented tradition in social work practice (Huss, 2019). Social workers, for instance, apply artistic means to motivate and engage people in processes of empowerment, identity formation, and social cohesion along with verbal or cognitive means or skills. Many social work curricula involve acquiring some forms of creative or arts-based skills. However, this often involves the instrumental use of art-based methods: art is used as a tool to enhance some other social process or asset that is of value (de Bruijn & Jansen, 2019; Jansen, 2018).

Our current argument for the application of the arts is based on the epistemic qualities of the arts. Art connects to ways of knowing other than verbal or propositional and in this way manifests epistemic resources that allow one to understand the circumstances and causalities of one's life (Jansen, forthcoming). Particularly in times of social complexity, it is vital for human wellbeing to understand and appreciate the circumstances and relationships with which one engages: if losing one's job amidst times of economic prosperity or having to flee a disaster-struck homeland was never an anticipated future, one needs to come to terms with this. Concepts and categories that adequately describe these situations form epistemic resources as sensemaking devices, enabling a person to understand what is happening to her/him while it is happening and thereby gaining control over matters of concern (Fricker, 2007). Additionally, Prinzhorn (1922) described the intrinsic human need to express and to interpret oneself as a constant factor in life and one of the six fundamental motives essential for the creative process. Furthermore, he also emphasised the desire to play, the need to decorate, the need to order, the desire to imitate, and the need to attribute meaning to the intangible (Prinzhorn, 1922). An example of this concept is provided in our case description to follow.

Moreover, in situations where some have structural access to epistemic resources to appreciate a complex world and others do not, rebalancing these ways of knowing for the benefit of the least well-off helps to counter epistemic injustice (see Fricker, 2007) and is therefore well within the action scope of social work. A good way to do this is to find the applicable concepts and causalities as they reveal themselves in the world along the way and get a handle on life while new things happen or old things fall apart. This, in essence, aligns with the special skill of improvisation.

Improvisation as exercising agency

How should we define improvisation? According to several authors (Cobussen, 2017; Goldman, 2016) there is no clear and agreed upon definition of (artistic) improvisation and each context will bring its own essential characteristics based on the substantive domain, which in the case of these authors is music. For instance, in the neuro-cognitive study of musical behaviour, improvisation tends to be viewed as consisting of the unique brain processes that constitute *novelty*, *spontaneity*, and *freedom* (Goldman, 2016). In the field of creativity research, it tends to be associated with specific problem-solving behaviours (e.g., Lemons, 2005), whereas when seen from the perspective of complexity studies, it is the process leading to a specific configuration of causal relations also referred to as an assemblage (Boutellier, 2007; Fox & Alldred, 2016). The commonality between these conceptions of improvisation seems to be their concern for balancing *freedom* and *autonomy* in the face of contextual limitation and constraint. Moreover, improvisation involves a way of real-time coping with circumstances. Or according to Iyer (2004, p. 164), improvisation is "the real-time interaction with the structure of one's environment". Environment can be interpreted in a broad or in a narrow sense: it may either involve all surrounding physical, social, and psychological structures, including the cognitive frames that define one's world view, or it may pertain to a specific artistic setting with limited materials and strict application rules. These context-specific conceptions notwithstanding, the reigning principle remains: balancing autonomy and freedom with contextual limitation in ways that are novel and spontaneous. By broadening the definition of improvisation in this way we can create scope for methodically designing situations in which improvisation can be practiced and learned at various levels of abstraction.

In a way, improvisation is a cornerstone of all forms of art (Cobussen, 2017), although some art forms (such as jazz music or some forms of drama) capitalise more strongly on improvisational behaviour. But what is the difference between improvisation and creativity? We see at least three differences. First, our definition of improvisation entails an in-action process aspect; creativity is not necessarily an inaction process. Second, in some definitions improvisation is associated with novelty, but it does not necessarily entail it. If one improvises, the solutions found need not be novel; it is sufficient if they are adequate for coping with circumstance. Third, what we generally call creativity may in fact be described better by improvisation, as the latter integrates both productive behaviour and the constraining contextual arrangements and thus includes an adaptive function. The concept of creativity does not necessarily entail such adaptivity, although of course, one can argue that creativity is fuelled by having limitations.

This conception of improvisation capitalises on balancing autonomy and limitation in novel and spontaneous ways and can be related to the broader concept of agency. Claassen (2016) considers *freedom* and *autonomy* as the core elements of human agency: whereas the former involves the conscious evaluation and weighing of options one has in one's daily life practice, the latter involves acting in accordance with one's desires or aims. In other words: as agents, human beings deal with what they perceive as circumstances, opportunities, and challenges. Thus, without cutting short life goals and aspiration as important drivers for what it means to be a human being, while pursuing these, we are confronted with having to balance our agency with opportunity offered by our surroundings. And this is also the basic pattern that we just described as improvisation. Thus, if one improvises in a specific artistic setting, one exercises agency in a micro-context. And this can easily be viewed as *rehearsing* for the real thing in the real world.

Furthermore, experientially, improvising often induces a mental state of flow in which one experiences agency to the fullest. This is illustrated by a phenomenological study by Csikszentmihalyi (2008) in which jazz musicians and basketball players report experiencing a heightened and enjoyable state of consciousness in similar abstract terms, while they are engaged in successful improvisation or jamming. Thus, improvising is also enjoyable and emphasises feeling competent.

This raises the question of how we can learn improvisational skills in practice. Smeijsters (2005) proposed an analogue process model for the art therapy, to indicate that experiences in the artistic domain can induce psychological processes that mirror processes in our everyday lives. Therefore, artistic experiences can form a micro-world in which we can gain knowledge about how things work. In new sociological materialist terms: in artistic space, we form assemblages or constructions as models for how things in the world operate (Fox & Alldred, 2016). Compare this to a child's play with Lego bricks, in which a Lego built model allows the child to recreate or anticipate real-life situations. Whereas with Lego we refer to concrete situations, artistic experiences (musical experiences in particular) often have ineffable qualities (Jankélévitch, 2003) – they express processes or ideas of an abstract nature that do not necessarily refer to objects in the real world but nonetheless signify meaning. Knowledge about these abstract qualities is indeed valuable and reflects the epistemic resources we seek, but it may be quite specific to the discipline of art. In other words, a certain degree of skill is required for any improvisation exercise in an artistic playing field.

Case study: mask-making

We illustrate our argument by describing a case from a Dutch intervention using social-artistic improvisation in which social workers supported refugees suffering from addiction who received intensive social care and housing assistance in a residential community. The case focuses on social-work education, more precisely a student placement with a final practical assignment.

Consider the following: as part of their obligatory visual arts education in the social work practical curriculum, second-year students were required to design a social-artistic activity during their placement. The practical skills they had to develop were: [1] increasing craftsmanship in visual art, [2] demonstrating the added value of this craftsmanship as a (future) professional, and [3] showing how these professional skills can be meaningfully applied in the practice of the social work. The point of departure in this case was that students themselves experienced creative thinking and acting, inspired by real-life examples. One of the activities the students had to plan was to apply a creative design to an addiction treatment intervention.

One student visited her clients at home on a regular basis. For this specific assignment, she had set herself two goals: first, to improve the self-confidence of two clients and second, to enable and encourage them to participate in the community. Prior to carrying out the assignment, this student discussed some of the possible ways to achieve these goals with her professor, but she felt incapable of starting off on the right track with the clients. Then the professor inquired about the student's own home interior, which led to an inspiring, reflective conversation about the role of art and artifacts in one's house and how raising this subject can initiate alternative ways of contact and enhance deeper modes of understanding.

With regained confidence, the student then asked clients to come to her office, in pairs, where she asked them to draw a self-portrait in the form of a mask. During the student's home visits, the clients had never spoken about why they had had to flee from their home countries, having endured serious traumas from the war they had experienced. The student's aim became to offer them the opportunity to open their hearts and to air their feelings about what they had experienced, expressing their experience in pictures, instead of words. While drawing the masks, clients told their stories and gave voice to their pasts. Afterwards, the clients shared their experiences about participating in the mask-making activity. As the student expressed it, "My clients opened up". By playing with her ingenuity and imagination, the student showed that she had developed skilful improvisation. She stated that her thinking and acting had shifted from focusing on a methodical routine to aiming for better understanding of the behaviour and needs of both clients and attuning her actions to what she deemed necessary, using artistic means along the way.

This case shows that the student learned to improvise by exploring the boundaries of her professional abilities as well as her conception of professional practice. By investigating what limited her in the situation, she was able to find novel ways to overcome those limitations. Inspired by a new way of observing and engaging via the use of physical materials and the mask-making, the student adopted a more relational attitude in her meetings with the clients. In other words, she "unmasked" her previous approach to practice. This worked well for the clients but also turned her feeling of methodical incapability into a deeper sense of professionality. She concluded that, from then on, she would engage her clients more holistically, irrespective of the substantive methodological goals.

The focus on materials, surroundings, and the creative activity of mask making were essential elements enabling the student to experience a transformative process and allowing her to improvise – or to jam her way through being stuck in the assignment. This enabled both student and professor to uncover the analogous patterns within the arts and the real world (Smeijsters, 2005), which required both their social and artistic skills and insights. A promising way of systematically uncovering such analogous patterns with art-based methods is the visual thinking strategies method (Yenawine, 2013) which we adapted to further focus on psycho-social processes (de Bruijn & Jansen, 2019) or the art dialogue and method by Muijen and Brohm (2018).

Conclusion

Because improvisation allows one to acquire epistemic resources that are so vital to surviving the current era of increasing complexity (van Ewijk, 2014) and allows one to deal with the constantly changing and insecure circumstances (Bauman, 2007), it is vital that individuals acquire improvisational skills as a means for dealing with complexity in their lives. Moreover, if this is what contemporary societies require, being unable to improvise will create new inequalities, and the increasing complexity in the world will continue to create an unjust divide between those who are able to deal with it and those who are not (van Ewijk, 2014). In fact, based on the rationale presented, we can extend this to assert that being unable to exhibit improvisational behaviour is an infringement of one's agency and therefore of one's humanity.

Further, we argued that improvisation involves being able to match autonomy with existing contextual structures for new purposes in novel, free, and spontaneous ways. Having this ability is not obvious and has always been distributed unevenly across the general population. Following our argument, we outlined a strategy of how art-based activities can provide opportunities to learn such skills collectively to counter forms of epistemic injustice. This can be done with an individual focus on the one hand – allowing one to come to terms with existential questions on the complexity of one's life – but also with a collective focus aiming to engage in transformative societal change.

How do social work and art fit in this picture? The social work profession deals with social matters of concern that call for social change. Epistemic injustice around complexity is one such matter of concern given that the great societal transformations ahead require humanity to respond by adopting collective action. The transformative power of art hides a constructive value that combines the value of art as art (the intrinsic meaning of art), as well as the external benefits art yields (the instrumental function of art), to typically affect how groups and individuals relate to each other and to their material environment.

Art makes people more sensitive to existential dimensions of life. Through art people are able to explore options. To reconcile with reality, using improvisation in the practice of art supports openness and sensibility, as well as engagement in working with people on existential questions (de Bruijn, forthcoming). This social side of art, in which existing social or cognitive structures are disputed and which requires participants to improvise, provides the main scope for its transformative powers.

Scope for transformational social work practice

What can this argument contribute to social work practice in using improvisation as a means for transformation? At the individual level, first of all, it could inspire social workers to gain insight into service-users' and community-dwellers' dilemmas and issues as symptomatic for reconciliation of life in the fast-changing liquid age. Second, improvisation-focused activities may reveal what kind of successful strategies for existential coping or solutions participants can come up with. Third, it offers alternative strategies for the less-abled and a transfer of skills and stimulation of their imagination, thereby expanding their capability. Improvisation activities, if well designed, will thus yield empowerment effects for individual participants. And, fourth, as we saw in our case example, this opens up novel strategies for social work practitioners.

By learning how to improvise in an artistic domain, the arts form a playground in which one can learn how to jam (improvise) through the troubles and complexities of one's life, as an upbeat method to collectively address the existential issues facing human life on earth.

References

Bauman, Z. (2007). *Liquid times: Living in an age of uncertainty*. Polity Press.

Boutellier, H. (2013). *The improvising society: Social order in a boundless world*. Eleven Publishers.

Boutellier, J. C. J. (2007). *Nodal order: Security and citizenship in a network society*.

Boutellier, J. C. J., & Trommel, W. A. (Eds.). (2018). *Emerging governance: Crafting communities in an improvising society*. Eleven Publishers.

Claassen, R. (2016). An agency-based capability theory of justice. *European Journal of Philosophy*, *25*(4), 1279–1304.

Cobussen, M. (2017). *The field of musical improvisation*. Leiden University Press.

Csikszentmihalyi, M. (2008). *Creativity: Flow and the psychology of discovery and invention*. HarperCollins Publishers Inc.

de Bruijn, P. (forthcoming). *The existential matters: The heart of art in social work*. Unpublished doctoral dissertation. National University of Ireland.

de Bruijn, P., & Jansen, E. (2019). Enhancing capabilities for social change with the arts. In E. Huss & E. Bos (Eds.), *Art in social work practice: Theory and practice: International perspectives*. Routledge.

Deleuze, G., & Guattari, F. (2005). *A thousand plateaus*. University of Minnesota Press.

Fox, N. J., & Alldred, P. (2016). *Sociology and the new materialism: Theory, research, action*. Sage.

Fricker, M. (2007). *Epistemic injustice: Power and the ethics of knowing*. Oxford University Press.

Goldman, A. J. (2016). Improvisation as a way of knowing. *Music Theory Online*, *22*(4), 1–20.

Huss, E. (2019). Arts in social work practice: From theory to practice, an introductory chapter. In E. Huss & E. Bos (Eds.), *Art in social work practice: Theory and practice: International perspectives*. Routledge.

Iyer, V. (2004). Improvisation, temporality and embodied experience. *Journal of Consciousness Studies*, *11*, 159–173.

Jankélévitch, V. (2003). *Music and the ineffable*. Princeton University Press.

Jansen, E. (2018). Art and creativity as capability: Utilizing art in social work education. *Social Dialogue*, *19*, 33–36.

Jansen, E. (forthcoming). *Art as capability*. Manuscript in preparation.

Kroese, W., & Jansen, E. (2016). Tussen vast en vloeibaar [Between fixed and fluid]. *Tijdschrift voor Vaktherapie*, *2016*(4), 21–29.

Latour, B. (2018). *Waar kunnen we landen? Politieke oriëntatie in het Nieuwe Klimaatregime* [Down to earth? Political orientation in the New Climatic Regime]. Octavo.

Lemons, G. (2005). When the horse drinks: Enhancing everyday creativity using elements of improvisation. *Creativity Research Journal*, *17*(1), 25–36. doi:10.1207/s15326934crj1701_3

Muijen, H., & Brohm, R. (2018). Art dialogue methods: Phronèsis and its potential for restoring an embodied moral authority in local communities. *British Journal of Guidance & Counselling*, *46*(3), 349–364.

Neiman, S. (2017). *Resistance and reason in post-truth times*. Lemniscaat.

Nussbaum, M. C. (2012). Who is the happy warrior? Philosophy, happiness research, and public policy. *International Review of Economics*, *59*(4), 335–361. https://doi.org/10.1007/s12232-012-0168-7

Prinzhorn, H. (1922). *Bildnerei der Geisteskranken: ein Beitrag zur Psychologie und Psychopathologie der Gestaltung* [Artistry of the mentally ill]. Verlag von Julius Springer.

Smeijsters, H. (2005). *Sounding the self: Analogy in improvisational music therapy*. Barcelona Publishers.

van Ewijk, H. (2014). *Omgaan met sociale complexiteit: Professionals in het sociale domein* [Dealing with social complexity: Professionals in the social domain]. SWP.

Yenawine, P. (2013). *Visual thinking strategies: Using art to deepen learning across school disciplines*. Harvard Education Press.

10 Social arts for recognition

Sociological perspectives on arts and youth identities

Anna Smirnova and Nina Poluektova

Introduction

The new risks in the modern world caused by economic and political crises, social problems, global changes in educational systems and labour markets have created new challenges that can be added to the traditional developmental tasks for young people. The most crucial personal task in young age is the development of identity in terms of better self-understanding and the ability to find one's own place in the world or 'stability constants'. Increased options for behaviour and lifestyles, conflicts between adolescent peer values and parental or societal values, increased diversity and pluralism, and immigration and globalisation all mean that symptoms of identity problems are on the rise (Arnett, 2004). Studies show that identity distress is a very real issue for many young people, with approximately 14% of youth in 'regular' school populations and 34% of youth in 'at-risk' school populations suffering from this issue, thereby making it a potentially important target for interventions (Gullotta & Bloom, 2014). In particular, this distress is often at its greatest during the transition from education to work. The high level of young unemployment all over the world and increasing number of NEET youth, who are Not in Education, Employment or Training (Otto et al., 2017), is evidence of how difficult youth are finding it to transition into the modern world. All of this makes identity harder to form, but a developed one can help young people to cope better with social transformations and to change under pressure but remain true to themselves.

Social arts effects on youth identities

It is widely accepted that arts hold the potential to provide therapy and to educate and to empower people and can be understood through both psychological and social epistemologies (Schwartzberg et al.,

DOI: 10.4324/9781003105350-11

2021). In youth studies and practice of youth work, arts-based methods are particularly effective for supporting participation, creating conditions for emotional connections, and delivering messages that are deeply embodied and difficult to express through words alone (Karkou & Glasman, 2004). Arts-based knowledge transfer and capacity-building strategies are also extremely valuable for bringing young people together to examine important and, at times, vexing questions about themselves and their wellbeing. Thus, arts can provide young people with a better understanding of themselves and the social context they live in, develop their personal and social identities, and promote agency. A consideration of how arts can be used in a social context with youth identities will be presented through a discussion of its therapeutic, educational, and empowering effects.

'Person-in-Context': therapeutic effects of arts and beyond. Traditional arts have been used in therapy, with a diverse range of tools and modalities of arts therapy having been created. Arts can go beyond pure therapy, integrating psychological and social theories and being 'an intense medium for embodying and concretizing the person-in-context'. They connect the subjective and objective, the micro and the macro, the individual and society, and enable both perspectives 'to appear together on the same page' (Huss & Bos, 2019, pp. 2–3). Furthermore, the most recent arts therapy trends like using digital arts-based methods and environmental/eco arts therapy can enhance the creative process and self-expression beyond the traditional methods of painting, music, drama, and dance. Thus, digital arts-based methods are especially accessible for young people thanks to their great contribution to psychosocial experiences and the important role that technology plays in individuals' worldviews nowadays (Malchiodi, 2018). Also, eco-art therapy expands therapeutic functions of arts by active usage of the salutogenic potential of natural factors, creating positive relationships with nature, and developing ecological awareness and eco-identity through personalisation and participation (Kopytin, 2017). From these perspectives, engaging young people in arts, raising and answering the questions: "Who am I?", "What am I for?", "Who will I be, and do I want to be?" help them to reveal their needs and emotions in relationship to themselves and to 'significant others' and to the broader environment whether inter-subjective, digital or ecological.

Arts as an educational tool. The incorporation of arts in its 'dialogic nature' (Bakhtin, 1997) into education has the potential to enhance experiential dimensions of learning. Arts as a significant part of 'embedding learning' can be more successful in the formation of identity and agency of adolescents, even young children, by inviting students to reflect on their creations, rewrite their experiences, and represent their culture in dynamic, local spaces (Bruner, 2006; Eaude, 2019). Marta Nussbaum argues that the involvement of arts at school and university cultivates capacities for play and empathy and creates 'citizens of the world' who possess 'inner eyes' and are capable of addressing particular cultural blind spots (Nussbaum, 2010, p. 125). Thus, it can be seen that using arts in educational settings not only promotes identification process but also produces capable active citizens who possess dignity and self-esteem and who can appreciate their own strengths and contribution to the community. In other words, citizens who are empowered.

The empowering effect of arts. Combining arts and critical theories can create methodology that empowers. Together, they aim to create a more embodied knowledge, create participatory practices and give voice to marginalised groups. In line with the Freire critical pedagogy, in which participants construct stories as they construct changes (Freire, 1998), arts can demonstrate the possibilities of overcoming the limitations of the 'banking' approach to education and the helping professions. Modern arts-based methods of self-expression such as Photo-Voice and Digital Storytelling are especially effective for young people thanks to their 'participatory' promise of enhancing opportunities to tell their stories and, thus, express their needs, providing participants new lenses on their experience and subjectively pertinent ways of representing shared realities (Botfield et al., 2018; Wendel et al., 2019). Promoting an agentic nature is crucial for youth identities to develop an active, integrated personality, which is capable of acting purposively and reflectively and of adapting to the quickly changing conditions of a 'liquid' turbulent world, which is characterised by weakened pressure of social norms, uncertainty and a shift of the responsibility for life onto the shoulders of 'atomistic individuals' (Bauman, 2006). Agency is also at the core of the capability approach, which asserts that social opportunities have to expand into the realm of human agency and freedom in order for wellbeing and "what a person is free to do and achieve in pursuit of whatever goals or values he or she regards as important" (Sen, 1992). Recent studies emphasise the close connection among arts, creativity and human wellbeing, with arts being a significant capability for individuals to gain wellbeing. (Jansen, 2018).

In the attempt to locate therapeutic, educational and empowering effects of social arts in the identity-formation of young people, a construction of a theoretical framework for the use of arts in the light of the theories of recognition of Paul Ricoeur and Axel Honneth will be offered in the next part of the chapter.

Recognition theory

Theorists from various fields, including psychological (Vygotsky, 1987; Cooley, 1998), philosophical (Fraser, 2000; Ricoeur, 2005; Decker, 2012), sociological (Mead, 1967, Honneth, 1995) and social work (Froggett, 2004; Webb, 2010; Houston, 2015), acknowledge the significance of social and political recognition in people's lives and the formation of their identities.

The last works of French philosopher Paul Ricoeur were dedicated to developing a phenomenology of the 'capable human being' in connection to recognition. According to the 'Dictionary of Paul Ricoeur', the concept of 'recognition' makes sense connected in its reference to objects, to self, or to inter-subjectivity (Vdovina, 2012). Recognition of objects is its identification in 'cognito' and memory; self-recognition is confirmation that we are agents of our own words and actions and, finally, mutual recognition is ascertained by approbation of others (Ricoeur, 2005).

In terms of laying 'the course of recognition', Ricoeur started from 'recognition as identification', which means recognition of the uniqueness of the individual as well as the relations that a certain person acquires. The next stage, 'to recognise oneself' is implied through the statement 'I believe that I can'. Herein self-identifying as a 'capable human being' Ricoeur distinguishes four capabilities in a hierarchical order that are each inextricably linked to identity. Thus, a 'capable human being' must be capable: to speak, to act, to narrate and of imputation. The final capability is the culmination of all the capabilities. When imputability is accepted by the person, they become a responsible agent, capable of ascribing to themselves the consequences of action; and where harm done to others is concerned, it underlies the possibility of reparation and final sanction. The course of self-recognition culminates in mutual recognition: 'the apogee of the otherhood is mutuality' (Ricoeur, 2005). Thus, Ricoeur argues that through intersubjectivity, a person relates to the self and to the other, recognising one's and other people's capabilities, so in order to be a dignified capable human being, it is necessary to be recognised.

Ricoeur discussed three 'spheres of recognition', suggested earlier as 'love', 'rights' and 'solidarity' by Axel Honneth (1995) for the positive foundation of identity-formation:

(1) *Receiving love, care and positive regard* from intimate, friendly and family relationships, which are supposed to be 'constituted by strong emotional attachments among a small number of

people' (Honneth, 1995; Ricoeur, 2005). Such attachments are inconsistent with direct violations of physical integrity (as Honneth stresses) or negations of approbation (as Ricoeur stresses) that indirectly affect a person's basic self-confidence (Laitinen, 2007).

(2) *Legal recognition of different kinds of rights*, such as Marshal's classic typology of civil, political and social rights – possession of which gives people a sense of equality, empowerment and citizenship. But this is the sphere in which there can be various specific forms of disrespect, such as denial of rights and social exclusion. To deal with this, a capability to advocate one's own rights needs to be developed.

(3) *Appreciating and valuing a person's skills and contribution to the community* taking into account that for positive self-esteem people need recognition of 'the importance of their individual qualities for the life of others' in accordance with shared goals and values (Ricoeur, 2005).

Ricoeur also emphasised the negative forms of disregard in the spheres of recognition as they 'give flesh and blood to the struggle for recognition' (Ricoeur, 2005, p. 188). Thus, work on identity-formation can be focused both on strengthening the positive 'practical relation-to-self' – such as self-confidence, self-respect and self-esteem – and on preventing or minimising the negative forms of disrespect in each sphere – abuse in the primary relationship of love, exclusion in rights and denigration and insult in community relationships.

Therefore, the process of identification develops in three spheres by means of self- and inter-subjective recognition of capabilities. In this context, arts can be considered as a very powerful tool not only in developing self-identity as capable to speak, to act, to narrate and to ascribe to self the consequences of action (imputation) but also in contributing to broader social effects in mutual recognition in respect to 'love, rights and solidarity'.

Based on the recognition theories of Ricoeur and Honneth and also the social work intervention model of Houston (2015), a model of arts-based intervention for identity-formation in the three spheres of recognition can be constructed (see Figure 10.1). To illustrate how it can work, the case study of a Photovoice project and a number of arts-based sessions with social work students of St. Petersburg State University are analysed. These activities aimed to help students better understand themselves, to reveal problems in their path of personal and professional identification and to learn about social work values,

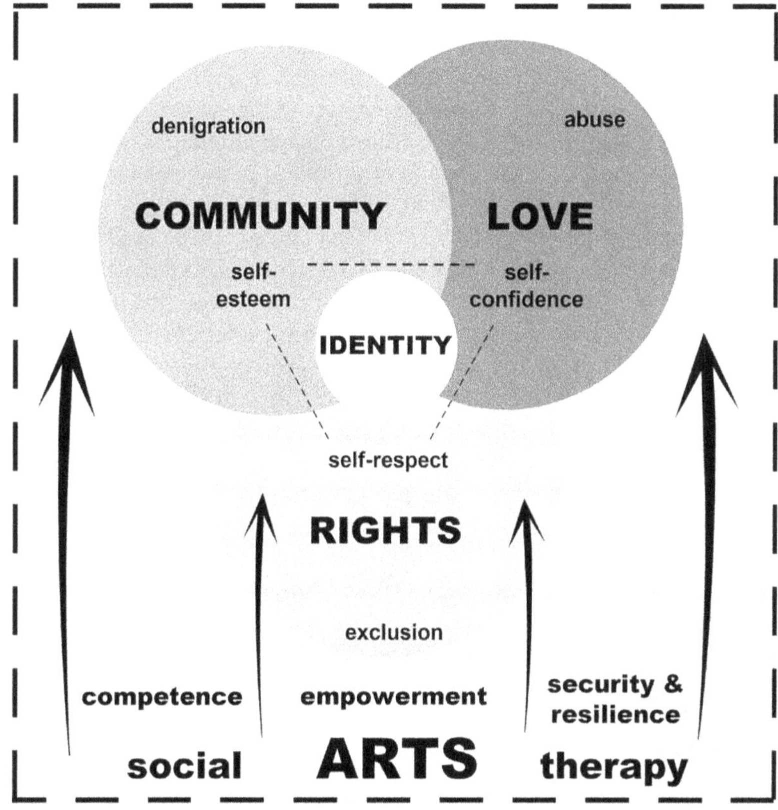

Figure 10.1 Model of arts interventions in different spheres of recognition

ethics and concepts more successfully by employing critical thinking skills and creative capacities. The sessions also aimed to 'raise voices' of students in developing the education programme.

(1) In the recognition sphere of *Primary relationships of love and regards* (*the targeted positive component of which is self-confidence and the negative is abuse*) arts interventions can be directed towards revealing the needs and emotions of young people in their relationships with family members and friends so that strong feelings of security and resilience can be built. This meaningful interpersonal experience of recognition, being a precondition of all further possibilities of respect and participation in public life, should be central to helping and educative relationships (Froggett, 2004). By incorporating psychodynamic approaches, e.g.

Winnicott object-relations theory, this sphere of recognition can be investigated and treated by traditional arts-therapy methods using dynamic potential and projective mechanisms. In our case creative genograms were used, which allowed us to explore how parental and other close relationships influenced students' choices of educational programmes and their identification with the social work profession and also family, gender and generational patterns related to career attitudes. In the creative process, an awareness of family history and its impact on students' professional decision-making and the acceptance of their choices were raised.

As an example, Figure 10.1, a creative genogram of a female student, illustrates how her choice of the social work profession was influenced by *parents* – '*you are very talented*', by siblings (*brother*) – '*development of responsibility*', by *love* (partner) – '*you are inborn leader*', by *friends* – '*you are a psychologist, you help us a lot*' and so on. During the session the student was reflecting on her educational choice in accordance with the recognition of her capabilities by 'significant others', and she noticed that her path to professional identification is much smoother than many other students thanks to this.

(2) In the recognition sphere of *Legal recognition of rights* (*the targeted positive component of which is self-respect and the negative is exclusion*) arts interventions can be directed towards providing moral standing and facilitating social integrity. The possibilities of arts to empower and provide advocacy of rights for young people are significant and such arts-based participatory methods as Photovoice, digital storytelling or theatre practices under the umbrella of the 'Theatre of the Oppressed' (Boal, 1993) can be used. In the Photovoice project, students used photos to reflect on the problems that social work deals with, the profession itself – including its limits – and any possible ways to improve work situation (e.g. low salary and bureaucracy). They also demonstrated their will to be heard throughout the educational programme and to be able to influence University policy.

> Students are listened to, but not heard. All kinds of surveys about 'education quality' do not make the situation better. They only give the illusion of change. After all, there are no positive changes. In fact, problems are often silenced due to fear. A clear example is that in 2018, a student of the faculty of International Relations, [NAME], started action against sexism towards students and was supported by many students. But it all ended at an ethics commission, where [NAME] was recognized as a violator of internal regulations, a violator of ethical standards, and the action was called offensive: 'The actions, in particular, of student [NAME], can be assessed as an attempt at some kind of self-promotion' and

'by the way, our conversation with [NAME], revealed that she has no clear idea of sexism as such.'

Discussion of one picture (Figure 10.2 – 'Students are listened to, but not heard') revealed the existence of a lack dialogue between the

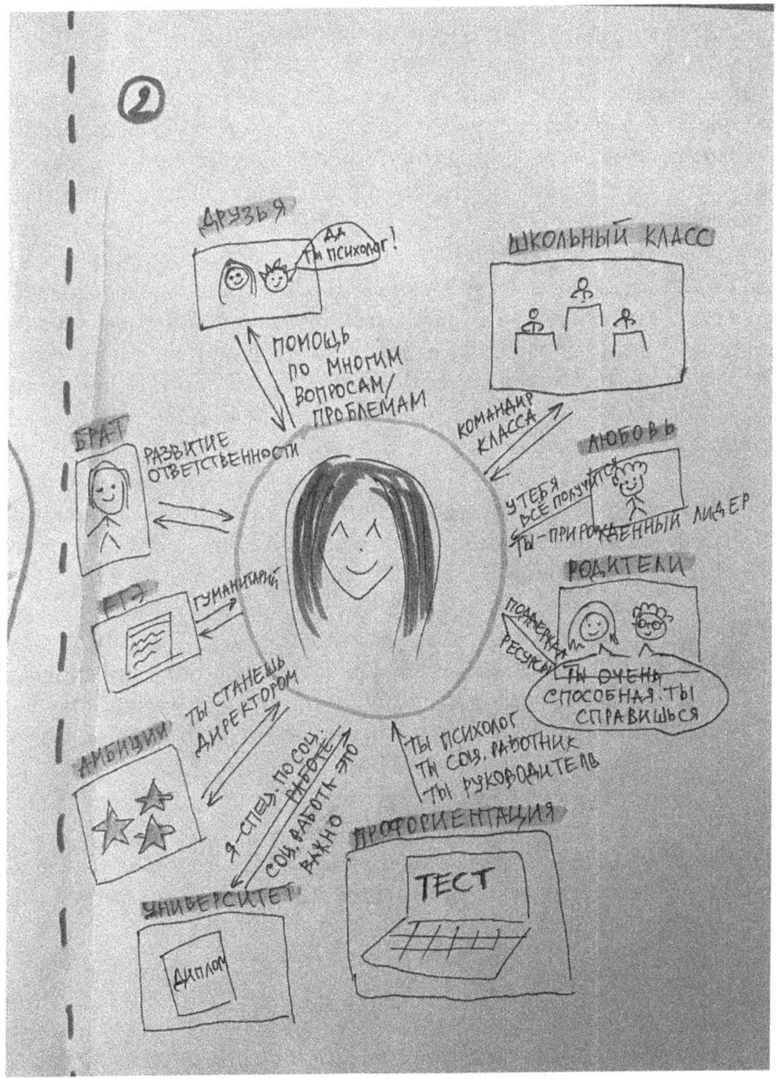

Figure 10.2 Drawing of a student – creative genogram of influence on choice for social work profession

university and students that made them feel that their rights were being denied and they did not have any power. During the project, feedback from the university on the particular case and other raised issues was provided, and thereby a bridge to the course of recognition of the students' rights was built.

(3) In the recognition sphere of *Valuing a person's skills and contribution to the community* (*the targeted positive component of which is self-esteem and the negative is denigration*), arts interventions can be directed towards sharing views on values and tasks in communities, dealing with social problems, and making changes in terms of people's roles in community, for instance as future specialists. As was already mentioned, students in the Photovoice project most commonly discussed the following topics: social problems they intended to solve; problems they were going to face, such as low salary of social work specialists and the bureaucracy of the profession, alongside ethical issues and professional roles and rules. According to the students' feedback, the discussion of their artworks allowed the participants to feel better about the impact they could have on their future work, to appreciate more their strengths and potential contribution to the community and to feel more positive about the development of their professional competence.

> A social worker, relying on theoretical knowledge and practical skills, and possessing information about a client and his/her problem situation, chooses the forms and methods of social work. The dice is NOT the LIFE of a CLIENT, but the WORK TOOL.
>
> Often social workers are overcome by doubts about the quality and effectiveness of their work, and the chosen forms and methods of that work, so s/he thinks "Will this be effective for a client, will I help him or her?" – this is seen in the second photo in the collage – looking to the future, forward with the question.
>
> The professional identity of the social worker is a subjective experience, expressed in taking responsibility for their life and activity, accepting professional values and roles, being willing to carry out certain types of activities and to work with certain categories of people.
>
> Attention should be paid to the ongoing support and development of social workers, in terms of their education, self-education, and self-development. Supervisions should be introduced in social services centers to discuss problems and difficulties in work, to share feelings, and to get recommendations for working with clients and working with oneself.

Figure 10.3 Photo and narrative of a student 'Your opinion is very important to us'

Figure 10.3 demonstrates a student's awareness of the responsibility taken by social workers and the potential impacts they can make on clients. Discussion on this and other pictures allowed students to develop their views on responsibilities, promote and visualise borders of professional competence, and to have experience of mutuality, belonging and solidarity within a community of value.

Figure 10.4 Photo and narrative of a student RESPONSIBILITY should be taken by social worker

Conclusion: lessons and perspectives

Social arts are broadly understood as innovative arts-based practices with focus on the social gains (Schwartzberg et al., 2021). They will be most relevant for individuals and groups who are suffering from disrespect in the spheres of recognition, such as abuse in the primary relationship of love, exclusion in rights and denigration in community. The chapter has attempted to provide a theoretical framework for arts-based practices as an insight into the cumulation of their therapeutic, educating and empowering social effects. The adoption of theories of recognition in the identify-formation of young people by means of social arts can have significant findings and lessons for detecting future perspectives (theoretical and practical) in youth studies and youth work.

Our case study demonstrated that applying model of arts interventions in the light of recognition theories for formation of identity, including professional, is significant due to the possibilities of:

- revealing blind spots e.g. in the denial of young people's rights, thus starting a dialogue and a path to empowerment;
- recognising the capabilities, expectations and limitations of a youth's potential contribution to the community, thus leading to solidarity;
- realising the influence of recognition by 'significant others', which can result in a smoother process of (professional) identification.

Moreover, involving young people in social arts on the basis of mutual regard and shared experiences gives them the experience of recognition. In short, arts-based methods can be used in the framework of recognition theories to understand young individuals and groups of young people in terms of their satisfaction with emotional bonds, their expectation of recognition of rights and the scope of their contribution to communities.

Furthermore, applying the model in educational settings develops new knowledge and provides students with a deeper understanding of a profession. In this way, enabling the readiness of social work educational institutes to use arts-based methods will ensure a new type of specialists who will realise the role of creativity in the profession and who are capable of forming their own identity in this light while also shaping the entire profession. Thus, these new professionals will be ready to provide the circumstances in which social transformation through the use of creative tools can occur.

Acknowledgements

We would like to thank the students who shared their experience in the Photovoice project and arts-based sessions and gave permissions to use their artworks in the study of social potential of arts. And special thanks to Michelle Cornick, Anna's partner, for her natural logic and native English, which strengthened the chapter significantly.

References

Arnett, J. J. (2004). *Emerging adulthood: The winding road from the late teens through the twenties*. New York: Oxford University Press.

Augusto, B. (1993). *Theater of the oppressed*. New York: Theatre Communications Group.

Bakhtin, M. (1997). The problem of text. In *The collected works of M.M. Bakhtin* (Vol. 5). Moscow: Russian Dictionaries. (in Russian).

Bauman, Z. (2006). *Liquid times: Living in an age of uncertainty*. Cambridge: Polity Press.

Botfield, J. R., Newman, C. E., Lenette, C., Albury, K., & Zwi, A. B. (2018). Using digital storytelling to promote the sexual health and well-being of migrant and refugee young people: A scoping review. *Health Education Journal*, *77*(7), 735–748.

Bruner, J. S. (2006). *In search of pedagogy: The selected works of Jerome S. Bruner* (2 Vols.). Abingdon: Routledge.

Cooley, C. H. (1998). *On self and social organization*. Chicago: Chicago University Press.

Decker, K. S. (2012). Perspectives and ideologies: A pragmatic use for recognition theory. *Philosophy & Social Criticism*, *38*(2), 215–226.

Eaude, T. (2019). The role of culture and traditions in how young children's identities are constructed. *International Journal of Children Spirituality*, *24*(1), 5–9.

Fraser, N. (2000). Rethinking recognition. *New Left Review*, *3*, 107–120.

Freire, P. (1998). *Pedagogy of freedom: Ethics, democracy, and civic courage*. Rowman & Littlefield Publishers.

Froggett, L. (2004). Holistic practice, art, creativity and the politics of recognition. *Social Work and Social Sciences Review*, *11*(3), 29–51.

Gullotta, T. P., & Bloom, M. (Eds.). (2014). *Encyclopedia of primary prevention and health promotion*. New York: Springer.

Honneth, A. (1995). *The struggle for recognition: The moral grammar of social conflicts*. Cambridge, MA: The MIT Press.

Houston, S. (2015). "When I look I am seen, so I exist to change": Supplementing Honneth's recognition model for social work. *Social Work & Society*, *13*(2). http://nbn-resolving.de/urn:nbn:de:hbz:464-sws-868

Huss, E., & Bos, E. (Eds.). (2019). *Art in social work practice: Theory and practice: International perspectives*. London: Routledge.

Jansen, E. (2018). Art and creativity as a capability: Utilizing art in social work education. *Social Dialogue*, *19*, 63–67.

Karkou, V., & Glasman, J. (2004). Arts, education and society: The role of the arts in promoting the emotional wellbeing and social inclusion of young people. *Support for Learning*, *19*(2), 57–65.

Kopytin, A. (2017). *Environmental and ecological expressive therapies: The emerging conceptual framework for practice in Environmental expressive therapies: Nature-assisted theory and practice* (A. Kopytin & M. Rugh, Eds.). New York: Routledge/Taylor & Francis.

Laitinen, A. (2007). The course of recognition. Review in *Redescriptions Political Thought Conceptual History and Feminist Theory*, 224–231.

Malchiodi, C. (Ed.). (2018). *The handbook of art therapy and digital technology*. London: Jessica-Kingsley-Publishers.

Mead, G. H. (1967). *Mind, self and society*. Chicago: Chicago University Press.

Moula, Z., Aithal, S., Karkou, V., & Powell, J. (2020). A systematic review of child-focused outcomes of arts therapies delivered in primary mainstream schools for children aged 5–12. *Children and Youth Services Review*, 112.

Nussbaum, M. C. (2010). *Not for profit: Why democracy needs the humanities*. Princeton, N.J.: Princeton University Press.

Otto, H.-U., Egdell, V., Bonvin, J.-M., Atzmueller, R., & Kepler, J. (Eds.). (2017). *Empowering young people in disempowering times: Fighting inequality through capability oriented policy*. Edward Elgar Publishing.

Ricoeur, P. (2005). *The course of recognition*. Cambridge, MA: Harvard University Press.

Schwartzberg, T. G., Huss, E., & Slonim-Nevo, V. (2021). Exploring the concept of social art through a single session art activity with asylum seekers. *The Arts in Psychotherapy*, 72. https://doi.org/10.1016/j.aip.2020.101729

Sen, A. (1992). *Inequality re-examined*. Oxford: Clarendon Press.

Vdovina, I. S. (2012). Dictionary of paul ricoeur. *Philosophical Sciences*, *1*, 91–105. (in Russian).

Vygotsky, L. S. (1987). Thinking and speech. In R. W. Rieber & A. S. Carton (Eds.), *The collected works of L. S. Vygotsky: Problems of general psychology* (Vol. 1, N. Minick, Trans.). Plenum Press.

Webb, S. (2010). (Re)assembling the left: The politics of redistribution and recognition in social work. *British Journal of Social Work*, *40*(8), 2364–2377.

Wendel, M. L., Jackson, T., Ingram, C. M., Golden, T., Castle, B. T., Ali, N. M., & Combs, R. (2019). Yet we live, strive, and succeed: Using photovoice to understand community members' experiences of justice, safety, hope, and racial equity. *A Journal of Community-Based Research and Practice*, 2(1), 9, 1–16.

11 Compassion embodied – the particular power of the arts

Eva Bojner Horwitz, Tero Heinonen, Anne Birgitta, and Monica Worline

Introduction: humans as embodied emotional beings

When we seek to understand something new, we activate inner images, emotions, and sensations from memory of situations that we have encountered previously. Our memory is more tied to our bodies and emotions than we tend to think. Knowledge acquisition involves multiple modalities; images, feelings, emotions, sensations, sounds, motor activities, and cognitions. Not surprisingly, this is one reason why art has been so successful as a teaching aid, including in complex areas such as empathy. Our societies require transformation and art has historically played an important role in that development. Inner transformation involves changes in our mindsets and has recently received growing attention (Wamsler, 2020). The arts may offer a route to inner transition, targeting compassion as a set of action-driven embodied processes.

This chapter elaborates three key elements: a) the meaning of emotions, particularly compassion, b) embodied humans and, c) the arts. The human experience is deeply rooted in emotions. Compassion is an example of a human emotion that is collective and self-transcendent. When we reflect on an act of kindness or a beautiful piece of art that evokes human warmth, our bodies react with physical signals of compassion. Compassion can therefore be an example of a powerful source of transformation.

Art facilitates, as part of the learning body, both biological and behavioral changes that can lead to improved health outcomes, better opportunities for knowledge acquisition, and enhanced compassionate processing (as well as other emotions). The reward-value of taking part in an artistic activity may contribute to brain plasticity (Fancourt & Finn, 2019). When we are moved by a piece of art or music, a set of emotional and non-emotional responses occur, and a range of

DOI: 10.4324/9781003105350-12

psychological operations are activated (Lindquist et al., 2012). Emotions also extend beyond the individual – they are culturally embedded and the arts reflect this: the arts vary with culture and its aesthetic properties and value are rooted in locally specific norms. The integration of the aesthetic into an experience of art requires cognitive elicitation and regulation of emotions (Goodman, 1976; Mead, 1934). The arts are therefore a powerful arena of embodied emotions, both individually and socially (Bojner Horwitz, 2018). Emotions are an important part of learning (Immordino-Yang & Damasio, 2007), and the emotional evocativeness of art, theatre, and music means that they likely serve as facilitators and transformers of learning at individual and social levels.

In order to benefit from the arts, several cognitive and emotional functions are required including working memory, audio memory, and selective attention. These can be trained and improved in the pursuit of artistic work. We know for instance that children who play instruments perform better in fine motor skills, rhythmic feeling, and hearing comprehension (Miendlarzewska & Trost, 2014) and that engagement with music, theatre, and arts are also beneficial for learning in a wider sense (Bojner Horwitz et al., 2021). Art can play a key role in societal transformation, and the compassion-embodiment-art axis, explored in the sections to follow, is an important part of this.

Emotions and embodiment

The term embodiment explains the relation between cognition and the physical body. Its theoretical focus, according to Niedenthal and colleagues (2005), is the brain´s modality-specific systems. These systems are constituted by a combination of different processes: a) the sensory systems, which regulate perception; b) the motor systems, which trigger actions; and c) the introspective systems, which govern conscious experiences of emotion and cognition. As Damasio asserted "We feel therefore we learn" (Immordino-Yang & Damasio, 2007); this describes how embodiment is part of a process where we start to reconnect through feelings and sensing and thereby start connecting to each other's knowledge. Embodiment is a major part of how we learn from each other and how we mirror one another via our own bodies.

Emotions are formed in conjunction with our sensemaking of the world, a process in which we attribute meaning and draw from our prior experiences (Lindquist et al., 2012). Learning depends on both emotions and cognitions, as well as motivation and intention. There are particular challenges that we face in learning about things of which we have no direct experience and that require empathy with – and compassion for – others. In order to attempt to bypass those obstructions, music, arts, and lyrics could be used to complement more traditional "cognitive" ways of teaching and learning (Fancourt et al., 2019).

Humans are deeply emotional beings – much more so than we tend to acknowledge, both in academia and in the everyday. Importantly, emotions are always embodied. Biological functions of the nervous system, stemming from sensory input, working memory, and cortical arousal, produce autonomic, hormonal, somatic, and visceral feedback (LeDoux, 1998). In contrast, feelings have been defined as mainly psychological reactions to aspects of sensory experience (Arnold, 1960). Emotions require psychological objects or antecedent situations that are perceived as a whole. The cognitive dimension of emotions consists of making value judgements concerning things that we find important in the context of our beliefs, values, and wellbeing (Moors et al., 2013).

Humans are not only deeply emotional beings individually but also in connection to each other. As infants, our first interpersonal relationships are based on emotions and are internalized as the foundation from which the self, our future affective identifications, and social connectedness develop (Harrow, 2002; Jacobson, 1964). The primary caregiver´s recognition and emotional availability are necessary for the development of selfhood, the capacity for symbolic prosocial behavior, and the ability to recognize emotional states of our fellow human-beings. We first relate to others by indicating our own emotional states (Izard, 1977; Sutherland, 1994; Winnicott, 1971). Throughout our lives, emotions emerge in social acts, in our reflective, embodied, and relational responses to social interaction, consciously altered and reconstructed with long-term memory (Denzin, 1984). Emotional learning requires the capacity to interpret expressive embodied cues as predictive information in socially meaningful experiences (Bandura, 1986; Izard & Buelcher, 1979).

Our embodied emotions are always bound by culture. Culture consists of shared meanings: interpretive schemes, values, and feeling rules internalized and activated through participation in social institutions and practices. Emotions are culturally scripted and shaped socially (Schweder, 1993). Emotional demands, resources, goals, or power rules are defined by social structure. What is deemed socially permissible in a particular situation influences whether and how we elicit, suppress, and regulate our emotional responses to others (Hochschild, 1979; Lazarus, 1991). As Riis and Woodhead (2010) underscore, we exist within the emotional regimes of our cultures. As emotional creatures, we are shaped by and can shape our social and societal structures.

Compassion embodied

We are rarely alone in our emotions. Emotions are socially and culturally bound and "contagious" in social networks: happiness, joy, and excitement are known to spread far and wide, as do negative emotions (Cacioppo et al., 2009). Emotions are transferred between individuals even without verbal information: emotion-specific vocal, facial, and postural expressions, mutual adjustment of attentional focus, and social appraisals function as a means of coding and decoding emotional information. They simultaneously trigger unintentional bodily synchronization of expressions and emotional sharing (Goldenberg et al., 2020; Parkinson, 2020; Witkower & Tracy, 2019).

Emotional contagion plays a role in the elicitation of collective emotions, which manifest in physical proximity to other individuals. Collective emotions tend to last longer than individual emotions. They also strengthen and activate emotions of others as a cascading reaction, forming emotional climates. Emotional cascades do not always require physical proximity in order to appear: the experience and expression of group-based emotions result from self-categorization as a member of a group and in a response to a situation appraised as relevant to the group with which one identifies, even if the events do not concern them personally (Goldenberg et al., 2020; Smith & Mackie, 2015).

Emotions can also transcend the self through compassion, elevation, admiration, awe, gratitude, and love. These are often called positive self-transcending emotions because they are elicited by other-focused appraisals, oriented toward the needs of others. Self-transcending emotions promote prosocial behavior and commitment to social relationships by diminishing the individual's focus on oneself and attuning one's sensitivity toward others. Self-transcending emotions build social resources by strengthening social ties necessary for overcoming social problems (Stellar et al., 2017).

Compassion is an emotion that epitomizes the interconnectedness of you and me, we and me. It is an emotion of both the self and of self-transcendence. Compassion refers to a complex four-part interpersonal process involving noticing, feeling, sensemaking, and acting that alleviates the suffering of another person (e.g., Dutton et al., 2014). Interestingly, compassion is often regarded as a positive emotion, yet it often involves an embodied experience of encountering suffering. Because of its complex relationship with both embodiment and collectivity, compassion offers an important window into the complexity of the interplay between self, other, and world. Following this line of thinking, compassion becomes "embodied" in many senses.

Pessi et al. (2017) have developed a conceptual mosaic based on literature and their own work to illustrate various angles of how compassion is embodied. The mosaic is five-fold and designed to stimulate further thinking by juxtaposing often separate ways of seeing. Of interest here, this mosaic view shows us that first, compassion can be understood as not only an emotion but also an embodied *virtue* – the roots of compassion lie in universal humanity and in the core of all world religions (e.g., Brown & Reimer 2013; Pessi, 2011, 2017; Ringu & Mullen, 2005). Second, compassion is embodied in *space* (see, e.g., Havik & Tielens, 2013) as well as in visual and performative arts. For instance, what kind of spaces inspire people to be more compassionate? Third, compassion is embodied in *self and other*. How does it, for example, feel bodily when you witness compassion? Fourth, compassion is embodied also in relation to nature and *ecology* (e.g., Acampora, 2006). Fifth, compassion is deeply embodied in the *arts* (e.g. Bojner Horwitz et al., 2021). Expanding our view of embodiment in this manner, juxtaposing physical human bodies with a wider lens on embodied culture, space, and performance, aids us in making the case that compassion is an essential element in understanding how the arts facilitate collective transformation.

Embodied compassion and the arts

In processes of social exchange, group members mutually entrain their focus during the execution of some shared task, and emotions tend to converge (Lawler et al., 2014; Parkinson, 2020). When shared meaning is constructed among in-group members, a joint action – such as professional musicians making music – becomes a relational space of emotional self-transcendence where group identity functions as a source of meaning, accomplishment, and engagement (Ascenso et al., 2017).

Music and embodied compassion

Music has a particularly strong influence on those parts of the brain that are important for emotional function, e.g. the corpus callosum (de Manzano & Ullén, 2018) and the reward system encompassing the insula, orbitofrontal cortex, amygdale, and hippocampus, i.e. those areas that are important for motivation, emotion regulation, and social communication. These emotional centers can have an impact on personality traits such as "openness to experience" (Miendlarzewska & Trost, 2014), which means that art can facilitate openness toward embodied compassion.

Knowledge concerts are an intervention that exploits the embodied nature of engagement with music. They address an important issue in our society around the need for knowledge dissemination around humanity, compassion, empathy, emotions, and integrity. It is especially important for young people to stimulate and raise awareness of responsibilities linked to embodied compassion, and music may create opportunities to deal with this. (Bojner Horwitz et al., 2021; Bojner Horwitz, 2021; Viper et al., 2020).

A second example is singing. For example professional singers report that they miss the aesthetic experiences, flow, and the physical aspects of embodied compassion during the COVID-19 lockdown periods (Theorell et al., 2020).

Dance and embodied compassion

Coordination of visual, auditory, and motor stimuli in the brain is affected by the bodily movements of dance. Dance training connects emotions with motor expressions that stimulate the embodied part of the state of compassion (Bojner Horwitz, 2004). There is a coherence between movement and emotion, which can be explained by both internal and external so-called mirroring mechanisms (Giacosa et al., 2016). During long-term dance training different stimuli can affect the whole body's nervous system where visual and auditory sensorimotor signals and the action observational network interact (Cross et al., 2009).

Art, theatre, and embodied compassion

We do not all share common vocabulary around emotions. Understanding how the body's signaling system can be translated into words can be crucial for mutual aid in emotionally charged situations. Theatrical play and art can establish links between our emotions i.e. compassion and our bodies (Bojner Horwitz, 2010). Through theatre and art, we can develop a vocabulary to express and communicate our emotions to others.

Nature and embodied compassion

Connecting to others with nature may facilitate authenticity and compassion where age, titles, and background have reduced influence (Bojner Horwitz et al., 2020). Nature sharing seems to evoke a deeper sense of connection than being inside a workplace: when activating our bodies in nature by walking, dancing, or contemplating, the awareness of our bodies and kindness toward each other increases. This wakefully relaxed state is a state that one could relate to openness and compassion through clarity of mind (Bojner Horwitz et al., 2020).

Toward transforming the society – how might compassion embodied inform novel leadership?

The arts can help to stimulate emotional activity and increase embodied receptivity to being reflective and compassionate. Based on this line of thought, five steps might serve as the first stepping stones to practical interventions in our societies and workplaces (Pessi et al., 2017).

First, ***take care of individual and organizational wellbeing, both the physical and the mental.***Wellbeing fosters compassion, and compassion fosters wellbeing. Compassion at work can be practiced and fostered, and practices of self and other oriented compassion can be also integrated into physical exercises. There are different methods to train and evaluate these embodied skills e.g. Video Interpretation Technique (Bojner Horwitz et al., 2003) and Self Figure Drawings (Bojner Horwitz, 2004).

Second, ***bring cultural and artistic activities into work,***or support individual cultural activities outside of workplaces. We know that in workplaces, which provide access to: a) cultural activities during working hours help to collectively protect their staff against burnout (Theorell et al., 2013) and b) arts based activities enhance the relationships in the workplace the arts can be seen to enhance quality of work experiences in the workplace (Bojner Horwitz et al., 2017).

Third, ***practice embodied exercises together at work.*** From twin studies we know that achievement in creative practices such as dancing, writing, performing theatre, and playing music seems to be connected to a lower level of alexithymia (Bojner Horwitz et al., 2017). Creative connection developed through artistic activities may help to improve the ability to empathize with others. Furthermore, when engaging in deliberate movement, we activate neural areas that correspond to the limbic system (Umilta et al., 2001), allowing mirroring in space by others. This kind of reflective feedback system through movement may help us to understand the other person's feelings.

Fourth, ***be aware of the power of emotions at work – and also of our inabilities.*** Nordic workplaces are not typically emotionally expressive. Embodied compassion at work may thus require some cultural change. In Greek, the word *alexithymia* means "no words for feelings" and the prevalence has been shown to be 5–10 % for women and 9–17% for men in a Finnish working age population (Mattila et al., 2007). Alexithymia is an impairment of both emotional awareness and emotional regulation (Lars-Gunnar et al., 2003). It is important to be aware of this because if we cannot recognize and regulate our own emotions, it is unlikely that we achieve full relationality with others and negotiate emotional contagion.

Fifth, ***pay attention to spatial structures and also their aesthetics.*** The spatial structures of workplaces should be planned in order to facilitate interaction and inspiration as well as to allow for solitude. The better the people know each other, the more compassion they will experience. A simple yet crucial fact is that losing contact with our bodies means that we lose our ability to perceive our body signals and therefore also the ability to read other people´s body signals. Perception and awareness are linked to each other and are skills that can be trained through the arts (Bojner Horwitz, 2004; Bojner Horwitz et al., 2010).

A beautiful triangle remains: body, art, culture – noticing, perceiving, encountering others – mental and physical wellbeing of individuals and of teams. Embodied compassion truly epitomizes the power of this entire triangle – and this asset could be put much more into action as we transform our societies' workplaces.

References

Acampora, R. R. (2006). *Corporal compassion: Animal ethics and philosophy of body*. Pittsburgh, PA: University of Pittsburgh Press.

Arnold, M. B. (1960). *Emotion and personality. Volume: Psychological aspects*. New York: Columbia University Press.

Ascenso, S., Williamon, A., & Perkins, R. (2017). Understanding the wellbeing of professional musicians through the lens of positive psychology. *Psychology of Music*, *45*(1), 65–81.

Bandura, A. (1986). *Social foundations of thought and action: A social cognitive theory*. NJ: Prentice Hall.

Bojner Horwitz, E. (2004). *Dance/movement therapy in fibromyalgia patients: Aspects and consequences of verbal, visual, and hormonal analyses*. Doctoral dissertation, Faculty of Medicine, Department of Public Health and Caring Sciences, Uppsala University, Sweden.

Bojner Horwitz, E. (2018). Humanizing the working environment in health care through music and movement: The importance of embodied leadership. In L. O. Bonde & T. Theorell (Eds.), *Music and public health: A Nordic perspective* (pp. 187–200). Springer Books.

Bojner Horwitz, E., Grape Viding, C., Rydvik, E., & Huss, E. (2017). Arts as an ecological method to enhance quality of work experience of healthcare staff: A phenomenological-hermeneutic study. *International Journal of*

Qualitative Studies on Health and Well-Being, *12*(1), 1333898. https://doi.org/10.1080/17482631.2017.1333898

Bojner Horwitz, E., Harmat, L., Osika, W., & Theorell, T. (2021). The interplay between chamber musicians during two public performances of the same piece: A novel methodology using the concept of "flow". *Frontiers in Psychology*, *11*, 618227. https://doi.org/10.3389/fpsyg.2020.618227

Bojner Horwitz, E., Kowalski, J., & Anderberg, U. M. (2010). Theatre for, by, and with fibromyalgia patients: Evaluation of emotional expression using video interpretation. *The Arts in Psychotherapy*, *37*, 13–19.

Bojner Horwitz, E., Rehnqvist, K., Osika, W., Thyrén, D., Åberg, L., Kowalski, J., & Theorell, T. (2021). Embodied learning via a knowledge concert: An exploratory intervention study. *Nordic Journal of Arts, Culture and Health*, *3*(1–2), 34–47. https://doi.org/10.18261/issn.2535-7913-2021-01-02-04

Bojner Horwitz, E., Spännäri, J., Langley, J., Jacobs, B., & Osika, W. (2020). Taking care of the researcher: A nature and art-related activity retreat: Sharing natural space puts humanity into perspective. *Work*, *67*(3), 535–548.

Bojner Horwitz, E., Theorell, T., & Anderberg, U. M. (2003). Fibromyalgia patients' own experiences of video self-interpretation: A phenomenological-hermeneutic study. *Scandinavian Journal of Caring Sciences*, *17*(3), 257–264.

Brown, W. S., & Reimer, K. S. (2013). Embodied cognition, character formation, and virtue. *Zygon: Journal of Religion & Science*, *48*(3), 832–845.

Cacioppo, J. T., Fowler, J. H., & Christakis, N. A. (2009). Alone in the crowd: The structure and spread of loneliness in a large social network. *Journal of Personality and Social Psychology*, *97*(6), 977–991. https://doi.org/10.1037/a0016076

Cross, E. S., Kraemer, D. J., Hamilton, A. F., Kelley, W. M., & Grafton, S. T. (2009). Sensitivity of the action observation network to physical and observational learning. *Cerebral Cortex*, *19*(2), 315–326. https://doi.org/10.1093/cercor/bhn083

de Manzano, Ö., & Ullén, F. (2018). Same genes, different brains: Neuroanatomical differences between monozygotic twins discordant for musical training. *Cerebral Cortex*, *28*(1), 387–394. https://doi.org/10.1093/cercor/bhx299

Denzin, N. K. (1984). *On understanding emotion*. San Francisco: Jossey-Bass.

Dutton, J., Workman, C., & Hardin, A. (2014). Compassion at work. *The Annual Review of Organizational Psychology and Organizational Behavior*, *1*, 277–304.

Fancourt, D., & Finn, S. (2019). *What is the evidence on the role of the arts in improving health and well-being? A scoping review*. Copenhagen: WHO Regional Office for Europe (Health Evidence Network (HEN) synthesis report 67). www.euro.who.int/en/publications/abstracts/what-is-the-evidence-on-the-role-of-the-arts-in-improving-health-and-well-being-a-scoping-review-2019

Fancourt, D., Garnett, C., Spiro, N., West, R., & Müllensiefen, D. (2019). How do artistic creative activities regulate our emotions? Validation of the Emotion Regulation Strategies for Artistic Creative Activities Scale (ERS-ACA). *PLoS One*, *14*(2), e0211362. https://doi.org/10.1371/journal.pone.0211362

Giacosa, C., Karpati, F. J., Foster, N. E. V., Penhune, V. B., & Hyde, K. L. (2016). Dance and music training have different effects on white matter diffusivity in sensorimotor pathways. *NeuroImage*, *135*, 273–286.

Goldenberg, A., Garcia, D., Halperin, E., & Gross, J. J. (2020). Collective emotions. *Current Directions in Psychological Science*, *29*(2), 1–7.

Goodman, N. (1976). *Languages of art: An approach to a theory of symbols* (2nd ed.). Indianapolis: Hackett.

Harrow, A. J. (2002). Towards a theory of the self: Fairbairn and beyond. In F. Perreira & D. E. Scharff (Eds.), *Fairbairn and relational theory* (pp. 183–196). New York: Karnac.

Havik, K. M., & Tielens, G. (2013). Atmosphere, compassion and embodied experience: A conversation about atmosphere with Juhani Pallasmaa. *Building Atmosphere, OASE*, (91), 33–53. www.oasejournal.nl/en/Issues/91/AtmosphereCompassionAndEmbodiedExperience

Hochschild, A. R. (1979). Emotion work, feeling rules, and social structure. *American Journal of Sociology*, *85*(3), 551–575.

Immordino-Yang, M. H., & Damasio, A. (2007). We feel, therefore we learn: The relevance of affective and social neuroscience to education. *Mind, Brain, and Education*, *1*(1), 3–10.

Izard, C. E. (1977). *Human emotions*. New York: Plenum.

Izard, C. E., & Buelcher, S. (1979). Emotion expressions and personality integration in infancy. In C. Izard (Ed.), *Emotions in personality and psychopathology* (pp. 445–472). Boston: Springer. https://doi.org/10.1007/978-1-4613-2892-6_16

Jacobson, E. (1964). *The self and the object world*. New York: International Universities Press.

Lars-Gunnar, L., Johnsson, A., Sundqvist, K., & Olsson, H. (2003). Alexithymia, memory of emotion, emotional awareness, and perfectionism. *Emotion*, *2*, 361–379. https://doi.org/10.1037/1528-3542.2.4.361

Lawler, E. J., Thye, S. R., & Yoon, J. (2014). The emergence of collective emotions in social exchange. In C. von Scheve & M. Salmela (Eds.), *Collective emotions: Perspectives from psychology, philosophy, and sociology* (pp. 189–203). Oxford University Press. https://doi.org/10.1093/acprof:oso/9780199659180.003.0013

Lazarus, R. S. (1991). *Emotion and adaptation*. New York and Oxford: Oxford University Press.

Ledoux, J. (1998). *The emotional brain*. New York: Touchstone.

Lindquist, K. A., Wager, T. D., Kober, H., Bliss-Moreau, E., & Barrett, L. F. (2012). The brain basis of emotion: A meta-analytic review. *The Behavioral and Brain Sciences*, *35*(3), 121–143. https://doi.org/10.1017/S0140525X11000446

Mattila, A. K., Ahola, K., Honkonen, T., Salminen, J. K., Huhtala, H., & Joukamaa, M. (2007). Alexithymia and occupational burnout are strongly associated in working population. *Journal of Psychosomatic Research*, *62*, 657–665. https://doi.org/10.1016/j.jpsychores.2007.01.002

Mead, G. H. (1934). The background of the genesis of the self. In C. W. Morris (Ed.), *Mind, self, and society: From the standpoint of a social behaviourist* (pp. 144–152). Chicago: The University of Chicago Press.

Miendlarzewska, E. A., & Trost, W. J. (2014). How musical training affects cognitive development: Rhythm, reward and other modulating variables. *Frontiers in Neuroscience*, 7, 279. https://doi.org/10.3389/fnins.2013.00279

Moors, A., Ellsworth, P. C., Scherer, K. R., & Frijda, N. H. (2013). Appraisal theories of emotion: State of the art and future development. *Emotion Review*, *5*, 119–124. https://doi.org/10.1177%2F1754073912468165

Niedenthal, P. M., Barsalou, L. W., Winkielman, P., Krauth-Gruber, S., & Ric, F. (2005). Embodiment in attitudes, social perception, and emotion. *Personality and social psychology*, 9(3), 184–211. https://doi.org/10.1207/s15327957pspr0903_1

Parkinson, B. (2020). Intragroup emotion convergence: Beyond contagion and social appraisal. *Personality and Social Psychology Review*, *24*(2), 121–140. https://doi.org/10.1177/1088868319882596

Pessi, A. B. (2011). Religiosity and altruism: Exploring the link and its relation to happiness. *Journal of Contemporary Religion*, *26*(1), 1–18.

Pessi, A. B. (2017). Dazed and amazed by moonlight: Exploring sense of meaning as the mediator of the effects of religion, belonging, and benevolence on well-being. *Nordic Journal of Religion and Society*, *30*(1), 24–42.

Pessi, A. B., Bojner Horwitz, E., & Worline, W. (2017). In A. B. Pessi, F. Martela, & M. Paakkanen (Eds.), *Myötätunnon mullistava voima* [The revolutionary power of compassion] (pp. 78–80). Jyväskylä: PS-kustannus.

Riis, O., & Woodhead, L. (2010). *A sociology of religious emotion*. Oxford: Oxford University Press.

Ringu, T. R., & Mullen, K. (2005). The Buddhist use of compassionate imagery in mind healing. In P. Gilbert (Ed.), *Compassion: Conceptualisations, research, and use in psychotherapy* (pp. 218–238). Abingdon, UK: Routledge.

Schweder, R. A. (1993). The cultural psychology of emotions. In M. Lewis & J. Haviland (Eds.), *Handbook of emotions* (pp. 417–431). New York: The Guilford Press.

Smith, E. R., & Mackie, D. M. (2015). Dynamics of group-based emotions: Insights from intergroup emotions theory. *Emotion Review*, 7(4), 349–354.

Stellar, J. E., Gordon, A. M., Piff, P. K., Cordaro, D., Anderson, G. L., Bai, Y., Maruskin, L. A., & Keltner, D. (2017). Self-transcendent emotions and their social functions: Compassion, gratitude, and awe bind us to others through prosociality. *Emotion Review*, 9(3), 200–207.

Sutherland, J. D. (1994). The autonomous self. In J. S. Scharff (Ed.), *The autonomous self: The work of John D. Sutherland* (pp. 303–330). London and New Jersey: Jason Aronson Inc.

Theorell, T., Kowalski, J., Theorell, A., & Horwitz, E. B. (2020). Choir singers without rehearsals and concerts? A questionnaire study on perceived losses from restricting choral singing during the covid-19 pandemic.

Journal of Voice. Advance online publication. https://doi.org/10.1016/j.jvoice.2020.11.006

Theorell, T., Osika, W., Leineweber, C., Magnusson Hanson, L. L., Bojner Horwitz, E., & Westerlund, H. (2013). Is cultural activity at work related to mental health in employees? *International Archives of Occupational and Environmental Health*, *86*(3), 281–288. https://doi.org/10.1007/s00420-012-0762-8

Umiltà, M. A., Kohler, E., Gallese, V., Fogassi, L., Fadiga, L., Keysers, C., & Rizzolatti, G. (2001). I know what you are doing: A neurophysiological study. *Neuron*, *31*(1), 155–165. https://doi.org/10.1016/S0896-6273(01)00337-3

Viper, M., Thyrén, D., & Bojner Horwitz, E. B. (2020). Music as consolation: The importance of music at farewells and mourning. *OMEGA Journal of Death and Dying*. https://doi.org/10.1177/0030222820942391

Wamsler, C. (2020). Education for sustainability: Fostering a more conscious society and transformation towards sustainability. *International Journal of Sustainability in Higher Education*, *21*(1), 112–130.

Winnicott, D. W. (1971). *Playing and reality*. New York: Tavistock.

Witkower, Z., & Tracy, J. L. (2019). Bodily communication of emotion: Evidence for extrafacial behavioral expressions and available coding systems. *Emotion Review*, *11*(2), 184–193.

12 The art studio as public health practice

Mitigating the negative impacts of social inequality through community care

Catherine Hyland Moon

Context

The current global context is rife with injustice dispensed according to intersections of social difference, with profound health implications. Wellbeing is socially produced, and the root causes of problems are more often injustice than misfortune (Evans et al., 2014; Friedli, 2009; Lawthom et al., 2007). We need accessible, effective public health care that centers the perspectives and needs of those who have historically been marginalized (Jeffery et al., 2019). Collective, art-based approaches to health have the potential to mobilize people across socio-cultural-political divides (Timm-Bottos, 2017) and to establish public spaces of creativity, solidarity, and mutual care.

ArtWorks, a community art studio in Chicago, is one such initiative. It has been in existence since 2007 at sites including a health and housing organization, a food pantry, and a shelter for homeless men. Since 2016, it has been hosted by the main branch of the Chicago Public Libraries. ArtWorks provides weekly three-hour art making sessions open to everyone, from local residents to international visitors. Over the years, it has been supported by a collective of art therapist facilitators, small grants, and donations of space, art materials, and labor. I have been involved in ArtWorks since its inception and currently partner with art therapist Jackie Bousek to coordinate the weekly studio.

Community art practices have existed in the art therapy field since its beginning, though primarily within the circumscribed environments of health care settings (Moon, 2016b; Ottemiller & Awais, 2016). Given that the public library that hosts ArtWorks sits on the unceded lands of the Ojibwe, Odawa, and Potawatomi Nations, it is important to acknowledge that Western art therapy's growing recognition of the importance of collective art practices was preceded by the traditional

DOI: 10.4324/9781003105350-13

practices of many Indigenous communities whereby the arts have long been integrated into a holistic approach to health and healing (Archibald et al., 2012). Likewise, it is essential to acknowledge the long unrecognized groundwork laid by early Black art therapists who contextualized their practices within their own communities, deviating from professional norms to literally meet people where they were at – in grocery store parking lots, at the Asbury Park riots in New York, and in their personal art studios (Gipson, 2019).

Art therapy community studios established apart from social service settings are based on a rejection of medical, pathologizing models of care in favor of aligning art making with health (Allen, 1995, 2008). Instead of private, confidential therapy sessions, the focus is on intersubjective, participatory encounters and co-creative processes (Leake, 2015). These public practices emphasize interdependence, shared expertise, solidarity, and critically conscious processes directed toward social change (Talwar, 2016; Timm-Bottos, 2006; Timm-Bottos & Chainey, 2015).

Artworks model

ArtWorks began in a slowly gentrifying neighborhood in Chicago where there was a heavy concentration of social service organizations. Some affluent neighbors in this racially, ethnically, and socioeconomically diverse locale objected to living among fellow residents who were homeless or struggling with mental distress or substance use. ArtWorks was developed as a space where people both housed and housing insecure, mentally stable and distressed, racially dominant and marginalized, cisgender and transgender, wealthy and poor, old and young, etc., could get to know one another. The model is based on research showing that stigma and discrimination are most effectively reduced when people have the opportunity to connect with one another through non-contrived mutual activities within informal settings (Moon & Shuman, 2013), such as those offered by participatory arts spaces (Howells & Zelnick, 2009; Welsh NHS Confederation, 2018).

Thus, unlike many community arts and art therapy practices in which *community* refers to people identified by their deviation from a white, middle-upper class, cisgender, nondisabled norm (Kester, 1995), ArtWorks was established to bring together people across socio-cultural differences. It employs a transformational approach to art therapy whereby participants collectively determine their engagement in social change processes, in contrast to an instrumental focus by which art is used as a "tool" for fostering individual adaptation to a broken society (Huss & Sela-Amit, 2018). We enact this transformational approach through cultivating community, taking a position of radical inclusivity, working to decenter power, maintaining a deglamorized view of our work, and fostering mutual care practices. In the following sections I address the strategies and challenges of enacting these transformational aims.

Cultivating community

One challenge to cultivating community is determining what we mean by *community*, an elastic, politicized term. Community is typically delineated over against the forces of oppression, associated with the "victimized yet resilient other" (Kwon, 2002, p. 147) and tied to concepts like trust, belonging, safety, and caring for one another. It is seldom conceived of as unfavorable, which hinders critical evaluation of its effects (Badham, 2013). The ideal of social closeness and comfort can obscure the fact that communities sometimes create divisions, borders, and exclusions (Young, 1986, p. 302). A more nuanced understanding of community and social inclusion/exclusion is called for. Today's uncertain, confusing, changeable world requires that people piece together fragments of life, reflexively building and rebuilding a coherent sense of self and community identities (Mulligan et al., 2008).

Because at ArtWorks we strive to bring together people from a wide spectrum of social, cultural, economic, and political identities, our collective identity is complicated. The ArtWorks 'community' is constantly negotiating the social terrain of belonging and alienation. There is a core group of people who have developed a sense of trust, camaraderie, and care for one another, but this very closeness can subtly function to exclude others. Our composition of participants is changeable, and due to socio-cultural-political differences there are limits to their ability to deeply understand each other's perspectives and experiences. Far from an ideal, our community is contingent, unstable, divergent, dynamic, and complex. At times, I long for a less ambiguous, more romanticized version of community, but I remind myself that such an ideal echoes the "same desire for social wholeness identification that underlies racism . . . ethnic chauvinism . . . and political sectarianism" (Young, 1986, p. 302). One defining characteristic of ArtWorks is a commitment to making art in the context of community, which enables us to continually reimagine and reinvent our collective identity based on the realities of our lived experiences.

Radical inclusivity

Radical inclusivity makes encounters across social divides possible. When people have the opportunity to learn about each other's experiences, hopes, struggles, skills, values, and perspectives, it becomes impossible to hold onto the thin, essentializing stories strangers often create about one another. Social identities are not erased at ArtWorks; rather, simplistic caricatures transform into real people under the relational scrutiny of working side-by-side.

Establishing a community-based arts practice does not, however, automatically foster questioning of taken for granted assumptions about oneself, other individuals, or groups of people. It is not enough to engage in a shared space and provide opportunities for the disenfranchised to be afforded voice. There must also be efforts to deconstruct normativity through an explicit examination of whiteness, ableism, transphobia, classism, and heteronormativity and to critically engage with marginalizing discourses that arise within the dynamics of participation (Ehlert, 2020; Madyaningrum & Sonn, 2011).

There are two primary challenges to radical inclusivity. First, who is included in the relational dynamic? Do we include the couple who makes art in an isolated corner of the room, the library staff and security personnel, the man who weekly sets up his laptop at the table where we congregate but remains absorbed in music playing through his headphones, or the curious onlookers who check out what we are doing as they wait their turn to use one of the music practice rooms around the perimeter of the space? Are they all part of this radically inclusive community?

Second, is *everyone always* welcome in the space? How about the person who is intoxicated and belligerent, or the man who repeatedly makes young women in the space uncomfortable through his use of sexual innuendo? Is the man caught stealing a phone from another person's backpack still welcome? Can we simply accept someone who is loud and disruptive when another participant who has difficulty screening stimuli is visibly distressed by the chaos and noise?

As participants and co-facilitators, Jackie and I use harm reduction, conflict mediation, critical dialogue, and collective problem-solving skills in addressing these thorny questions. We encourage consideration of how social identities may impact the way behaviors are interpreted. We challenge oppressive narratives. Who is and is not 'normal'? Who is permitted to be loud, disruptive, quirky, to take up space and time, to dominate an environment? When is behavior unsafe and when is it really just uncomfortable? When does one person's behavior impinge on the rights of another person? As difficult as these questions are, collectively engaging with them is essential to fostering a vibrant, inclusive community.

Working to decenter power

As a white, cisgender, heterosexual, currently non-disabled, middle class, female-identified art therapist and university professor, I benefit tremendously from privilege. While Jackie and I continually work to shed the role of experts (Yi, 2019), we recognize that we hold positions of subtle power. We are allowed in the staff office area, order supplies and materials, and are called upon by internal staff and external professionals to be the representatives of ArtWorks and set the tone for what happens in the studio space.

Thus, it is an ongoing project to decenter power and foster a co-constructed art practice. Small tasks such as setting-up and putting away materials or orienting new people to the space are shared by everyone. An ongoing exchange of skills and knowledge occurs informally as well as through participant-led workshops. Similarly, we all take collective responsibility for material and emotional resources. When we needed sewing machines, one participant used social media to resource three donated machines. When it is someone's birthday, any one of us might bring a special treat.

When conflicts in the studio arise, we engage in collective problem-solving. For example, when a young child's behavior had, on more than one occasion, disrupted the ability of other participants to enjoy their experience in the studio, we had a group discussion about how to resolve the situation, with the goal of remaining both a broadly inclusive environment and a space conducive to artmaking and conversation.

In these ways and others, we co-create our own miniature utopia (Drass, 2016), our nontraditional subculture of aesthetic experience (Hickey-Moody, 2016) and mutual care.

Maintaining a deglamorized view

Much of the art therapy literature about community art studios extols their virtues. At their best, community art studios are indeed small utopias, and it is a joy to take part in them. Yet, they are not a panacea that can solve all the problems of this complex and deeply troubled society.

Art therapy students and professionals sometimes think all one has to do is show up to a community studio, make art with participants, and experience positive results (Nolan, 2019). There is a misguided notion that community-based practices are little bubbles of warm fuzzies and that their very existence assumes engagement in social justice work. In this romanticized scenario, social justice is falsely viewed as the domain of heroes (Toporek, 2018) and words like *empowerment* or *inclusion* are used with little effort to unpack what they really mean (Lawthom et al., 2007; Lentz, 2008). In reality, participatory art practices can mask uncritical, exploitative actions that reinforce the very injustices they purport to combat (Robertson & Vinebaum, 2016).

Understanding and negotiating power within collaborative relationships is messy work (Talwar, 2019). ArtWorks is particularly challenging because of the lack of a cohesive, consistent community composition. Multiple levels of relationships, from acquaintances to intimates, must be navigated on any given day, making for a dynamic but at times exhausting relational terrain.

Given differences in identity, affiliations, motivations, and intentions, it is no surprise that misunderstandings and conflicts erupt from time to time. Jackie and I attempt to bridge cultural differences, sort out conflicts, and be the itinerant empaths, all while trying to take into account our own socio-cultural-historical privileged and marginalized positionalities. The fact is, sometimes we are worn out and don't want to be there at all. And sometimes we want to be there only to quietly work on our art, without attending to the social dynamics. What helps Jackie and I stay centered in our practice is our belief in its value.

Fostering mutual care

Whenever I begin working in a new place as an art therapist, I want to know: What health and healing practices are already working well here? How have people come together to support and care for one another over time? This, I know, is the foundation of the work we will do together.

My experience with various ArtWorks sites affirms that each community has its own unique identity, knowledge of wellbeing strategies, and methods for engaging in mutual care. At the food pantry, there was a well-established group of people from the neighborhood who exhibited a sense of belonging, trust, and caregiving. In contrast, at the men's shelter, it was initially difficult to discern how care was enacted. Gradually, I began to see how caring was offered by one individual to another, as if it were a precious commodity. One person helped set up the art tables, another person taught how to make folded paper chains with gum wrappers. When we (at that time, a group of six art therapists) had already decided to end ArtWorks programming at the shelter due to a lack of participation from the broader community, one guest revealed that he would have been able to promote the studio in the community if he had only known we needed his help. In hindsight, I realize we were not at the shelter long enough to understand its intricate, resourceful structure of care. For the poor, often disabled, predominantly people of color who were living there, the skill of individual resourcefulness was a necessity, part of the injustice of a social system set up to distribute resources inequitably (Ahmed, 2014).

In establishing mutual care practices at ArtWorks, I acknowledge the labor of Black, Brown, Indigenous, queer, and disabled activists, artists, art therapists, healers, and scholars who have provided the scholarship, praxis, and inspiration behind this work (for example, Anderson, 2021; Brown, 2019; BAVH, 2013; Piepzna-Samarasinha, 2018; Talwar, 2016; Tillet & Tillet, 2019; Yi, 2021). As co-participants in an arts-based public health practice, we foster an environment of honoring and learning from the many ways people fight back against injustice and develop their own methods for healing and resilience (Iman et al., 2009).

Currently, the need to be resilient in an inhospitable world produces people acclimated to prolonged periods of precarity and instability. Embracing a relational aesthetic in which the focus is on enhancing intrapersonal, interpersonal, and social connections (Moon, 2002, 2016a), the community studio becomes a place where everyone is viewed as having healing capabilities and potentials (BAVH, 2013), all of which are part of the living care practice we concoct together.

A challenge to community care is tied to the radically inclusive nature of the practice. We have had participants make sexist remarks, interpret other attendees' behavior on the basis of racial stereotypes, behave in a manner that some people found disturbing or intimidating, and use humor to make disparaging remarks about people passing through the space. The wider social context of power relations doesn't disappear in a community studio (Lewis & Spandler, 2019). If everyone is welcome, what do we do when one person's presence or behavior threatens other people's sense of being safe and cared for? How do we attend to structural inequalities that play out in the space so that they aren't reinforced? While Jackie and I strive to create an environment of mutual care and accountability, sometimes we have to lean into our facilitator roles to put a stop to harmful behaviors, foster consciousness raising, promote reparative actions, and engage the collective in fighting for mutual respect and dignity.

Summary

We are grateful to have found a home for ArtWorks at the Chicago Public Library. It is a dynamic, vibrant, inclusive social space that provides the perfect context for a public arts and health practice aimed at radical inclusivity, community cultivation, decentered power, and mutual care.

ArtWorks is a perfectly imperfect space where we "chart, experimentally, what it feels like to be in mixed company . . . and the horizon is not safety, calmness, smoothness, but the moment when the smoothness breaks toward an Other" (Kuppers, 2019, p. 54). Though my efforts in this chapter have been to present ArtWorks with all its rough edges and challenges, there are those moments of unscripted magic when that *breaking toward an Other* occurs. For example, there was the day that two men made music together. One of them was typically talkative but with a private logic that was impossible to follow, and the other was mostly silent but with occasional bursts of abrupt, loud, awkwardly enunciated words. As a result, they rarely talked or even acknowledged each other's presence. On that day, I turned around to find them crouched together on the floor, leaning over a third person's phone on which an app was playing a percussive rap-style beat. The two men spontaneously began improvising, making beats, playing off of each other. It was an example of "homeopathies of intimacy, small inclusions of new forms of closeness and tenderness, in public space, inoculating publics by exposing them, bit by bit, to new futures" (Kuppers, 2019, p. 55). Or, to put it more simply, it was a bit of magic in our midst.

References

Ahmed, S. (2014, August 25). Selfcare as warfare. *Feministkilljoys*. http://feministkilljoys.com/2014/08/25/selfcare-as-warfare/

Allen, P. B. (1995). Coyote comes in from the cold: The evolution of the open studio concept. *Art Therapy: Journal of the American Art Therapy Association*, *12*(3), 161–166.

Allen, P. B. (2008). Commentary on community art studios: Underlying principles. *Art Therapy: Journal of the American Art Therapy Association*, *25*(1), 11–12.

Anderson, M. (2021). Queer ethos in art therapy. In L. Leone (Ed.), *Craft in art therapy: Diverse approaches to the transformative power of craft materials and methods* (pp. 218–236). New York, NY Routledge.

Archibald, L., Dewar, J., Reid, C., & Stevens, V. (2012). *Dancing, singing, painting, and speaking the healing story: Healing through creative arts*. Aboriginal Healing Foundation. www.ahf.ca/downloads/healing-through-creative-arts.pdf

Badham, M. (2013). The turn to community: Exploring the political and relational in the arts. *Journal of Arts & Communities*, *5*(2+3), 93–104.

BAVH, B. (2013). "A babe-iliscious healing justice statement" from the BadAss Visionary Healers (BAVH). *Nineteen Sixty Nine: An Ethnic Studies Journal*, *2*(1), 1–12. https://escholarship.org/uc/item/1z61z54j

Brown, A. M. (2019). *Pleasure activism: The politics of feeling good*. Chico, CA Press.

Drass, J. M. (2016). Creating a culture of connection: A postmodern punk rock approach to art therapy. *Art Therapy: Journal of the American Art Therapy Association*, *33*(3), 138–143.

Ehlert, R. (2020). A little less alone: Surviving sanism in art therapy. *Art Therapy: Journal of the American Art Therapy Association*, *37*(2), 99–101.

Evans, S. D., Kivell, N., Haarlammert, M., Malhotra, K., & Rosen, A. (2014). Critical community practice: An introduction to the special section. *Journal for Social Action in Counseling and Psychology*, *6*(1).

Friedli, L. (2009). *Mental health, resilience and inequalities*. World Health Organization. www.euro.who.int/__data/assets/pdf_file/0012/100821/E92227.pdf

Gipson, L. (2019). Envisioning Black women's consciousness in art therapy. In S. Talwar (Ed.), *Art therapy for social justice: Radical intersections* (pp. 96–120). Abingdon, UK Routledge.

Hickey-Moody, A. (2016). Being different in public. *Continuum: Journal of Media & Cultural Studies*, *30*(5), 531–541.

Howells, V., & Zelnik, T. (2009). Making art: A qualitative study of personal and group transformation in a community art studio. *Psychiatric Rehabilitation Journal*, *32*(3), 215–222.

Huss, E., & Sela-Amit, M. (2018). Arts in social work, do we really need it? *Research on Social Work Practice*, *29*(6), 721–726.

Iman, J., Fullwood, C., Paz, N., W, D., & Hassan, S. (2009). *Girls do what they have to do to survive: Illuminating methods used by girls in the sex trade and street economy to fight back and heal*. Young Women's Empowerment Project. https://ywepchicago.files.worpress.com/2011/06/girls-do-what-they-have-to-do-to-survive-a-study-of-resilience-and-resistance.pdf

Jeffery, L., Palladino, M., Rotter, R., & Woolley, A. (2019). Creative engagement with migration. *Crossings: Journal of Migration & Culture*, *10*(1), 3–17.

Kester, G. (1995). Aesthetic evangelists: Conversion and empowerment in contemporary community art. *Afterimage: The Journal of Media Arts and Cultural Criticism*, *22*(6), 5–11.

Kuppers, P. (2019). Public intimacies: Water work in play. *Canadian Journal of Disability Studies*, *8*(1), 32–57.

Kwon, M. (2002). *One place after another: Site-specific art and local identity*. Cambridge, MA MIT Press.

Lawthom, R., Sixsmith, J., & Kagan, C. (2007). Interrogating power: The case of arts and mental health in community projects. *Journal of Community and Applied Social Psychology*, *17*, 268–279.

Leake, J. (2015). Women re-imagining life through art: A/r/tographical discoveries in a community expressive arts studio. *Journal of Applied Arts & Health*, *6*(3), 291–306.

Lentz, R. (2008). What we talk about when we talk about art therapy: An outsider's guide to identity crisis. *Art Therapy: Journal of the American Art Therapy Association*, *25*(1), 13–14.

Lewis, L., & Spandler, H. (2019). Breaking down boundaries? Exploring mutuality through art-making in an open studio mental health setting. *Journal of Applied Arts & Health*, *10*(1), 9–23.

Madyaningrum, M. E., & Sonn, C. (2011). Exploring the meaning of participation in a community art project: A case study on the Seeming Project. *Journal of Community and Applied Social Psychology*, *21*, 358–370.

Moon, C. H. (2002). *Studio art therapy: Cultivating the artist identity in the art therapist*. London, UK Jessica Kingsley Publishers.

Moon, C. H. (2016a). Relational aesthetics and art therapy. In J. A. Rubin (Ed.), *Approaches to art therapy* (3rd ed., pp. 50–68). Abingdon, UK Routledge.

Moon, C. H. (2016b). Open studio approach to art therapy. In D. Gussak & M. Rosal (Eds.), *The Wiley handbook of art therapy* (pp. 112–121). Hoboken, NJ Wiley Blackwell.

Moon, C. H., & Shuman, V. (2013). The community art studio: Creating a space of solidarity and inclusion. In P. Howie, S. Prasad, & J. Kristel (Eds.), *Using art therapy with diverse populations: Crossing cultures and abilities* (pp. 297–307). London, UK Jessica Kingsley Publishers.

Mulligan, M., Scanlon, C., & Welch, N. (2008). Renegotiating community life: Arts, agency, inclusion and wellbeing. *Gateways: International Journal of Community Research and Engagement*, *1*, 48–72.

Nolan, E. (2019). Opening art therapy thresholds: Mechanisms that influence change in the community art therapy studio. *Art Therapy: Journal of the American Art Therapy Association*, *36*(2), 77–85.

Ottemiller, D. D., & Awais, Y. J. (2016). A model for art therapists in community-based practice. *Art Therapy: Journal of the American Art Therapy Association*, *33*(3), 144–150.

Piepzna-Samarasinha, L. L. (2018). *Care work: Dreaming disability justice*. Vancouver, Canada Arsenal Pulp Press.

Robertson, K., & Vinebaum, L. (2016). Crafting community. *Textile*, *14*(1), 2–13.

Talwar, S. (2016). Creating alternative public spaces: Community-based art practice, critical consciousness and social justice. In D. Gussak & M. Rosal (Eds.), *The Wiley handbook of art therapy* (pp. 840–847). Hoboken, NJ Wiley Blackwell.

Talwar, S. (2019). "The sweetness of money:" The Creatively Empowered Women (CEW) design studio, feminist pedagogy and art therapy. In S. Talwar (Ed.), *Art therapy for social justice: Radical intersections* (pp. 178–193). Abingdon, UK Routledge.

Tillet, S., & Tillet, S. (2019). "You want to be well?" Self-care as Black feminist intervention in art therapy. In S. Talwar (Ed.), *Art therapy for social justice: Radical intersections* (pp. 123–143). Abingdon, UK Routledge.

Timm-Bottos, J. (2006). Constructing creative community: Reviving health and justice through community arts. *Canadian Art Therapy Association Journal*, *19*(2), 12–26.

Timm-Bottos, J. (2017). Public practice art therapy: Enabling spaces across North America. *Canadian Art Therapy Association Journal*, *30*(2), 94–99.

Timm-Bottos, J., & Chainey, R. (2015). Art hives how-to guide. *Art Hives*. https://arthives.org/resources/art-hives-how-guide

Toporek, R. L. (2018). Strength, solidarity, strategy and sustainability: A counseling psychologist's guide to social action. *The European Journal of Counseling Psychology*, *7*(1), 90–110.

Welsh NHS Confederation. (2018). *Arts, health, and well-being*. www.social-partnershipforum.org/media/124797/Literature-review-of-arts-and-health-and-wellbeing.pdf

Yi, C.-S. (S.). (2019). Res(crip)ting art therapy: Disability culture as a social justice intervention. In S. Talwar (Ed.), *Art therapy for social justice: Radical intersections* (pp. 161–177). Abingdon, UK Routledge.

Yi, C.-S. (S.). (2021). Demystifying the individualistic approach to self-care: Sewing as a metaphorical process for documenting relational and community care in disability culture. In L. Leone (Ed.), *Craft in art therapy: Diverse approaches to the transformative power of craft materials and methods* (pp. 72–89). New York, NY Routledge.

Young, I. M. (1986). The ideal of community and the politics of difference. *Social Theory and Practice*, *12*(1), 1–26.

13 MOMU

A multiprofessional response to a multifaceted reality

Emilio J Gómez-Ciriano and Hugh McLaughlin

Introduction

This chapter will report on the findings and experiences of a European-funded Erasmus+ Project between 2015 and 2018 involving Turku University of Applied Sciences (TUAS) Finland, Manchester Metropolitan University (MMU) United Kingdom, University of Tartu Viljandi Culture Academy (UT VCA) Estonia, and Universidad de Castilla-La Mancha (UCLM) Spain. The project sought to work towards three major outputs. First, bringing together lecturers and students of social work and art to explore how they could work together to develop a programme with young people addressing youth unemployment, alienation and precarity. The second output consisted of the development and implementation of a teaching module based on a previously constructed competencies framework and, last, disseminating the results (Gómez Ciriano et al., 2018).

Three years after the end of the project, two of its members reflect on its potentialities for the present and for the future of what was entitled MOMU (Moving Towards Multiprofessional Work) project.

This chapter is structured into three sections. First, we contextualise the socio-economic and academic grounds on which MOMU was erected (particularly when referring to youth unemployment). Second, we explain and reflect on the common competencies framework, the training module. And last, the conclusion will reflect on the importance of the outcomes of MOMU and its follow up at international and national levels.

DOI: 10.4324/9781003105350-14

Part 1: building the foundations of MOMU

Why youth unemployment matters

Young people, youth unemployment, and MOMU

The idea of MOMU was built on the premise of EU Youth Strategy 2010–2018, which proposed cross-sectorial approaches with both short- and long-term actions involving all key policy areas that affect and empower young people in Europe: education and training, employment and entrepreneurship, social inclusion, health and wellbeing, participation, culture and creativity, volunteering, and youth and the wider world. The emphasis of MOMU's activities lay in understanding and promoting social inclusion, health and wellbeing, and culture and creativity in particular. The strategy emphasised cooperation at different levels in order to promote solidarity and social inclusion and doing it in a multiprofessional way.

Together with this, the 'New Skills for New Jobs initiative' (NSNJ) launched in 2008 by the EU Commission, became a source for the development of one of the main outputs of MOMU: a competencies framework in arts and social work developed after analysing surveys and national professional competencies frameworks and collecting 'best practices' of arts and social work collaborations by the different country members. The common framework paved the way for two subsequent steps: the production of an experimental training module for lecturers and practitioners and the implementation of pilot sessions that involved users, practitioners, and lecturers. These results can be found in the project handbook (Gómez Ciriano et al., 2018) that has been translated into English, Spanish, Estonian, and Finnish.

Unpacking some of the terminology

How can art and social work intersect? How do they enlarge the definitions of both? And how do they open up new professional and treatment options for youth?

For many, the term multiprofessional may appear strange, as they may be more familiar with interprofessional practice. Multiprofessional working can be understood as two or more professionals working alongside each together where each discipline contributes to a fuller understanding of the issue. However, in some nations, as Banks (2010, p. 281) notes, it has been replaced by interprofessional working signifying 'different professionals coming together with shared roles and interchangeability of roles.' Without wishing to get bogged down in terminological quagmires, the two terms are often used interchangeably, and one may be more acceptable in some countries than others. One of the features we discovered while working across nations is the power of language to express and define ideas, particularly as for three of the four countries in the project English was not their first language. This was illustrated keenly when as we were making an argument for collaborative practice we were told that in Estonia 'collaboration' meant traitorous cooperation with either the Germans (WW2) or more recently with the Russians. We should not assume that what we call art or social work in one country will map across the same as what another country includes in its description of art or social work. Thus, building common understandings brings with it a humbleness in not taking for granted the same meaning for the same word and concept in the different cultural contexts.

There is also a debate about whether you can – or should – consider artists and social workers as professionals. Do they meet the traditional criteria (Giddens, 2001) of having restricted entry into the profession via identified criteria or qualifications? Do they have a professional association that registers and manages conduct and performance? Last, is social work or art practice restricted only to those who are licensed? You could also ask whether this definition matches the accepted use of terms like 'professional footballers,' 'dancers,' or 'soldiers.'

Whilst Payne (2000) has argued that groups like social workers, nurses, or physiotherapists may be viewed as semi-professions or aspiring professions, this neglected the issue that such claims also act as a means of exclusion and exclusivity. Importantly, they also neglect issues of power (McLaughlin, 2012b), ignoring how certain occupational groups seek to corral areas of expertise for their members and by definition exclude other professions. Professions are not natural entities and they are not necessarily benign or harmless, but rather they represent occupational boundary claims where changes in one may have consequences for others. However, for the purposes of this chapter in discussing artists and social workers it may matter less whether these are professions or not; what matters is that the social workers and artists act professionally by being reliable, respectful, and competent in how they act and what they do.

Artists and social workers together

WHAT DIFFERENCES DO THEY HAVE? WHAT COMMONALITIES?

In thinking about artists and social workers working together there is no requirement that the relationship should always be equal. In reality it is likely to be more of a continuum where at one end all the power resides with the social worker who has commissioned an artist to work with young people to create a cartoon film, YouTube clip, dance, poem, performance, or comic book based on their experiences. At the other end of the continuum an artist may recruit the help of a social worker to help understand the experiences and legal situation of young people in care to help inform a sculpture they are creating. Last, there are other more equal positions in the continuum where both are committed to a joint project sharing a common vision of what is to be achieved and why it is important in both artistic and social terms. In an editorial for a special edition of *Social Work Education (2012)* on arts-based approaches, the co-editors claimed:

> Crossing boundaries between the social sciences with the arts and humanities can help to communicate service users' and carers' experiences more powerfully.
>
> (Hafford-Letchfield et al., 2012, p. 683)

Two social work academics working alongside an artist curated the first UK public exhibition of social workers using art to explore the lived experience of 'doing' and 'being' a social worker (Leigh et al., 2019, p. 271). Tonteri (2013) claimed that some artists are willing to work in new environments; similarly there are social workers who are willing to apply art particularly in work with children or with those with learning difficulties where alternative modes of communication need to be developed. Boehm and colleagues (2016) noted that artists may feel that they cannot access the world of social work or if they do their artistic integrity might be viewed as compromised. They may also be concerned that they are not trained to respond to safeguarding risks, whilst social workers may feel that they do not have the confidence, knowledge, or expertise to apply artistically based approaches. Social workers may also feel that their work is complicated enough in having to work interprofessionally with health, education, and police colleagues (McLaughlin et al., 2011).

It is in situations like these that interprofessional practice approaches can provide a way forward to benefit service users and communities. As Gómez Ciriano and colleagues (2018) identified, although there are examples of interprofessional work between artists and social workers, there is a lack of learning frameworks to support how best artists and social workers can negotiate joint projects, identify roles, implement actions, and evaluate the effectiveness of any strategy within this collaborative process. It is also worth considering when such interventions can be considered a success. If they produce an excellent artefact but fail to address the social problem, is it success? Is it a failure if the work addressed a social problem, but the artistic production was poor? As social workers the authors might claim that addressing the social problem is more important, but would an artist necessarily agree? And would they be wrong?

One of the aims of MOMU was to clarify the roles of different social care and arts professionals in order to promote interprofessional practice. In order to do this the MOMU academics were challenged to undertake a range of experiential embodied activities to take them out of their comfort zone and to free them up to new learning opportunities. These included: dance, a concept card game to identify the formula for effective interprofessional work, designing occupational maps, photographic representations, and liberarte activity (further information on all these activities can be found in Gomez Ciriano et al., 2018).

In one of the activities developed by MOMU, students of the School of Fine Arts were asked to draw a picture in which they described themselves at their present moment and their labour expectations for the future. One of the options that many of them had in mind was migrating abroad due to lack of opportunities. This art activity was developed to be used as a way of expressing hopes and frustrations. The forum that followed the activity, in which students, practitioners, and lecturers of social work and arts were represented, contributed to the chance to empathise and learn one from another and to realise the importance of combining skills, competences, and knowledge in a synergic way (see drawing the journey to find a job in the blog: https://blog.uclm.es/momu/2017/05/06/drawing-the-journey-to-find-a-job/MOMU-Spain).

Part II: MOMU in motion

The project created a common competencies framework that could be adapted to: a) an international context, b) different national contexts, and c) arts and social work academics and professionals, and this proved to be a challenge. It took almost a year to complete and was structured into 5 guidelines, resulting in 23 competencies. On reflection we may have overcomplicated the process (Gómez-Ciriano et al., 2018, p. 34)!

Once the framework had been created it was time to prepare the training package for the multiprofessional teaching for arts and social work lecturers. Pilot sessions were organised by MOMU in the different countries. Two of the models to support this dialogue between the different professionals included the ACCeSS model and the CAST model. The ACCeSS model was undertaken in pairs (although it could be done in groups) and sought to identify basic knowledge and techniques for working with arts approaches with communities identifying core experiences, skills, and perspectives of the arts and social work students that supported interprofessional working and experiential learning.

A – **Aims,** can include government initiatives, funding bodies targets etc.
C – **Competencies,** experiences, skills, perspectives (this links very closely to the CAST model mentioned later)
C – **Communities,** getting to know communities, groups, or individuals and consultation
S – **Setting Goals**, SMART – specific, measurable, assignable, realistic, and time specific
S – **Setting Roles,** what, who, where, when, and how will we know if it has worked?

The CAST model aims to support a structured conversation between arts and social work professionals and was also used in pairs to explore experiences and competencies between artists and social care students within a structured dialogical framework.

C – **Communities**, clients, or participants they wished to work with.
A – **Arts approaches** they could use
S – **Stakeholders** who needed to be included and how
T – **Themes** what were the themes, challenges, and issues they wanted to work on?

The feedback was compiled from the lecturers who participated in the MOMU training seminars as well as creating material for the training that would later be delivered. This group included 40 lecturers, 200 students, and 20 working life representatives (practitioners). It is noteworthy that during some of the teaching sessions in each country, members of the project from other countries were present and actively participated, and this enriched the process with an international perspective. Part of the tested materials and the educative resources were included in the MOMU handbook and online. The MOMU process can be followed in the blog: https://blog.uclm.es/momu.

Part 3: reflections on MOMU

These reflections are very much our own, as two of the participants in MOMU. We do not claim to be representative or claim that these thoughts are shared by our colleagues, although we would hope they would agree with much we have written. The reflections are split into reflections in relation to the academics working together, the national projects undertaken by the different university teams, and some reflections at the European level.

Academic reflections

Working in an international project as academics in arts and social work provides a dual dynamic between academic disciplines and national identities. As such it provides opportunities to challenge one's own taken-for-granted assumptions and encourages you to be clearer about what you think and why. It also provides an opportunity for greater diversity than previous experiences, creativity, and a need to be aware of the differing cultural roots and norms of others participating.

Whilst cultural competence is embedded in social work professional mandates, policy guidelines and educational curricula Fisher-Borne and colleagues (2015) critique it. Its focus on comfort with 'others' functions as a proxy for racial group identity in emphasising knowing and becoming competent in another's culture, while it neglects to address social justice and social inequalities. In contrast cultural humility explicitly acknowledges power differentials in seeking to cultivate self-awareness of how cultural forces interact with structural forces and includes three components: 'reflection, institutional and individual accountability, and the mitigation of systemic power imbalances' (Fisher-Borne et al., 2015, p. 173). As such, cultural humility can be seen as important in MOMU while working between the teams from the different countries, between the different disciplinary preferences, and between the students and young people. It is less about mastery of someone else's position but more about an accountability for one's own. How things are done within the arts and social work may have similarities as well as differences and we needed to accept these as starting points for discussion and not assume that artists should master social work or vice versa. Whilst within this there was also awareness about different nationalities needing to work according to a more specific timetabled programme with others being more laissez-faire than others. Some countries have more individualistic cultures than others. In some nations there was also a greater acceptance of academic hierarchy than others and some favoured a more 'blunt' approach in their communication than others. Some of these differences may also have been exacerbated by not being able to use their first language in the MOMU project. All the meetings were held in English resulting in the other three nations having to speak to an international meeting in a second language that some members were obviously more confident to use than others. This resulted in some of the participants being unable to fully participate.

To promote effective international co-operation it is important to have time with shared opportunities get to know your fellow workers; games and creative activities are great for this. Having fun together really helped whilst one of the authors will never forget a cultural experience in Finland when they went to a sauna, ran along a pier in the snow, broke the ice, and then went for a 'short swim,' before getting out and running back through the snow to an outside hot tub and repeating the experience as it was so enjoyable! In all of this it is essential to communicate, communicate, and communicate again.

Student learning and reflections

The implementation of the project worked much better in two of the countries whilst the other two struggled to implement the programme fully. In one country the geographical distances proved problematic and working with arts and social work students was impossible to organise within the university schedules, which resulted in an inability to undertake joint projects. In the other country the university disbanded its community arts programme whilst the arts students were on a different campus 30 minutes away by train. The professional social work curriculum had no space for such a programme and so it had to be delivered voluntarily as part of a summer school.

The other two countries were much more successful. In these countries they were able to recruit arts and social work students and lecturers. The team in one country delivered a three-session programme focussing on migration as an option for young unemployed people. In completing the evaluation of the programme there was a feeling that interprofessional work would be easier if they 'could acquire more practice skills' and 'If only I had more time, I would dedicate more time to this.' The students also commented in looking towards the future that they now had:

> The possibility of new ways of action, not just at the personal level, but also as a way of collaborating with different subjects in social work and art studies. Many nice future projects in mind.

Overall, the student group in this country identified the need for interprofessional working between social work and arts-based students – more so now than ever before – and were open to developing work between the two professions.

In the final country, the team arranged the most successful and longest programme of five sessions and included practitioners from the field. In terms of interprofessional work the students noted,

> Everyone got something new from the workshop. The line between who were the social work students and who were the theatre students was not as clear as you would have expected.

At the end of the programme one student reflected that,

> For the future students, I wish this kind of multiprofessional project will become even more common. . . . I think that in working life, they need people that are open to multiprofessionality or even take it for granted.

And

> I have gained a huge amount of knowledge and shared understanding from the functional methods courses in my own studies, but the different theoretical viewpoint made me see the issue in a different light.

Reflections at the European level

The MOMU project proved to be a key experience of working in a non-traditional multiprofessional partnership for those academics and students who participated. The project helped to open boundaries and minds to new possibilities and thinking 'outside the box.' It has been useful to help identify competencies relevant for your own practice and to create others. However, the follow up of this project should not be ignored. It is critical now that the funding has ended to consider whether the gains made by the project have now been embedded in the four countries or are now lost. Have the different universities been able to continue to promote these non-traditional types of interdisciplinary learning in order for multiprofessional learning and teaching to achieve better outcomes for communities and service users? At best we can say that this is a mixed result and depends as much on the individual champions involved in the project as the willingness of universities to think outside the box.

Conclusions

Within both the notions of multiprofessionals and interdisciplinary practice is the belief that 'the whole is greater than the sum of the parts' and thus by bringing different professions together you would necessarily get a better solution. Such a perspective is obviously flawed, and just because you have an intelligent, well-meaning artist and social worker using the most up to date practices to work with young people does not necessarily mean that the situation will improve: they could actually make it worse! In bringing together various professions to create a better understanding between professionals in order to bring about transformation for service users on a micro, meso, or macro level this should be taken into account.

The project set out to promote multidisciplinary work between art and social work students in developing a framework for mutual cooperative learning. In particular, this was an international project with countries at different points in the multidisciplinary process with differing professional and curricular requirements who were able to collaborate effectively at the pedagogic and theoretical levels. This became more difficult when the project attempted to put these theories into practice in the different countries resulting in differing levels of success. At best the project can be seen as a partial success, but probably more importantly for the promotion of arts and social work there was need for a longer evaluation period to find out whether the programme had influenced any of the participants, in particular whether they sought out collaborative opportunities between the arts and social work or whether any of the artists became social workers or social workers developed artistic skills. Last and most importantly for social work, it would be critical to evaluate whether such ventures had a positive impact for service users. This is the big challenge for social workers and artists working together and more evidence is needed to encourage such collaborations.

Acknowledgements

We would like to acknowledge our colleagues from the University of Castilla-La-Mancha, Manchester Metropolitan University, University of Tartu, and Turku University of Applied Sciences. In particular the authors of this chapter would like to thank Suvi Kivela from TUAS for being the project manager in the development of the project.

References

Banks, S. (2010). Interprofessional ethics: A developing field? Notes from the ethics and social welfare conference, Sheffield UK. *Ethics and Social Welfare*, 4(3), 280–294.

Boehm, C., Lilja-Vilherlampi, L. M., Linnossuo, O., Mc Laughlin, H., Gómez Ciriano, E. J., Martínez Martín, O., Mercado García, E., Kivela, S., Maännamaa, I., & Gibson, J. (2016). Contexts and approaches to multiprofessional working in arts and social care. *Journal of Finnish Universities of Applied Sciences* (UAS journal), EAPRIL. https://uasjournal.fi/in-english/contexts-and-approaches-to-multiprofessional-working-%E2%80%8Ein-arts-and-social-care/%20%E2%80%8E

Brueghel Think Tank. (2020). *The scarring effect of Covid-19: Youth unemployment in Europe.* Retrieved December 1st, 2020 from www.bruegel.org/2020/11/the-scarring-effect-of-covid-19-youth-unemployment-in-europe/

European Commission. (2015). *European semester thematic factsheet: Youth unemployment.* Retrieved January 13th, 2021 from https://ec.europa.eu/info/sites/default/files/file_import/european-semester_thematic-factsheet_youth_employment_en.pdf

European Commission. (2018). *Communication from the commission to the European parliament, the council, the European economic and social committee and the committee of regions: Connecting and Empowering young people: A new EU Youth Strategy COM(2018) 269 final.*

European Commission. (Europe 2020). *A European strategy for smart, sustainable and inclusive growth.* Retrieved January 13th, 2021 from https://ec.europa.eu/eu2020/pdf/COMPLET%20EN%20BARROSO%20%20%20007%20-%20Europe%202020%20-%20EN%20version.pdf

European Commission. EU youth strategy. (2010–2018). *EU Youth Strategy 2010-2018 | European Youth Portal (europa.eu).* Retrieved January 31th, 2021 from https://europa.eu/youth/strategy/strategy-2010-2018_en

Eurostat. (2021). News release euroindicators 16/2021. *Euro Area Unemployment.* Retrieved February 22nd, 2021 from https://ec.europa.eu/eurostat/documents/portlet_file_entry/2995521/3-01022021-AP-EN.pdf/db860f10-65e3-a1a6-e526-9d4db80904b9

Fisher-Borne-M., Caine, J. M., & Martin, S. L. (2015). From mastery to accountability: Cultural humility as an alternative to cultural competence. *Social Work Education*, *34*(2), 165–181.

Giddens, A. (2001). *Sociology*. Bristol: Polity Press.

Gómez Ciriano, E. J., Kivela, S., Araste, L., Gibson, J., Herranz de la Casa, J. M., Lilja-Viherlampi, L. M., McLaughlin, H., & Männamaa, I. (Eds.). (2018). *Handbook for moving towards multiprofessional work.* Course Material from Turku University of Applied Sciences 113. TUAS.

Hafford-Letchfield, T., Leonard, K., & Couchman, W. (2012). "Arts and extremely dangerous": Critical commentary on the arts in social work education. *Social Work Education*, *31*(6), 683–690. https://doi.org/10.1080/02615479.2012.695149

Leigh, J., Morriss, L., & Morriss, M. (2019). Making visible an invisible trade: Exploring the everyday experiences of doing social work and being a social worker, *Qualitative Social Work*, *19*(2), 267–283.

McLaughlin, H. (2012a). *Understanding social work research*. London: SAGE.

McLaughlin, H. (2012b). Keeping interprofessional practice honest: Fads and critical reflections. In B. Littlechild & R. Smiths (Eds.), *Interprofessional and inter agency practice in the human services: Learning to work together* (pp. 50–61). Harlow: Pearson Education.

McLaughlin, H., Reubsaet, H., & Vanhanen, S. (2011). Introduction. In E. Heikkilä, M. Danker, E. J. Gómez-Ciriano, H. Mclaughlin, & H. Reaubsaet (Eds.), *Working together or better integration: Immigrant, police and social work*. Turku: Institute of Migration.

Payne, M. (2000). *Teamwork in multiprofessional care*. London: Palgrave Macmillan.

Tonteri, A. (2013). Developing multiprofessional working skills in art and social work. In A. Lehto (Ed.). *Deepening the CARPE dimension:* TUAS papers from the second CARPE networking conference in Manchester on 4–6 November 2013. *Comments from Turku University of Applied Sciences*, *82*, 22–29.

14 Using reader's theater to enhance reflexive social work practice, research, and education

Izumi Sakamoto and Shelley Cohen Konrad

Introduction

The heart of the human service professions takes place in relationships. For example, in social work, it is the human relationships that form the context where its core values of service, social justice, dignity, and worth of the person are expressed, a context that also encompasses attentiveness to differences, discrimination, and diversity (National Association of Social Work, 2008). In order to learn these core values, habits of the mind such as critical, reflective thinking are essential. In sum, critical, reflexive, and relational learning is at the core of our practice and learning.

Despite its importance, helping students become engaged in critical, reflexive, and relational learning is challenging. This is especially true when students confront their own biases and assumptions, encounter difficult conversations, and grapple with complex and unjust situations in their internships. Difficult emotions such as anxiety, shame, guilt, and frustration can disrupt learning and impact cognitive and affective processing (Pitner & Sakamoto, 2005, 2016). We have observed, however, that the development of relationships and becoming aware of the development processes of critical consciousness through the arts can help learners identify and analyze these disrupters, making it 'less likely that they will impose their values and beliefs onto their clients' (Pitner & Sakamoto, 2005, p. 6).

Relational learning and critical consciousness are synergistic concepts that cultivate students' capacities to learn with and from others while simultaneously gaining a deeper awareness of themselves. They share many of Freire's (1970) conceptualizations as well as feminist leanings. This chapter makes a case for the integration of the arts in the education of social workers and other human service professions as a mechanism to strengthen relational learning and foster critical consciousness.

DOI: 10.4324/9781003105350-15

There are myriad definitions and applications of the arts. For our purposes we are drawing from a wide range of forms including storytelling, music, visual arts – in fact, any form identified by the artist as art. Both authors have witnessed learners (including practitioners and educators) individually and collectively express, analyze, and effect meaningful exchange through art-infused methodologies. We have come to appreciate how art bridges disconnecting barriers between people and across communities, opening possibilities for learning from others (Escueta & Butterwick, 2021; Huss & Sela-Amit, 2019). Used in concert with multiple liberating educational theories, the arts provide a mechanism to raise the unspoken, learn deeply from those whose values and perceptions are different from our own, address racial and cultural differences, and collaboratively imagine the future. To support our synergistic perspective, we will first explore two bodies of social work literature; relational learning theory (Cohen Konrad, 2010, 2019) and critical consciousness in anti-oppressive practice (Pitner & Sakamoto, 2005, 2016; Sakamoto & Pitner, 2005), which then will be followed by case examples and discussions.

Relational learning

Relational learning is a preferred pedagogy for teaching social work practice, synthesizing multiple theories to inform the 'what, why, and how' of teaching. It promotes a process of conscious instruction whereby selected subject matter is reflexively studied to ensure its coherence with social work values and the ethos of practice. Content is contextualized, meaning that there is no one way to understand any given concept – knowledge and its applications must be responsive to culture, milieu, and stakeholder desire. The effort to understand other's perspectives motivates learners to listen deeply and think critically. The arts can facilitate this process well, as the arts by their very nature contextualize knowledge. How one instructs is similarly conscious, prompting intersubjective and empathic learning, bolstered by the addition of the arts as a pedagogical method. Relational educators foster cognitive and affective human exchange that engages with vulnerability and oftentimes disruptive content. Psychological safety (the shared belief that the learning environment is safe for risk-taking and free of judgment) is foundational; instructors set the stage by modelling and facilitating radical curiosity, intellectual and emotional risk-taking, courageous conversations (Singleton, 2014), and mediating power differentials.

Relational learning builds upon Freire's theory of 'education with people' (1970, 2000). His favored pedagogy, liberating education, promotes facilitated critical inquiry with the objective of both conveying what is known and analyzing existing knowledge, while creating new knowledge to apply to individual and societal change. He used the term 'banking education' to describe traditional pedagogy that is monolithic, unexamined, and authoritarian in nature (Freire, 2000). Freire's concept of liberating education promoted facilitated critical inquiry, which equitably transfers what is known (facts/content) while at the same time cultivates new knowledge through a shared process of learning with and from each other.

Like Freire, feminist learning theories espouse multiple ways of knowing (Belenky et al., 1986) and promote knowledge interrogation and critical pedagogy (Sharma, 2019). Feminist theorists expose implicit curriculum and inequitable power relations in all spheres of education, noting that what is taught and how it's taught historically disenfranchises people of color, the poor, the uninsured, non-English speakers, and 'anyone who is not a possessor of some kind of power, authority, or financial security' (Wear, 1997, p. 100). Feminist-inspired learning produces what some have called connected knowing (Belenky et al., 1986). Connected knowing critically explores the complexities and intersectionalities[1] of human experience; it challenges traditional learning models where reason is privileged over intuition (Foster, 2007). Understanding is balanced by humility, so that feminist learning theory values curiosity in contrast to passive acceptance of status quo.

Feminists such as Belenky and colleagues (1986) viewed empathy as essential to connected knowing. Although it's impossible to fully appreciate another's experience or circumstance, the effort to try to understand – to suspend assumption – is characteristic of relational learning models. Experiencing empathy leads to affective and cognitive change – changes observed by Pitner and Sakamoto (2016) to be essential to identifying one's own biases, knowing oneself, and gaining multicultural awareness and cultural humility. Empathy is a cornerstone of cultural humility, which unlike cultural competence assumes that we can never truly know another but should duly try. A relational learning community accepts that there are myriad perspectives and multiple truths and is more apt to reflect upon and re-examine their assumptions (Dean & Rhodes, 1998). Critics of empathy in education argue that it 'has to be considered in the context of institutions and power' (Gaines, cited in Worthen, 2020). Then, empathy must go beyond an effort to understand another; it must also incorporate the context and circumstances. Relational and feminist learning theories espouse 'the need to learn with, rather than learn about' (Sharma, 2019, p. 574) others. Listening and responsiveness, tenets of empathy, antiracism, and humility, are construed as meaningful and necessary, and complementary rather than contradictory to evidence-based facts and scientific findings.

Critical consciousness

While the importance of self-awareness, reflexivity, critical consciousness and similar concepts have traditionally informed social work and other human service professions, researchers also point out that there is a relative dearth of literature describing *how* to raise critical consciousness (Ferguson, 2018; Yu, 2018); in fact, many recognize that teaching how to raise critical consciousness is not easy (Azzopardi & McNeill, 2016; Bransford, 2011; Glover Reed et al., 2011; Suarez et al., 2008).

Drawing from Freire's concept of conscientization (1970), Sakamoto and Pitner (2005) discussed critical consciousness as a process of continuously reflecting upon one's power relations with others (privilege and marginalized statuses) and, further, taking actions to correct them. These actions are targeted toward transformation of themselves (e.g., noticing and correcting their racist assumptions and behaviors), which then leads to the transformation of their interpersonal relationships. The accumulation of these changes could eventually lead to gradual changes in communities and society. At the same time, Pitner and Sakamoto (2005) pointed to the difficulty of raising critical consciousness, which stems from specific roadblocks in engaging cognitive and affective process in doing so. In order to address these limitations, the authors developed the *Critical Consciousness Conceptual Model* (CCCM; Pitner & Sakamoto, 2005, 2016). CCCM involves the processes of raising awareness of the power relations at the personal level as well as the structural level. These processes are facilitated by the action at the core – the action is 'the catalyst by which a person comes to critically examine personal- and structural-level dynamics' (Pitner & Sakamoto, 2005, p. 691). Knipe (2020) applied this model in their undergraduate social work education and aptly described this process:

> In practise, this action, in turn, defines the way in which social workers will likely act toward clients. If students are engaged in critical examination at the personal and structural levels, they not only will act toward clients (and classmates) with more humility, they also will be motivated to address societal injustices through action. In short, the classroom becomes a laboratory for modeling and experiencing the challenges, obligations, and commitments required for critical consciousness development. Action is at the core of the Critical Consciousness Conceptual paradigm.
>
> (p. 377)

In order for the action to follow the development of critical consciousness, it is important to note that this process likely takes place out of positive relationships among learners (practitioners) and between learners (practitioners) and the teacher (facilitator). In the previous example, students in Knipe's classroom become a community in which critical consciousness development is facilitated, and together they can explore taking actions 'to address societal injustices' (Knipe, 2020, p. 377).

On another note, critical consciousness may be raised out of difficult encounters and relationships. Award-winning social work leader and activist Notisha Massaquoi calls them 'transformative disruptions' (2017, p. 293). Transformative disruptions are identity-based experiences in which the individual experiences high tension, confusion, frustration, emotional pain, and/or self-doubt. These moments can either stall or halt the learning process or alternatively provide the opportunity for intense, vivid learning, pushing practice knowledge to a new, critical, and important level (Massaquoi, 2017, p. 293).

In one example, she – a Black woman – describes her experience of being rudely undermined by a white fellow professor while teaching a class, being asked 'where is the professor?' (Massaquoi, 2017, p. 298). The supposedly safe, privileged social location of being a professor did not protect her from this humiliating racist behavior, which was a transformative moment for her. She writes: '[w]hile disturbing, this experience caused me to rethink the way that various kinds of borders and barriers restrict service users and communities while privileging others' (Massaquoi, 2017, p. 300). For Massaquoi, it conceptualized a way to engage in anti-oppressive practice, a form of scholar-activism leading to the transformation of others (cf. Cann & DeMeulenaere, 2020).

Relational and critically conscious learning: meeting at the crossroads of the arts

Relational and critically conscious methodologies deploy the arts in myriad ways. Art deeply engages learners on neurological and phenomenological levels that bypass barriers imposed by traditional methods of instruction (Huss & Sela-Amit, 2019). Let's take storytelling as an example. Individual and communal storytelling offers students opportunities to see inside the terms and concepts that they are learning in the classroom. It moves them from 'learning about' (cognitive) to 'learning with' (affective) aspects of human vulnerability, oppressive/exploitive practice, and circumstance. It provides opportunities to hear people speak for themselves rather than being spoken for or about.

Dramatic storytelling about human trafficking

In one of the author's social work classrooms (Cohen Konrad), dramatic storytelling was used to introduce students to the lived experience of human trafficking. One of the students had been given permission by a young playwright, a survivor, to preview her play. The play was richly descriptive and cleverly used humor to engage the audience without overwhelming them. Using a reader's theater model,[2] individual students volunteered to be readers, selected roles, and then read the script aloud to classmates. The instructor facilitated discussion. Counseling support from university services was made available should someone be triggered by the difficult content. Students reported that being immersed in a story of human trafficking made its reality palpable – not something that could be easily dismissed or blamed on the victim. As one student reflected, 'Storytelling helps to empower individuals, especially in communities that are often forced into silence'.

Yael Harlap's (2006) *Seven Meanings of Social Change*,[3] though designed to map out elements of community enacted transformation through art, well describes the aims and outcomes of arts and social work learning activities:

1 Working toward equity and justice;
2 Raising consciousness and awareness;
3 Fostering individual empowerment and participation;
4 Bringing people together and building relationships among individuals and groups;
5 Creating dialogue;
6 Giving voice and telling stories;
7 Creating new vision and opening new imaginations for what the world could be.

For the learner audience, the play vividly raised awareness of how human traffickers insidiously insert themselves in the lives of vulnerable youth who are frightened into compliance (2 and 3 of Harlap's Seven Meanings). For the author, storytelling enabled them to tell their truth and reclaim power, control, and resilience (3 and 6). Altogether, the relational learning environment created a forum for learners, survivors, and teachers to explore feelings in response to the plight of youth forced into invisible servitude in their own backyards (2, 3, 4, and 6). Following the performance, students engaged in powerfully open dialogue and then debriefed its emotional impact (5). Altogether these activities reinforced the value of using the arts to urge affective and cognitive learning.

Figure 14.1 Presenting together

Students took Reader's Theater to the next level by presenting the play to a broader audience of social work field instructors, interprofessional faculty and students, and community providers (7). Their collective action was not for course credit or part of an assignment. It was motivated by their desire to use art to disrupt myths about human trafficking and to transform knowledge to promote real world change (1). They did so in community with collaborative leadership and common vision (4). They enhanced their critical thinking and engaged the audience through the arts to do the same (2). In the end, they utilized art to perform a version of Massaquoi's 'transformative disruption' (2017) to foster a deeper, critical, and perhaps more painful understanding of human trafficking obliterating stereotypes and assumptions that too often render victims invisible within communities and to social and human services providers.

Engaging audience about immigrant employment discrimination

The next example took place in the context of public engagement and education, rather than in classrooms. While the contexts differ, we believe that the lessons drawn align well and are relevant to our discussion.

Figure 14.2 Rehearsing together 1

While Canada is known to be an open, inclusive society, persistent employment barriers exist for immigrants (Wilson et al., 2017). One of these common barriers is called 'Canadian (work) experience' (CE). Often highly qualitied immigrants were told 'we can't hire you because you don't have Canadian experience'. At the same time, paradoxically, many found CE to be difficult to articulate as there is a tacit cultural dimension to it (Sakamoto et al., 2010). Our research showed that CE is used to exclude immigrants in a 'nice' Canadian way, for being 'different' from the white middle-class (Bhuyan et al., 2018; Ku et al., 2019; Sakamoto et al., 2013).

Recognizing the limits of traditional research approaches to succinctly communicate the meanings and problems of CE, the research team (Sakamoto and colleagues) collaborated with a theater specialist (Jessica Bleuer) and used theatrical techniques in focus groups to elicit tacitly held knowledge about CE from research participants (Bleuer et al., 2019; Chin et al., 2014). The resultant 'data' were then orchestrated into a reader's theater script, and the actors, including some skilled immigrants themselves, re-enacted the challenges skilled immigrants face when trying to find and retain jobs. In one of the performances, the audience included human resource professionals, service providers, and politicians at a half-day event that our research team organized.

Figure 14.3 Rehearsing together 2

After the play, participants had time to discuss and respond to the theater presentation. Overwhelmingly, the responses were positive; attendees commenting on memorable scenes raising their awareness on the implicit assumptions behind CE and CE's exclusionary outcomes (2 of Harlap's 7 Meanings). They further appreciated the problem-solving learning approach as opposed to lecture (5). In sum, watching the performance gave many participants opportunity to reflect on their own identities and standpoint if they hadn't already (2; personal level reflections in MCCC), connect the issue to broader structural issues through different presentations (structural level reflections), and engage in interactive problem solving through small and large group discussions (deepening reflections in groups and trying on actions), leading to a development of critical consciousness on the issue. Some even articulated planned actions to address the issue further. In fact, the university-community collaborative research team went on to collaborate with the provincial human rights commission, which then led to the research team helping with the creation of the human rights policy by the *Ontario Human Rights Commission* (2013; structural level reflections & action; Wilson et al., 2017).

One limitation to this example is that, to some audience members, some of the ideas we presented led to negative reactions. These viewers might have experienced transformative disruptions, but instead of raising critical consciousness, this led to stopping their learning process (Massaquoi, 2017) and resorting back to their existing ideas of immigrants. At the same time, whether they liked the play's message or not, the audience can't 'unsee' what they saw in the play, so the fact that CE is a difficult issue was conveyed to them either way. Still, the research team concluded that an optimal aesthetic distance must be struck for the message to be effective for different audiences, which was a new learning for us (for fuller discussions, see Bleuer et al., 2019).

Summary and lessons learned

We have reviewed how art can be utilized in relational learning and critical-consciousness-raising in classroom and community learning through theory and examples. Taken together, when used in the context of relational learning to facilitate the development of critical consciousness, art can help transform people's views and call them to action. The potential impact of art in social work education can include helping learners:

1. Take note of social issues;
2. Create space to reflect on them;
3. Develop critical consciousness while learning in relation with others;
4. Take on action.

Facilitating factors may include aesthetic quality in itself to command attention, as well as emotional reactions to grab people's attention (e.g., surprise). These emotional reactions include 'negative', 'positive', and ambiguous emotions such as disgust, frustration, uncertainty, anger, empathy, sadness, and warmth. These emotions can make people uncomfortable and turn away from the social issue or the art that invokes a particular social issue (e.g., Wong, 2004). Used in a relational context, however, learners/practitioners have more opportunities to process complex emotions and engage in a meaningful and connected dialectic process. Art makes difficult social issues palatable when there is a sufficient 'aesthetic distance' (Bleuer et al., 2019) which, in turn, leads to recognition of knowledge and viewpoints that may otherwise have been avoided or dismissed (e.g., Sakamoto et al., 2008, 2009, 2015). Safe enough space allows us to maintain a sustained interest on a possibly difficult issue, which could lead to envisioning a hopeful future and collectively identifying actions for social justice, as was shown in the examples.

Notes

1 While the scope of this chapter does not allow for a fuller discussion of the theory of intersectionality applied in social work, see, for example, Chapple (2019), Gibson (2018), and Mehrotra (2010).
2 Reader's theater is a style of theater in which the actors present dramatic readings of narrative material while seated, without costumes, props, scenery, or special lighting.
3 Also see Sakamoto, 2014 for the application of this thoughtful model.

References

Azzopardi, C., & McNeill, T. (2016). From cultural competence to cultural consciousness: Transitioning to a critical approach to working across differences in social work. *Journal of Ethnic & Cultural Diversity in Social Work*, *25*(4), 282–299. doi:10.1080/15313204.2016.1206494

Belenky, M. F., Clinchy, B. M., Goldberger, N. R., & Tarule, J. M. (1986). *Women's ways of knowing*. New York: Basic Books.

Bleuer, J., Chin, M., & Sakamoto, I. (2019). Why theater-based research works? Psychological theories from behind the curtain. *Qualitative Research in Psychology: Creative Representations in Research*, *15*(2–3), 395–411. doi:10.1080/14780887.2018.1430734

Bransford, C. L. (2011). Integrating critical consciousness into direct social work practice: A pedagogical view. *Social Work Education*, *30*(8), 932–947. doi:10.1080/02615479.2010.534449

Bhuyan, R., Valmadrid, L., Panlaq, E.L., Pendon, N.L., & Juan, P. (2018). Responding to the structural violence of migrant domestic work: Insights from participatory action research with migrant caregivers in Canada. *Journal of Family Violence, 33*, 613–627. https://doi.org/10.1007/s10896-018-9988-x

Cann, C. N., & DeMeulenaere, E. J. (2020). *The activist academic: Engaged scholarship for resistance, hope and social change*. Gorham, ME: Myers Education Press.

Chapple, R. L. (2019). Toward a theory of Black deaf feminism: The quiet invisibility of a population. *Affilia*, *34*(2), 186–198. https://doi.org/10.1177/0886109918818080

Chin, M., Sakamoto, I., & Bleuer, J. (2014). The dynamics of show and tell: Arts-based methods and language ideologies in community-based research. *Journal of Community Practice*, *22*(1/2), 256–273.

Cohen Konrad, S. (2010). Relational learning in social work education: Transformative education for teaching a course on loss, grief and death. *Journal of Teaching in Social Work*, *30*, 15–28.

Cohen Konrad, S. (2019). Art in social work: Equivocation, evidence, and ethical quandaries. *Research on Social Work Practice*, *29*(6), 693–697.

Dean, R. G., & Rhodes, M. L. (1998). Social constructionism: What makes a "better" story? *Families in Society*, *79*, 254–263.

Escueta, M., & Butterwick, S. (2012). The power of popular education and visual arts for trauma survivors' critical consciousness and collective action.

International Journal of Lifelong Education, *31*(3), 325–340. https://doi.org/10/1080/02601370.2012.683613

Ferguson, H. (2018). How social workers reflect in action and when and why they don't: The possibilities and limits to reflective practice in social work. *Social Work Education*, *37*(4), 415–427. doi:10.1080/02615479.2017.1413083

Foster, V. (2007). The art of empathy: Employing the arts in social inquiry with poor, working-class women. *Social Justice*, *34*(1), 12–27.

Freire, P. (1970). *Pedagogy of the oppressed*. New York, NY: Seabury Press.

Freire, P. (2000). *Pedagogy of the oppressed: 30th Anniversary Edition*. New York: Bloomsbury Academic.

Gibson, M. F. (2018). Predator, pet lesbian, or just the nanny? LGBTQ parents of children with disabilities describe categorization. *Journal of Homosexuality*, *65*(7), 860–883. https://doi.org/10.1080/00918369.2017.1364565

Glover Reed, B. G., Newman, P. A., Suarez, Z. E., & Lewis, E. A. (2011). Interpersonal practice beyond diversity and toward social justice: The importance of critical consciousness. In B. Seabury, B. Seabury, & C. D. Garvin (Eds.), *Foundations of interpersonal practice in social work: Promoting competence in generalist practice* (pp. 60–98). Thousand Oaks, CA: Sage.

Harlap, Y. (2006). *Toward training: The meanings and practices of social change work in the arts*. Vancouver, Canada: Judith Marcuse Projects. Retrieved January 1st, 2012 from www.ccl-cca.ca/CCL/Reports/OtherReports/report1.html.

Huss, E., & Sela-Amit, M. (2019). Art in social work: Do we really need it? *Research on Social Work Practice*, *29*(6), 721–726. https://doi.org/10.1177/1049731517745995

Knipe, M. R. (2020) Promoting critical consciousness in undergraduate social work classrooms. *Journal of Teaching in Social Work*, *40*(4), 372–384. doi:10.1080/08841233.2020.1790471

Ku, J., Bhuyan, R., Sakamoto, I., Jeyapal, D., & Fang, L. (2018). "Canadian experience" discourse and anti-racialism in a "post-racial" society. *Ethnic and Racial Studies*, 1466-4356. https://doi.org/10.1080/01419870.2018.1432872

Massaquoi, N. (2017). Crossing boundaries: Radicalizing social work practice and education. In D. Bains (Ed.), *Doing anti-oppressive practice: Social justice social work* (3rd ed., pp. 289–303). Halifax & Winnipeg: Fernwood.

Mehrotra, G. (2010). Toward a continuum of intersectionality: Theorizing for feminist social work scholarship. *Affilia*, *25*(4), 417–430. https://doi.org/10.1177/0886109910384190

National Association of Social Workers [NASW]. (2008). *Code of ethics of the national association of social workers*. Retrieved January 1st, 2021 from www.socialworkers.org/LinkClick.aspx?fileticket=KZmmbz15evc%3d&portalid=0

Ontario Human Rights Commission. (2013). *Policy on removing the "Canadian experience" barrier*. Toronto: Ontario Human Rights Commission.

Pitner, R., & Sakamoto, I. (2005). The role of critical consciousness in multicultural practice: Examining how its strength becomes its limitation. *American Journal of Orthopsychiatry*, *75*(4), 684–694. doi:10.1037/0002-9432.75.4.684

Pitner, R., & Sakamoto, I. (2016). Cultural competence and critical consciousness in social work pedagogy. In *Encyclopedia of Social Work* (20th ed.). Online publication. Oxford University Press. http://socialwork.

oxfordre.com/view/10.1093/acrefore/9780199975839.001.0001/acrefore-9780199975839-e-888

Sakamoto, I. (2014). The use of arts in promoting social justice. In M. Reisch (Ed.), *International handbook of social justice* (pp. 463–479). New York: Routledge.

Sakamoto, I., Chin, M., Chapra, A., & Ricciardi, J. (2009). A "normative" homeless woman? Marginalisation, emotional injury, and social support of transwomen experiencing homelessness. *Gay and Lesbian Issues and Psychology Review*, *5*(1), 2–19.

Sakamoto, I., Chin, M., Wood, N., & Ricciardi, J. (2015). The use of staged photography in participatory action research with homeless women: Reflections on methodology and collaboration. In D. Conrad & A. Sinner (Eds.), *Creating together: Participatory, community-based and collaborative arts practices and scholarship across Canada*. Waterloo, ON, Canada: Wilfrid Laurier University.

Sakamoto, I., Jeypal, D., Bhuyan, R., Ku, J., Fang, L., Zhang, H., Genovese, F. (2013). *An overview of discourses of skilled immigrants and "Canadian experience": An English-language print media analysis* (CERIS Working paper No. 98). CERIS–Metropolis Centre, Toronto, Canada.

Sakamoto, I., Khandor, E., Chapra, A., Hendrickson, T., Maher, J., Roche, B., & Chin, M. (2008). *Homelessness: Diverse experiences, common issues, shared solutions: The need for inclusion and accountability*. Toronto: Factor-Inwentash Faculty of Social Work, University of Toronto. ISBN: 978-0-9811128-0-0 (book). www.wellesleyinstitute.com/publications/homelessness-solutions-from-lived-experiences-through-arts-informed-research/

Sakamoto, I., & Pitner, R. (2005). Use of critical consciousness in anti-oppressive social work practice: Disentangling power dynamics at personal and structural levels. *British Journal of Social Work*, *35*(4), 420–437. https://doi.org/10.1093/bjsw/bch190

Sharma, M. (2019). Applying feminist theory to medical education. *The Lancet*, *393*, 570–578.

Singleton, G. E. (2014). *Courageous conversations about race: A field guide for achieving equity in schools*. Thousand Oaks.

Suarez, Z., Newman, P., & Glover Reed, B. (2008). Critical consciousness and cross-cultural/intersectional social work practice: A case analysis. *Families in Society: The Journal of Contemporary Social Services*, *89*(3), 407–417. doi:10.1606/1044-3894.3766

Wear, D. (1997). *Privilege in the medical academy: A feminist examines gender, race, & power*. New York: Teachers College.

Wilson, R., Sakamoto, I., & Chin, M. (2017). The labour market and immigration. In M. C. Yan & U. Anucha (Eds.), *Working with immigrants and refugees: A handbook for social work and human services* (pp. 111–132). Don Mills, ON, Canada: Oxford University.

Wong, Y.-L. R. (2004). Knowing through discomfort: A mindfulness-based critical social work pedagogy. *Critical Social Work*, *5*(1). https://ojs.scholarsportal.info/windsor/index.php/csw/article/view/5636

Worthen, M. (2020, September 4). The trouble with empathy: Can we really be taught to feel each other's pain? *New York Times*. Retrieved December 25th from www.nytimes.com/2020/09/04/opinion/sunday/empathy-school-college

15 Harnessing structure and support in music-based activities

Brian L. Kelly

Harnessing structure and support in music-based activities

Art and music-based activities have been used throughout the history of the social work profession (Nissen, 2019). From the early years of the Settlement House Movement and the Charity Organization Societies (Addams, 1910; Lanza, 2016), to mid-20th century social group work and summer camps for youth and their families (Kelly & Doherty, 2016, 2017; Kelly & Fleming, 2016), to current mindfulness and decolonial approaches (Coholic et al., 2020; Khorana, 2021), social workers use art and music-based activities to engage with individuals, groups, and communities. In my research with emerging adults experiencing homelessness and other forms of unstable housing (Kelly, 2019, 2017), participants described music production, education, and appreciation as important opportunities to engage and develop their talents, strengths, and interests. In a related project (Kelly, 2021, 2015; Kelly & Hunter, 2016), participants noted the importance of structure and support in co-producing an audio documentary. While existing literature provides examples of how social workers engage music-based activities in their practice, less is known about how they provide structure and support in assisting folks in reaching their goals in music-based activities.

In this chapter, I revisit three related research studies I conducted over the last decade. These studies explore the use of music-based activities with emerging adults experiencing homelessness and other forms of unstable housing. They highlight useful practices in providing participants structure and support in meeting their music-related goals. In my review, I address some of the outcomes and challenges encountered in these practices. Throughout the chapter, I also discuss the importance of social workers engaging their talents, strengths, and interests in the arts, forging collaborations with community-based arts

DOI: 10.4324/9781003105350-16

practitioners, and explicitly bringing the benefits of all of this into their practice. I envision this as an important way for social workers and the profession to engage with the arts and share their transformative powers with individuals, groups, and communities.

Social worker-artists and building collaborations

In recent conceptual work, my co-authors and I proposed a vision for engaging the arts in social work practice (Kelly et al., in press). An integral part of our vision is acknowledging and honoring our identities as artists (e.g., dancers, musicians, DJs, and poets). Rather than refusing these identities entry into our 'professional' roles as social work practitioners, researchers, and educators, we contend that it is essential to bring these parts of ourselves together to create synergized identities as social worker-artists. We also promote collaboration with community-based artists, some of whom may perceive of themselves as artist-social workers (i.e., community-based artists engaged in social justice praxis). In doing so, we imagine social worker-artists and artist-social workers engaging the arts in strengths-based, participatory, socially just, and anti-oppressive practice to foster collectivity, community, and conscientization with individuals, groups, and communities. Our conceptualization of the social worker-artist builds on Travis' (2019) call for 'triple threat professionals' (i.e., artist, practitioner, and researcher) or even 'quadruple-threat professionals' (i.e., artist, practitioner, educator, and researcher) to realize the full potential of the arts.

My interest in advancing a social worker-artist identity is grounded in over three decades of experience in music composition, production, and performance and feeling the consistent pull within the social work profession to separate the two. I grew up in the underground music scenes of the 1990s, forming bands, organizing and playing basements shows, and attending warehouse parties throughout the 'Chicagoland' area. Music provided a means to cope with the challenges of adolescence and early adulthood, as well as providing important opportunities to engage my talents, strengths, and interests. These experiences were bolstered by adults and mentors in these scenes who provided structure and support to help me reach my music-related goals, including receiving a degree in the recording arts in the late 1990s. Music remains an important part of my life and I am continually excited about the potential for engaging music in social work practice, research, and education.

Over the last decade, I have had the privilege of conducting three related research studies that explore the use of music-based activities with emerging adults experiencing homelessness and other forms of unstable housing. Each of these studies provided me with opportunities to engage my social worker-artist identity and collaborate with other practitioners who sit at the intersections of social worker-artists and artist-social workers. In the following sections, I review these studies and highlight the practices of social worker-artist and artist-social workers who provided participants structure and support in meeting their music-based goals.

Study one: a music studio for emerging adults experiencing homelessness

From summer 2011 to summer 2012, I conducted a study that explored whether involvement in a music studio in a transitional living program (TLP) engaged and promoted the strengths of emerging adults experiencing homelessness. Using an ethnographic approach, data were collected to explore their experiences using the studio and the meanings they attached to their experiences. In Kelly (2017), I noted how participants experienced the studio as space to engage in music production, education, and appreciation. They described these experiences as opportunities for connection and creative expression. Participants also described experiencing challenges and frustrations in the studio but ultimately framed these experiences as opportunities for growth and development.

As part of the study, I was also interested in exploring the processes involved in developing and sustaining the studio. In Kelly (2019), I noted how the agency's organizational commitment to a strengths-based, positive youth development (PYD) informed approach to working with emerging adults, the development of in-house holistic supportive services, specifically recreational services, the inclusion of residents' voices in recreational program development, and the role of a studio advocate within the TLP played a vital role in the development of the studio and its ongoing maintenance. While observations and interviews highlighted emerging adults' interest in the studio and their voices in advocating for it, it was clear the studio would not have existed if it were not for the studio advocate.

Hired as a recreational specialist for the TLP in the early 2000s, the studio advocate brought his own talents, strengths, and interests in music composition, production, and performance to his role within the agency. He facilitated creative writing groups and music lessons for residents. Over time, residents voiced a desire for groups that were reflective of their interests in rap and spoken word. The studio advocate redesigned the groups and provided residents with opportunities to explore their interests, which eventually evolved into residents expressing an interest in producing and recording their own beats and raps. In response, the studio advocate loaned his personal recoding equipment to some of the residents. Within weeks they had produced multiple demos. Inspired by their diligence and productivity, the studio advocate approached the TLP executive team about purchasing recording equipment and providing dedicated space for a studio for the residents, and the team agreed.

Through this collaborative and dynamic process, the studio advocate brought his personal talents, strengths, and interests in creative writing and music to recreational program development at the TLP. Upon learning about residents' interests in elements of hip-hop culture (e.g., rap and spoken word), he revised recreational programming to match their interests. Taking it a step further, when he learned of their interests in producing their own beats and raps, he loaned his recording equipment to some of the residents. Hearing their recordings, he quickly recognized that residents were not only interested in music production but that they had musical strengths and talents as well. Using his power and position within the agency, he advocated for the TLP to invest in a music studio for the residents. In doing so, the studio advocate provided financial and physical structure and strong support through his programming and advocacy efforts for emerging adult residents to engage in music composition and production and take some important steps in meeting their music-based goals.

Over the next several years, residents and the studio advocate experienced several challenges when the studio was robbed twice. There was a tension within the agency after each robbery, a complicated process of mourning the loss of the equipment and damage to the space, grappling with the resultant effects of the theft and the related feelings of violation of trust, doubts over replacing the equipment and rebuilding the studio due to residents' safety and the safety of the equipment, as well as the desire to continue providing residents with a space to work on music. Through the combined efforts of residents' interest in music and the studio and the studio advocate's efforts to provide increased accountability and security measures around the studio equipment, the studio was rebuilt twice. At the time of this study (i.e., 2011–12), the studio advocate continued to play an important role in the ongoing maintenance of the studio by providing training and mentorship through orientation sessions with new residents and lessons on use of studio equipment.

Circling back to the findings from Kelly (2017), where TLP residents used the studio for music production, education, and appreciation and experienced the studio as a space for connection and creative expression, I wish to underscore the vital role the studio advocate's structure and support played in facilitating these experiences. While it is possible residents may have located means to produce their own music outside the agency studio, these experiences would likely not have been possible if the studio advocate had not brought his talents, strengths, and interests into his work within the agency. In engaging his talents, strengths, and interests in music and perhaps unknowingly leaning into his role as a social worker-artist, the studio advocate provided residents structure and support in meeting their music-based goals. This collaborative and supportive spirit helped residents produce original music and spoken word work and served to transform the studio into a lifeline for several emerging adults experiencing homelessness.

Study two: co-producing an audio documentary with emerging adults experiencing homelessness

As part of the ethnographic study detailed in the previous section, I co-produced an audio documentary with a select group of study participants. As noted in Kelly (2015), I engaged in this project for several reasons.

> First, given the sonic nature of the research site (i.e., the music studio), it seemed particularly useful in providing an aural representation of the research findings. Second, it provided a means to incorporate young people's original music productions and spoken word work that would be otherwise impossible with a solely written account. In other words, the reader may listen to the music and spoken word work the young people created instead of just reading a description about or a transcription of it. Third, it provided an opportunity to engage young people and their talents, strengths, and interests in the research process (e.g., production and engineering skills, rap freestyle, spoken word, and writing skills). Finally, it brought a socially just, activist dimension to the project by creating opportunities for young people to expand their relationship with media production and collaboratively tell their stories of strength and resilience in and beyond the music studio.
> (p. 70)

Analyses and findings from the project are spread across multiple publications. Kelly (2015) provided an overview of our co-production process, a full transcript of the audio documentary, and a link to the recorded documentary. Kelly and Hunter (2016) explored the development of group dynamics through our creative process (i.e., communication and interactions patterns, cohesion, social integration and influence, and culture). Kelly (2021) examined the inherent nondeliberative and participatory nature of our work. A less explored aspect of the project was my role as a social worker-artist and the structure and support that lent to our process.

After spending the better part of a year in the music studio with the participants, I was surprised to learn at the conclusion of our work that the audio documentary was the first project they completed in the studio. As noted in Kelly (2015), the audio documentary:

> provided an opportunity for the development of a youth – adult partnership in the music studio between the young people and me. This partnership provided us with an opportunity to work collaboratively and experience each other's strengths in the process of developing the audio documentary. Young people commented on the importance of this partnership in completing the co-constructed audio documentary, noting that it was the first project any of them had completed in the studio, suggesting that both parties (i.e., the young people and me) were needed to realize the documentary.

While Kelly (2019, 2017) clarified the role of the studio advocate in developing and maintaining the studio, the co-produced audio documentary project demonstrated the benefit of developing a partnership with the participants, through which I was able to provide them with increased structure and support in reaching – and completing – their music-related goals.

Prior experience and training in audio production and social work practice and research methods provided me with an intersectional lens to recognize the aural the nature of the studio and the potential for a co-constructed sonic representation of the study findings. I embraced my identity as a social worker-artist and brought my talents, strengths, and interests in audio production and my training as a social work practitioner and researcher to the project. As a result, I provided the participants with additional structure and support they needed to complete the audio documentary and successfully reach their music-related goals. The process was not without challenges. Co-producing an audio documentary required a significant time commitment, which was difficult given the often unpredictable nature of participants' school and work schedules. In addition, group dynamics bristled and chafed at times as participants found their way to a unified vision for the final product.

As a final event, we hosted a premiere party at the TLP. Participants invited their family and friends, and most of the agency staff and residents were in attendance. In watching the participants engage with the audience following the premiere of the audio documentary, it was clear that our collaborative work transformed them and the agency. Participants were TLP residents *and* audio documentary producers, and the agency was a space where creative approaches to social justice flourished.

Study three: group-based music education residencies with emerging adults experiencing homelessness and other forms of unstable housing

Beginning in 2016, I had the opportunity to longitudinally evaluate a partnership between the TLP described in the previous sections – which now also ran a drop-in center for emerging adults experiencing homelessness and other forms of unstable housing – and a mid-sized, mixed instrumentation music ensemble. The ensemble performs nationally and internationally and is a recognized leader in audience engagement. In addition, the ensemble facilitates group-based music education residencies with social service agencies working with a variety of populations, including emerging adults and women experiencing homelessness and other forms of unstable housing. Classically trained ensemble musicians serve as teaching artists (TAs) for the residencies. While TAs are skilled music educators who often lack formal training in social service provision, they each have a passion for bringing the power of music composition, experimentation, and performance to historically marginalized groups. This passion is a key part of the ensemble's lived mission. As I explain later, TA's sit at the intersection of the artist-social worker, where artists engage in social justice praxis.

I had the opportunity to observe TAs facilitate residencies with TLP residents and drop-in center clients for multiple years. I also interviewed and conducted focus groups with TAs and participants from each residency. Form this work it was clear that TAs offered structure and support to residency participants in reaching their music-related goals, including assisting them in lyrical and musical composition, working with participants to develop hybrid audio-visual scores, training them in using audio production software and digital audio workstations, and serving as accompanying musicians for performances of participants' original compositions at agency hosted talent shows. Through all of this, one of the more impressive attributes of the TAs was their capacity to adapt to the ever-changing nature of the agency environment. In Kelly and Neidorf (2021), I described this phenomenon as TA adaptability and argued it was 'important and integral' to the residencies. TA adaptability was defined in three unique and interrelated ways.

- Flexibility – TAs' ability to pivot and make changes on the fly, adapting to the residency environment
- Role adaptability – TAs straddling multiple roles throughout the residencies, often changing and blending roles to serve the needs of the curriculum and participants' interests and needs
- Meeting participants where they are – TAs' accessibility and capacity to capitalize on participants' talents, strengths, and interests (p. 6)

As I noted earlier, while TAs were trained in music composition, education, and performance, few were formally trained in working in the often unpredictable and chaotic environments of residential and drop-in programs for emerging adults experiencing homelessness and other forms of unstable housing, let alone facilitating groups with residents and clients. This proved to be challenging for some TAs as lesson plans were consistently in flux due to the ever-changing needs of the agency and the clients it served. Lack of training, however, never stopped TAs from developing relevant content and programming for group lessons, facilitating lessons, and pivoting as needed to meet the interests of participants and the logistical needs of the agency, lending an ear before and after lessons to participants with additional questions about music composition or performance, or supporting an emerging adult going through a particularly challenging time.

It was in these moments, when TAs extended beyond their role as 'music educator,' enacted adaptability, transcended the discrete roles of 'artist' and 'social worker,' and instead leaned into a hybrid role of artist-social worker, that the transformative power of music education in their hands became strikingly apparent. While participants certainly appreciated the knowledge gained from the group-based music education residencies, as well as the structure and support offered by the TAs, they also witnessed the power of TAs' composition skills, musicianship, and live performances. In witnessing this power, participants experienced TAs as artist-social workers who met them where they were and provided the structure and support they needed to meet their music-related goals and, perhaps, reach beyond them.

Summary and conclusion

While social workers have used music-based activities throughout the history of the profession, less is known about how they provide participants structure and support in meeting their music-related goals. In this chapter, I analyzed three related research studies conducted over the last decade to identify specific practices that provided participants with such structure and support. These practices include social service providers and social work researchers explicitly engaging their talents, strengths, and interests in music in their work with individuals, groups, and communities. Rather than separating our interests in the arts and music from our professional endeavors as social work practitioners, educators, and researchers, it is time to embrace a social worker-artist identity. In doing so, we may assist folks in meeting their art and music-related goals and building transformative spaces and models of practice.

The analysis also demonstrates the power of social service agencies forging collaborations with community-based arts practitioners. Communities are rich with indigenous arts and cultural practices, and as this analysis demonstrates, some artists and musicians are interested in collaboration and equipped to manage the challenges of serving historically marginalized and oppressed groups. This is not to say that social workers are not needed in these spaces to support this work. On the contrary, it is imperative that social workers and artists collaborate in this work, with each field bringing their passion for the arts and social justice into hybridized spaces where the arts and social work support each other in assisting individuals, groups, and communities to realize and reach their fullest potential.

References

Addams, J. (1910). *Twenty years at hull house*. New York: Macmillan.

Coholic, D., Schwabe, N., & Lander, K. (2020). A scoping review of arts-based mindfulness interventions for children and youth. *Child and Adolescent Social Work Journal*, *37*, 511–526. https://doi.org/10.1007/s10560-020-00657-5

Kelly, B. L. (in press). Art and music-based activities as participatory research methods to build connection and community. In E. Bos & E. Huss (Eds.), *Social work research using arts-based methods*. Bristol, UK: Policy Press/Bristol University Press.

Kelly, B. L. (2015). Using audio documentary to engage young people experiencing homelessness in strengths-based group work. *Social Work with Groups*, *38*(1), 68–86. https://doi.org/10.1080/01609513.2014.931665

Kelly, B. L. (2017). Music-based services for young people experiencing homelessness: Engaging strengths and creating opportunities. *Families in Society*, *98*(1), 57–68. https://doi.org/10.1606/1044-3894.2017.9

Kelly, B. L. (2019). Positive youth development: Developing, implementing, and sustaining music-based services for emerging adults experiencing homelessness. *Emerging Adulthood*, *7*(5), 331–341. https://doi.org/10.1177/2167696818777347

Kelly, B. L., & Doherty, L. (2016). Exploring nondeliberative practice through recreational, art, and music-based activities in social work with groups. *Social Work with Groups*, *39*(2/3), 221–233. https://doi.org/10.1080/01609513.2015.1057681

Kelly, B. L., & Doherty, L. (2017). A historical overview of art and music-based activities in social work with groups: Nondeliberative practice and engaging young people's strengths. *Social Work with Groups*, *40*(3). https://doi.org/10.1080/01609513.2015.1091700

Kelly, B. L., & Fleming, J. (Eds.). (2016). Group work camp: Reflections and learning [Special issue]. *Groupwork*, *26*(3). https://doi.org/10.1921/gpwk.v26i3.1037

Kelly, B. L., & Hunter, M. J. (2016). Exploring group dynamics in activity-based group work with young people experiencing homelessness. *Social Work with Groups*, *39*(4), 307–325. https://doi.org/10.1080/01609513.2015.1061962

Kelly, B. L., Lanza, C., Travis, R., & Ellis, T. (in press). A vision for engaging the arts in social work practice. In M. Sela-Amit & S. Cohen Konrad (Eds.), *Social work and the arts: Grounds for new horizons*.

Kelly, B. L., & Neidorf, J. (2021). Teaching artists' adaptability in group-based music education residencies. *Social Work with Groups*, 1–16. https://doi.org/10.1080/01609513.2021.1896165

Khorana, S. (2021). How to make arts-based interventions appropriate for young refugees? Towards a decolonial framework. *Journal of Youth Studies*, 1–14. https://doi.org/10.1080/13676261.2021.1929885

Lanza, C. (2016). *"Truth plus publicity": Paul U. Kellogg and hybrid practice, 1902–1937*. Seattle: University of Washington.

Nissen, L. B. (2019). Art and social work: History and collaborative possibilities for interdisciplinary synergy. *Research on Social Work Practice*, *29*(6), 698–707. https://doi.org/10.1177%2F1049731517733804

Travis, Jr., R. (2019). All awareness and no action: Can social work leverage creative arts' potential? *Research on Social Work Practice*, *29*(6), 708–720. https://doi.org/10.1177/1049731517735178

16 Madrid, city of women

A project to empower the social participation of women in the city

Marián López Fdz. Cao, Juan Carlos Gauli, and Nacho Moreno Segarra

1 Introduction

1.1 Artivism and citizenship

Milena Dragićević Šešić, head of the UNESCO Chair in interculturalism, defines artivism as a neologism based on the merger of two concepts: art and activism. Dragićević and colleagues (2015) refer to the theatre theorist and sociologist Aldo Milohnić (2005), for whom artivism is a form of social intervention in which techniques featured in cultural expressions, specifically in artistic expressions, are used to constitute or shape action in the political arena either because those techniques are logical and causal for the action or for purely external reasons.

This classic definition of artivism points to an organic relationship between art and activism and which has been emphasised by later theorists such as Sandoval and Latorre (2008). It is closely linked with what Ginwright and Cammarota (2002) describe as critical civic praxis from their work with young people living in under-privileged neighbourhoods in the United States. For these researchers, critical civic praxis refers to the organisational processes that promote civic relations and elevate activism for social justice based on a greater critical awareness. This critical awareness is understood as the recognition of the systematic forms of oppression that limit the capacity "for self-determination and thus ability to take action to address the conditions of oppression" (2007, p. 968). Svetlana Hristova (2015) used similar ideas, discussing the concept of Urbactivism. What is interesting about Hristova's definition is how she broadens the concept of urban activism by relating it to European institutions. She compares it to participatory governance as a two-way process: from the institutional to the collective and from the collective to the institutional.

DOI: 10.4324/9781003105350-17

1.2 *Memory and city: urbanism and storytelling*

All the aforementioned cases are an example of the fusion among activism, art, and institutional social intervention as a practice that has been carried out and promoted in different cultural contexts like Europe or the United States since the 1990s to breathe new life into cities and is known by different names.

Christine Boyer (1994) describes how the only way that memories have acquired spatial form has been to insert architectural elements or remains from the past in the city of the present, thereby creating a difference between history and memory. In light of these reflections, Reena Tiwari (2010) explains in her book on performativity and memory how the objectification of the past succumbs to touristification and the alienation of its citizens, describing how those rebuilt historic spaces fail to acknowledge the "lived aspect of memory":

> Memory is an orientating experience for the individual, strengthening the links between the past and the present and links between different times and different spaces. When memory does not have a link to the lived experience, it is reduced to history or a fragmented re-construction of the past. Boyer thus differentiates between history and memory on the basis of lived experience. This lived aspect of memory has coincidence with Lefebvre's third space, the lived space.
> (Tiwari, 2010, p. 76)

Both Boyer and Tiwari base their discussions on Walter Benjamin's (2008) reflections on the loss of real experiences in the city and in modern life, especially in relation to the detrimental effect on traditional storytelling sourced in the exchange of experiences and whose leading role is losing ground to tourist information. Equally, as urbanist Dolores Hayden (1995, p. 46) argues, social memory is based on narratives – what philosophers such as Edward S. Casey (1987) call "place memory" – that can be activators of memory through the urban landscape. For Casey, places are containers of experiences that contribute to building their intrinsic memorability, which leads Hayden to state that "place memory encapsulates the human ability to connect with both the built and natural environments that are entwined in the cultural landscape" (Hayden, 1995, p. 56).

In this respect, choreographer and activist in the #blacklivesmatter movement, Rodney Diverlus (2016), emphasised in his article "Re/imagining artivism" the role of artists as storytellers based on their ability to "actively document and archive our collective experiences and histories". In a very similar vein, Jill M. Chonody (2014) discusses the virtues of storytelling, describing this as our natural way of communicating with each other and of finding a form of self-expression that connects us with that otherness and empowers us (Chonody, 2014, pp. 3–4). This storytelling mechanism has clear applications in urban planning as a story of the future (van Hulst, 2012), and can also be open to discussion about the present, as Cara Courage explains, [Storytelling] "is part of a micropublic place-attaching process or enactment, where the discussion of ideas publically can reinforce positive community aspects, as well as change community narrative and include marginalized voices, leading to increased intra- and inter-awareness of the community"(Courage, 2017, p. 45).

This way of using storytelling has been applied, for example, in artivist projects like *Sustainable Thinking and Expression on Public Space* (STEPS) in Canada, which fostered civic ties between young people through public art, using tools such as storytelling (Solanki et al., 2014).

1.3 New narratives on the city: emotional geography and feminist geography

As Owain Jones says (2007) emotional geography has a clear relationship with memory and space. For this author, who defines emotions as "intensely political, gendered, and spatially articulated" (2007, p. 207) and emotional geography as the way of thinking connections "between memory and our geographical imagination", memory "must play a key, formative role in the construction of our ongoing emotional and imaginative geographies" (Jones, 2007, p. 210).

Not only does memory have a spatial element, but gender does too. According to Linda McDowell (1999), feminist geography is based on the idea that men and women do not experience space in the same way because of hierarchical differences of power and that these differences are then reflected in space. In other words, we could consider feminist geography as the study of gender defined by space or through space, an academic field that, like all feminist ventures, is destined to have an impact on and change society. Both McDowell and Sharp, when defining one of the main purposes of this discipline, said it was to "demonstrate the ways in which hierarchical gender relations are both affected by and reflected in the spatial structure of societies, as well as in the theories that purport to explain the relationships and the methods used to investigate them" (McDowell & Sharp, 1997, p. 4).

For McDowell and Sharp (2014), although these kinds of studies focus in principle on reflecting inequalities in the way space is experienced across the world, they are currently based more on linguistics and on the analysis of symbolic or representational aspects in order to analyse the spatial construction of subjectivity, identity, and the body. This highlights that cultural ideas affecting gender are spatially and historically defined. Because of this, one of the specific aims of feminist geography is to "investigate, make visible and challenge the relationships between gender divisions and spatial divisions, to uncover their mutual constitution and problematise their apparent naturalness" (2014, p. 91). McDowell and Sharp (1997) highlighted how this cultural side of gender and space affects a series of considerations, such as:

> images and representations of this environment and of the 'natural' world, ways of writing about it, as well as our bodily place within it. The spaces in which social relations occur affect the nature of those practices, who is 'in place' and who is 'out of place' and even who is allowed to be there at all. But the spaces themselves in turn are constructed and given meaning through the social practices that define men and women as different and unequal.
>
> (McDowell & Sharp, 1997, pp. 2–3)

The feminist geography tools we have used were mainly those of life stories, a qualitative method apt to recover "lost geographies" (McDowell & Sharp, 2014, p. 153) in spatial studies. Another useful tool for this project has been the feminist critique of cartography (Huffman (1997), as maps were the predominant tools used in the "Madrid, city of women" project. Last, when applying these two methods, we chose to make use of different strategies from feminist geography and feminism, such as highlighting the ethics involved in representations of space, as well as the use of situated or relational knowledges (Haraway, 1998).

1.4 *Women, arts, and political artivism*

For the past few decades, several initiatives have denounced the reclaiming of the city of Madrid by its female citizens. Artivism is in debt to the critical urbanism developed from the theorised urban walks formalised by Canadian urbanist and activist Jane Jacobs who, in her work, developed fundamental concepts such as "social capital" and the "spontaneous self-organization of urbanism", as well as the idea that urban space is a public space that must be reclaimed in order to promote coexistence and the achievement of a good quality of life for its citizens (Jacobs, 1961).

There have been many such initiatives starting in the 1970s, continuing until now, when the engineer Aruna Sankaranarayanan generated an algorithm for Mapbox, a provider of custom online maps, which shows the city's streets in different colours for men and women denoting that "streets named after men are more numerous and more centrally located than streets named after women in the metro areas we analyzed" (Sankaranarayanan, 2017).

For decades, subaltern practices of the art world considered feminine and therefore marginal, such as knitting and sewing, have been vindicated as a path to political involvement for women. For example, the Riot Grrrl feminist punk movement of the 1990s brought new political significance to private female culture, encouraging feminists and others to take up crafting in order to resist corporations. Today, women artivists practicing "urban knitting" appeals to womens' sense of collaboration and social awareness. Examples of these types of actions are knitting together in public squares, holding workshops in which people of all ages and origins participate, and crocheting urban furniture and clothing for trees (also known as yarn bombing).

The absence of women in the city of Madrid

In major Spanish cities, as well as in the rest of the world, there are at least three times as many streets dedicated to men than there are dedicated to women (Llaneras, 2017). Since 2000, Madrid has incorporated around 350 people's names for streets, with only about 25% constituting women's names. Only 1% of all of streets with female names in Madrid are named for real women; the other names being symbols, saints, virgins, or other religious titles such as "our lady" (Llaneras, 2017).

We see this as evidence of a clear gender inequality that is hard to understand in a society and common European framework that supposedly supports and defends gender equality.

2 Methods and materials

2.1 How did the "Madrid, city of women" project come about?

Based on the alarming data described earlier and the initial theoretical premises, Divercity – an umbrella project for "Madrid, city of women" – arose from an initiative by seven European organisations aiming to advance inclusion in cultural and urban spaces and who wished to put these activist citizen participation strategies into practice in the city of Madrid.

The EARTDI Research Group (Art Application for Social Integration), together with the Feminist Research Institute of the Complutense University of Madrid, the leading partner of the Divercity project, had been involved since 2003 in an art-as-therapy social and educational project. Other participating partners of Divercity were the French Elan Interculturel, the Hungarian Artemiszio Foundation, the Austrian Stand 129, the Hungarian Museum of Ethnography, the Finnish Art Museum of Helsinky, and the Portuguese REDE.

The methodologies used to define the project "Madrid, city of women", organise its development, and subsequently evaluate the results were predominantly qualitative (see Figure 16.1) In the first instance, a file of good practices was compiled on diversity in museums

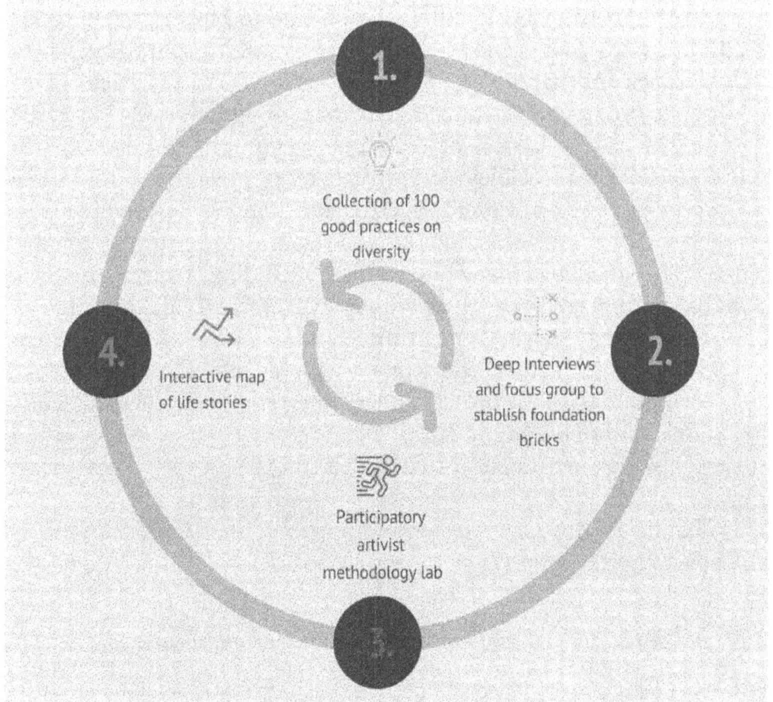

Figure 16.1 Phases of the project

and the city. More than a hundred good practices were collected in various spheres of action (Jermyn, 2001; López Fdz. Cao, 2016; Matarasso, 1997; Morgan, 1995; Palacios, 2009). Based on this, a compilation and analysis process of the basic intervention methodologies used in working with diversity in museums and the city through art was initiated. The team used qualitative methods such as brief interviews, alongside longer, in-depth face-to-face interviews with experts and focus groups. Their findings led to a report, articles in scientific journals, and a website (https://divercitysite.weebly.com/) (Bernárdez Rodal, 2015; Semova, 2015).

The "Madrid, city of women" project has a dual purpose:

- First, by means of an itinerary that enshrines women's memory in the form of a mobile app connected to videos that explore and follow the traces left by women in the city of Madrid. Viewing of the videos triggers historical, social, aesthetic, political, and educational debate and revisits Tiwari's concept of the "living aspect of memory" (Tiwari, 2010, p. 76), providing channels through which past and present can meet in different moments and spaces and creating, in line with what Lefevre (1974) sees as a third space (see: www.youtube.com/channel/UC-nroLMlxJy2h4X50oYqALA/videos).
- Second, to create an interactive map of life stories, "storytelling", as in the notion of emotional geography put forward by Jones (2007) and Sibley (1995). This map, woven from life stories recorded between September 2015 and June 2016, emerged from participative art workshops. These sessions were run by collaborating with a wide range of women, including women in vulnerable circumstances, such as women with mental health problems, migrant women, female prostitutes, and homeless women, and also with students, artists, and women who, as individuals, wanted to collaborate with the project and tell their life stories. All the workshops had a common goal of showing a map of stories (written, audiovisual, artistic, etc.) that linked city spaces with emotions.

This chapter will focus in the second purpose, life stories mapping to link spaces and emotions.

2.2 *"Madrid, city of women", a political and emotional map*

For the participatory workshops, the basic method of Participatory Action Research (PAR) was used (García-Ramírez & Suárez-Balcázar, 2003; see Figure 16.2). In this case, the idea was not only to express

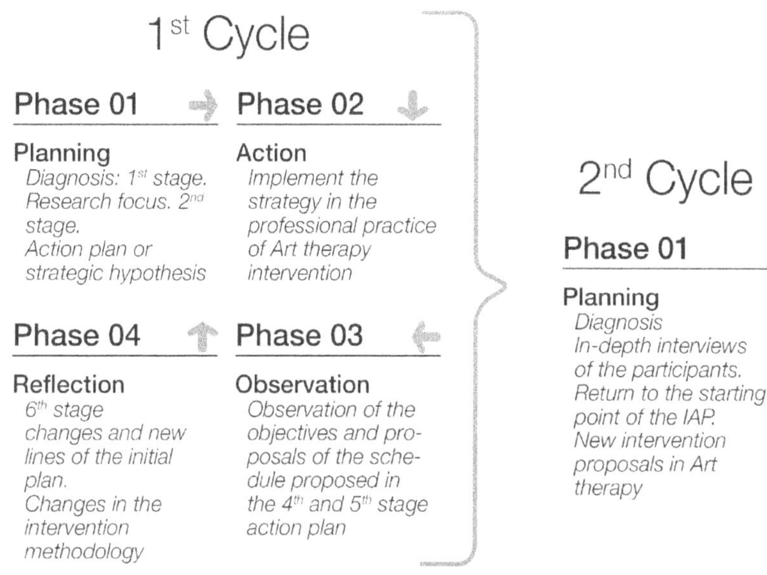

Figure 16.2 Cycles of participative action research methodology

Madrid women's living memories but also to conceive of the city as a living, organic space receptive to change through its citizens, where there is a joint commitment in terms of the work of social researchers and programme participants. This was based on the premise of PAR, by which the knowledge that an individual or group can generate is much more educational (enriching and profound) than that which it consumes (Ander-Egg, 2003). In this sense, the joint construction of narratives linked to space enabled the reconstruction of a collective history as a catalyst not only for awareness-raising but also for reinforcing the collective imagination towards new goals.

The duration of the workshops varied, ranging from 5 to 30 hours depending on the characteristics of the group, participants' availability, and their interest in deepening certain concepts. Five workshops were held, with a total of 52 participants and an average duration of 30 hours per workshop. The workshops had as a common axis the situation of social vulnerability (migrants, a workshop for street prostitutes, women with mental health problems, among others). To enable workshop participants to share their stories, we used intervention

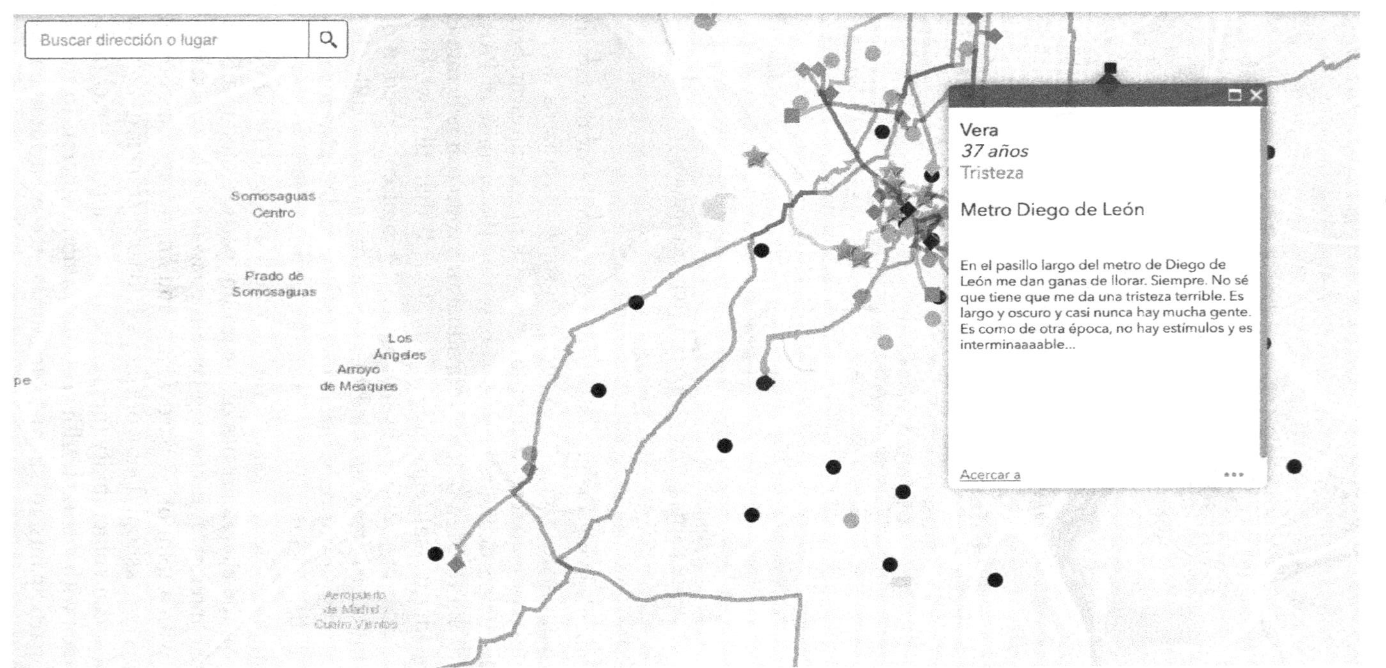

Figure 16.3 and 16.4 Madrid political-emotional map of women's narratives

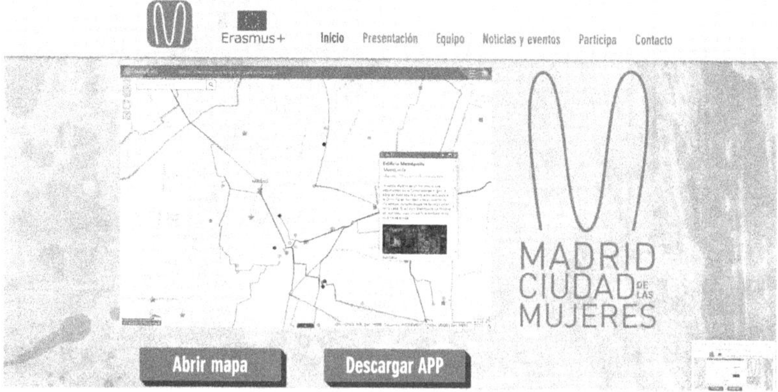

Figure 16.3 and 16.4 (Continued)

methodologies from art therapy, which sought to create a safe space, a potential space of trust, connection, and empathy where participants felt free to connect places in the city with emotions and with their own experiences through storytelling. Gradually, through the establishment of a safe bond with the facilitators, trust-building exercises, ensuring a confidential space, and active listening, the participants opened up to the group and were able to tell highly intimate personal narratives related to the city. The long duration of some workshops – with weekly meetings for more than three months – allowed the development of a transferential link that enriched the results and the emergence of personal narratives.

The outcomes of all the workshops, held between October 2015 and May 2016, were uploaded into a map using the Arc Gris tool, where personal stories could be geolocated (see: http://madridciudaddelas-mujeres.es, https://ucmadrid.maps.arcgis.com/apps/webappviewer/index.html?id=ebfd757372884065b5fd02337f10eff3). The end purpose of this emotional mapping process was, in the second instance, to make visible "other" discourses present in the city. It comprises the written, audio, and audiovisual narratives from the collectives described, individually and as a group, including the geolocation of murdered women who had become victims of sexist violence in the previous ten years in the city of Madrid, to put it negatively, the city's stolen narratives (see Figures 16.3 and 16.4).

The process described earlier was carried out alongside a series of events connected with the dissemination of the project products,

Figure 16.5 Lab about "What is Madrid for you?"

including various "open days" and discussions with participants and experts in the different cities involved (Paris, Budapest, Vienna, Helsinki, Lisbon, and Madrid; see Figure 16.5), as well as a project multiplier event in the form of an international conference held in Madrid that was replicated in Spanish in a number of educational locations across the community.

3 Analysis and results

The data collection technique used in workshops and labs was participatory observation, with the main tools being a field diary, a grid record of the sessions, and visual recording of artworks produced. In the latter stages, audio and audiovisual recording tools were added, plus the technique of semi-structured guided interviewing (see results: www.ucm.es/divercity/diversidad-en-la-ciudad). The grid record included indicators relating to the body, exploration of the female identity, and self-image. This was used to extract categories connected with bond, identity, and the connection with artistic techniques and creativity. Likewise, subcategories were analysed, such as in/security, relation with illness, confidence, decision making, autonomy, and identification.

Completing the stages and case study analyses on the categories described earlier led to visible changes in participants' confidence and security in the space, giving them greater autonomy and freedom in their artistic creations and highlighting the formation of attachment boundaries that had been the aim since the start of the sessions. The connection created through participatory action gave them the chance to tackle the fear and feelings of invisibility they experienced in their family and social environments, with the workshop space providing a place to feel free, strong, and above all, creative (García Castro, 2017). All these results were approved by participants of the workshops and led to the conclusion that there was a clear increase of agency and empowerment in relation to themselves and urban spaces, along with a feeling that they could and had the right to re-inhabit urban spaces as their own and to transform them.

3.1 *Delphi 01 group: Madrid, city of women, a political and emotional map*

Final evaluation of the quality and scope of the project was conducted using the Delphi analysis methodology. A total of 24 relevant experts were contacted. The Delphi group focused on the global project "Madrid, city of women, a political and emotional map", based on 16 questions.

Most experts assessed the project as having a high degree of innovation (71%) and participatory design (75%). In relation to the emotional and spatial connection, some experts made a range of comments such as: "The city comes alive" or "the emotional relationship between people and urban spaces is achieved by reconstructing memory and visibility". Other experts stated that they thought the project had made participants rethink their relationship with the city and can be considered "a vessel of real women's stories", "participatory reflection", "giving power to women and empowering them", and "offering voice and identity to people who normally have none". The three adjectives highlighted from the project, after making a word cloud of experts' feedback, were "participatory", "integrating", and "inclusive". A majority of the experts (86%) stated that the project should be expanded to include more collectives, and there was agreement to recommend proposing greater defence of anonymous women and "less visible groups". Also, some experts thought it could be used as a tool against social stigma (50%). On the potential of the study in the sphere of social inclusion, the experts said the project was "a tool for the city's urban redesign" and showed "potential for working in neighbourhoods and improving inclusion". In relation to the project's potential in the field of art and citizen participation, some experts commented in their feedback that "the potential lies in work done in the neighbourhoods" or "art as a driver". When it came to strengths and opportunities, the most prominent suggestions were innovation, inclusion, trigger for reflection, channel for recovering historic memory, and breaking away from hegemonic discourse. As for weaknesses, threats, and limitations, some expert feedback remarked that the lack of financial support for the project to continue being developed might be limiting.

4 Discussion and conclusions

Feminism has been partly responsible for the so-called crisis of representation (McDowell & Sharp, 2014) in geographic studies based on questioning the scientific and aseptic nature of certain representations of space such as mapping, a discipline that, according to Haraway, uses "the god-trick of seeing everything from nowhere" (Haraway, 1998, p. 189). In other words, feminist geography – applied in this chapter – has analysed how maps are representations of power and how a male, individual gaze hides behind that anonymous universality. This approach has been particularly important for us because of the way in which, in the resulting project, the political and emotional map, the use of maps commonly accepted by mapping technology came into conflict with the forgotten personal or collective stories.

Together with the use of art as an activist and memorialist mechanism, the "Madrid, city of women" project undoubtedly implemented two aspects of geographic studies that were essential for producing both the political and emotional map: emotional geography and feminist geography. As Bondi and colleagues (2007) point out, geographic studies are experiencing an emotional turnaround in relation to the analysis of the symbolic importance of places and their sentimental associations. Emotional geography, worked out through workshops in our project, "attempts to understand emotion – experientially and conceptually – in terms of its socio-spatial mediation and articulation rather than as entirely interiorized subjective mental states" (Bondi et al., 2007, p. 3). Three concepts have arisen, according to these authors, in the emotional approach to geography: Location of emotion in both bodies and places, the emotional relationality of people and environments, and representations of emotional geographies. The fluid and intrinsically relational nature of emotions (Bondi et al.,

2007) is one of the ways in which these phenomena construct social identities, as shown by David Sibley (1995) in which the non-material value of feelings of fear or of rejections appear in the construction of the other and how these feelings are encoded in places and, as revealed in our project, in the different workshops where many urban nodal points encoded senses of fear, loneliness, or lack of safety for many women. Similarly, geographies of connection, based on feelings such as love, desire, and company, widely studied by geographers of family, like Jamieson (1998), as well as in various studies on geographies of love and sexuality (Bell & Valentine, 1995), are present in the emotional mapping which emerged from the workshops where female friendship, love, and happiness linked to urban places also appeared.

The relationship between art, activism, memory, and storytelling has been essential to the "Madrid, city of women" project. It has shown the capacity that stories have in the construction of collective memory and the way in which art, placed in relation with activism – artivism – can serve as a narrative driver of those stories, connecting them organically with urban landscapes to reveal them as cultural and emotional landscapes.

As pointed out throughout this text, the use of artivism, artistic processes in social intervention and participation, has been revealed as a linking tool that brings participants into relationship with each other through the safe and playful space that implements creation, acting in a distinctive way on the reality it addresses. In this way, hidden and silenced narratives, claims, and demands emerge, which, through art, become cultural and artistic practices that modify the way of understanding the territory and its inhabitants.

References

Ander-Egg, E. (2003). *Repensando la Investigación-Acción Participativa* [Rethinking participatory action research]. Barcelona: Lumen.

Bell, D., & Valentine, G. (1995). *Mapping desire: Geographies of sexualities.* London: Routledge.

Benjamin, W. (2008). *La obra de arte en la época de su reproductibilidad técnica* [The work of art at the time of its technical reproducibility]. Madrid: Abada Editores.

Bernárdez Rodal, A. (2015). Discursos y paradojas de la intermediación cultural: una práctica profesional entre la élite y la pobreza cultural [Discourses and paradoxes of cultural intermediation: A professional practice between the elite and cultural poverty]. *Arteterapia. Papeles de arteterapia y educación artística para la inclusión social*, *10*, 247–268.

Bondi, L., Davidson, J., & Smith, M. (Eds.). (2007). Introduction: Geography's "emotional turn". In *Emotional geographies* (pp. 1–19). Hampshire: Ashgate.

Boyer, C. (1994). *The city of collective memory: Its historical imagery and architectural entertainments*. Cambridge: The MIT Press.

Casey, E. (1987). *Remembering: A phenomenological study*. Bloomington: Indiana University Press.

Chonody, J. M. (2014). Approaches to evaluation: How to measure change when utilizing creative approaches. In J. M. Chonody (Ed.), *Community art: Creative approaches to practice* (pp. 1–22). *Champaign*. Common Ground Publishing.

Courage, C. (2017). *Arts in place: The arts, the urban and social practice*. London: Routledge.

Criado Pérez, C. (2019). *Invisible women*. Abrams Press.

Diverlus, R. (2016). Re/imagining artivism. In D. Elliott, M. Silverman, & W. Bowman (Eds.), *Artistic citizenship: Artistry, social responsibility, and ethical praxis* (pp. 189–213). New York: Oxford University Press.

García Castro, P. (2017). *Cuerpo e imagen femenina. hacia una exploración de la identidad en una experiencia arteterapéutica con mujeres de un CRPS* [Body and feminine image: Towards an exploration of identity in an art therapy experience with women of a CRPS]. Trabajo Fin de Máster, Facultad de Educación: Universidad Complutense de Madrid.

García-Ramírez, B., & Suárez-Balcázar, Y. (2003). *Internet y cambio comunitario en un barrio empobrecido de Chicago. Implicaciones para Andalucía* [Internet and community change in an impoverished Chicago neighborhood: Implications for Andalusia]. *Apuntes de Psicología*, *21*(3), 533–548.

Ginwright, S., & Cammarota, J. (2002). New terrain in youth development: The promise of a social justice approach. *Social Justice*, *29*(4), 82–95.

Haraway, D. (1998). Situated knowledges: The science question in feminism and the privilege of partial perspective. *Feminist Studies*, *14*(3), 75–599.

Hayden, D. (1995). *Power of place: Urban landscapes as public history*. Cambridge: The MIT Press.

Hristova, S. (2015). We, European cities and towns: The role of culture for the evolving European model of urban sustainability. In S. Hristova, M. D. Šešić, M. D. Evi, & N. Duxbury (Eds.), *Culture and sustainability in European cities: Imagining Europolis* (pp. 42–55). London: Routledge.

Huffman, N. H. (1997). Charting the other maps: Cartography and visual methods in feminist research. In J. P. Jones, H. J. Nast, & S. M. Roberts (Eds.), *Thresholds in feminist geography: Difference, methodology, representation* (pp. 255–284). Lanham, MD: Rowman & Littlefield.

Jacobs, J. (1961). *The death and life of great American cities*. New York: Vintage Books.

Jamieson, L. (1998). *Intimacy: Personal relationships in modern societies*. Maiden: Polity Press.

Jermyn, H. (2001). *The arts and social exclusion: A review prepared for the Arts Council of England*. The Arts Council of England.

Jones, O. (2007). An ecology of emotion, memory, self and landscape. In L. Bondi, J. Davidson, & M. Smith (Eds.), *Emotional geographies* (pp. 1–19). Hampshire: Ashgate.

Lefebvre, H. (1974). La production de l'espace [The production of space]. L'Homme et la société Année 1974 31–32 pp. 15–32. Fait partie d'un numéro thématique: Sociologie de la connaissance marxisme et anthropolgie. Translation in 1991 by Donals Nicholson-Smith. The production of space. Basil Blackwell.

Llaneras, K. (2017, January 7). Ellos son doctores, ellas vírgenes y santas [They are doctors, they are virgins and saints]. *El País*.

López Fdz. Cao, M. (2016). Indicadores sobre prácticas artísticas comunitarias: algunas reflexiones [Indicators on community art practices: Some reflections]. *Arteterapia. Papeles De Arteterapia Y educación artística Para La inclusión Social*, *10*, 209–234. https://doi.org/10.5209/rev_ARTE.2015.v10.51693

Matarasso, F. (1997). *Use or ornament? The social impact of participation in the arts*. Comedia: Stroud.

McDowell, L. (1999). *Gender, identity, and place: Understanding feminist geographies*. Minneapolis: University of Minnesota Press.

McDowell, L., & Sharp, J. P. (1997). *Space, gender, knowledge: Feminist readings*. London: Arnold.

McDowell, L., & Sharp, J. P. (2014). *A feminist glossary of human geography*. London: Routledge.

Milohnić, A. (2005). Artivism. *Maska*, *20*(1–2), 15–25.

Morgan, S. (1995). Looking back over 25 years. In M. Dickson (Ed.), *Art with people* (pp. 16–27). Sunderland: AN Publications.

Palacios, A. (2009). El arte comunitario: origen y evolución de las prácticas artísticas colaborativas [Community art: The origin and evolution of collaborative art practices]. In *Revista Arteterapia. Papeles de Arteterapia y educación Artística para la Inclusión Social*, *4* (pp. 197–211). Madrid: Servicios de Publicación de la Universidad Complutense de Madrid.

Sandoval, C., & Latorre, G. (2008). Chicana/o artivism: Judy Baca's digital work with youth of color. In A. Everett (Ed.), *Learning race and ethnicity: Youth and digital media* (pp. 81–108). Cambridge: The MIT Press.

Sankaranarayanan, A. (2017, June 29). Mapping female versus male street names. *Medium*. Retrieved May 20th, 2020 from https://blog.mapbox.com/mapping-female-versus-male-street-names-b4654c1e00d5

Semova, D. (2015). Valorization of cultural diversity through good practices: Dissemination on art mediation. *Arteterapia*, *10*, 235–246.

Sibley, D. (1995). *Geographies of exclusion: Society and difference in the West*. London: Routledge.

Solanki, A., Kane Speer, A., & Huang, H. (2014). Youth ARTivism: Fostering civic engagement through public art. *Journal of Urban Culture Research*, *9*, 38–51.

Tiwari, R. (2010). *Space-body-ritual, performativity in the city*. Plymouth: Lexington Books.
Van Hulst, M. (2012). Storytelling, a model of and a model for planning. *Planning Theory*, *11*(2), 299–318.

Web resources

http://madridciudaddelasmujeres.es and https://ucmadrid.maps.arcgis.com/apps/webappviewer/index.html?id=ebfd757372884065b5fd02337f10eff3

17 Oh, what a tangled web we weave!

The transformative intentions of socially engaged art

Leanne Schubert and Mel Gray

Artists and social professionals use socially engaged art practices (SEAP) to help communities with shared goals generate conversation about – and raise awareness of – social issues. They use democratic forms of social engagement and engage in acts of rebellion and resistance to improve people's physical, psychological, and social conditions. Bishop (2006a) wrote, "[The] expanded field of relational practices currently goes by a variety of names: socially engaged art, community-based art, experimental communities, dialogic art, littoral art, participatory, interventionist, research-based, or collaborative art". Some practitioners, like Bishop (2006a), equated relational practices with artistic gestures of resistance. Her stance raised important questions on this entangled field of art practice: Were "the creative rewards of collaborative activity" more important than artistic quality or forms of relational engagement? What did she mean when she talked about "working with pre-existing communities or establishing one's own interdisciplinary network"? What frameworks do artists use for their community engagement? How do they evaluate the impact of their relational practices? This chapter argues that there has been little attention to the development of adequate philosophical and theoretical frameworks for SEAP or their evaluation and measurement. It highlights several theoretical attempts to explain the intent of SEAP and ways in which to evaluate their impact. In so doing, it provides examples of artistic practices that have raised ethical concerns about means and ends.

Theorists, like Bishop (2006a), suggest that relational or dialogical art necessarily involves contention or antagonism (Miller, 2016) with activism central to the artist's intent. This raised ethical questions of whether the means (relational art practice) justified the ends (changing social attitudes or raising awareness). It also raised empirical questions about the measurement of the social impact of artwork produced

DOI: 10.4324/9781003105350-18

through relational or collaborative engagement between artists and their participants.

Most, however, see socially engaged art as *art with a social purpose* best achieved through collaborative or participatory means (Kester, 2004; Miller, 2016). Its social purpose is inherent in its intent to attain social improvement through action, whether that be collaboration, agitation, activism, awareness raising, or antagonism (Miller, 2016). Though participation could take many forms, there appeared to be an emphasis on open dialogue and democratic interaction (Miller, 2016). Kester (2004), for example, talked about conversational art.

Bishop (2006a) suggested SEAP involved an "expanded field of relational practices" (p. 1) that included: socially engaged art (Helguera, 2011), community-based art (De Bruyne & Gielen, 2011), experimental communities (Basualdo & Laddaga, 2009), dialogical or collaborative art (Kester, 2004), littoral art (Barber, 1997, 1998), participatory art (Bishop, 2006b), interventionist art (Thompson et al., 2004), and research-based art (Foster, 2016), with new practices constantly emerging (Thompson, 2011). A common thread undergirding democratic forms of artistic engagement was Habermas's theory of communicative action (1984).

Another aspect of SEAP was the context in which they took place: They moved art from galleries to public spaces. Examples were Nicolas Bourriaud's (1998) relational aesthetics and Barber's (1997, 1998) littoral art. All forms of socially engaged art emphasised the interaction between artists and their audience, spectators, or participants; even viewing art was a form of participation. Suzanne Lacy (1991, 1995) referred to this wide-open field as New Genre Public Art. In surveying this wide field, this chapter examines relational aesthetics and social impact; activism, resistance, and politics; the creative rewards of collaboration; and location of engagement. It argues that artistic practice has outstripped the development of adequate philosophical and theoretical frameworks for SEAP that occur in contexts where evaluation and measurement are crucial. Few of these authors placed specific emphasis on social transformation.

Relational aesthetics and social impact

Suzi Gablik (1991) foreshadowed relational aesthetics when she proposed "connective aesthetics" as the basis for developing relationship between artists and their participants. For her, this relationship was central to participatory art making. In an interview in the *L.A. Times*, Carolina A. Miranda said, "You have to spend years developing relationships. . . .

It'd be an arrogant disregard of a community to come in and think you can grasp all the complexities of a place in a short time" (2014). The originator of relational aesthetics, Nicholas Bourriaud (1998), saw an inextricable link between aesthetics and relationships. He proposed that relational aesthetics comprised a "set of artistic practices which take as their theoretical and practical point of departure the whole of human relations and their social context, rather than an independent and private space" (p. 113). He saw artists as catalysts or facilitators and art as the exchange of information between artists and viewers. Together, connective and relational aesthetics served as the forerunners of the rapidly expanding field of relational SEAP.

Artistic quality and social impact aggressively railed against one another in the expanding field of relational aesthetics. Without specific reference to artistic quality or social impact, Bourriaud (1998) argued that artists *created temporary social relations using aesthetic objects* in response to emergent forms of control and alienation; power and change were central to the work of art. He highlighted the art of Liam Gillick, Pierre Huyghe, Carsten Holler, and Rirkrit Triavanija as artists pursing a relational aesthetic. For these artists and theorists, *the aesthetic embedded within the relationships* were central to the artwork; artists used art spaces to create social relations. Unlike conventional art that remained securely embedded in the sacred space of the institutions of art, such as museums and galleries, relational aesthetics took art outside into the public arena, using it to highlight social issues (Rasmussen, 2017). In time, there was a shift in terminology from relational aesthetics to socially engaged art.

However, confusion about – and resistance to – SEAP has given rise to ongoing questions about relational practices and the conditions necessary for the production of participatory artworks (Blanche, 2014), their aesthetic quality, social value, and impact (Belfiore & Bennett, 2008). Without clear signals of intent from artists or objective evaluative criteria, it was impossible to determine artistic quality or measure social impact. This was further confused by the fact that funding bodies conflated quality and impact by framing measurements of quality around social impact rather than artistic outcomes.

Clements (2007) referred to the contested, ambiguous process of impact measurement that, nevertheless, was a means of securing funding noting that bureaucratic, top-down approaches rather than aesthetic quality tended to influence project aims and social impact objectives. He warned of the potential to use evaluation as a tool of control. Thus, transparency was important. Artists needed to ensure participants understood the unpredictable nature of art-making processes, what participation involved, how their interests would be factored into the artmaking, and what the artist's intentions were. This called for high levels of political awareness among participants, as well as artist reflexivity, to ensure accountability (Helguera, 2011).

Schubert (2012) framed these as ethical issues, which the researcher-artist addressed through the research-ethics approval process. This required explicit information for participants about what participation involved and the risks involved.

Mounting international evidence from diverse disciplines linked art and cultural participation with increased democratic engagement and enhanced community wellbeing in addition to aesthetic value and the quality of art (Badham, 2010). How to evaluate the artistic quality of socially engaged art remained important to justifying something as an artistic activity (Miller, 2016). Several authors highlighted the need for increased attention to the artistic merits of SEAP (Badham, 2010; Cohen-Cruze, 2016). For Badham (2011) overlooking artistic quality or the artistic merit of socially engaged art meant the risk of losing its social impact. For Cohen-Cruze (2016), questions about whether this work was art stretched the "understanding of its scope, for other artists, funders, policy makers and the general public" (n.p.). She believed a work's evaluation as art increased its social impact. In short, philosophical confusion and resistance surrounded socially engaged art situated at "the complex interface of sociality, politics, ethics, and aesthetics" (Miller, 2016, p. 166). Miller (2016) concluded that there might be no "*aesthetic* basis" (p. 170 original emphasis) on which to evaluate relational art.

Badham (2011) observed that, in the absence of strong arts-based conceptual frameworks and effective strategies for analysis, evaluation, and measurement, practice had outrun philosophy and theory. Hence, no matter the approach or ethical position, these works would continue to be difficult to ground as legitimate art forms. Further, Thompson (2015) advised there were no answers as to whether these works should be interpreted as art or activism. He argued one could be critical of any form of connoisseurship related to this work. He described relational works as "living as form". He problematised relational practices and proposed that their focus was not aesthetics but change. For him, this was political and, on occasion, associated with the politics of the Left (Holmes, 2012). He located social art practices within the realm of spectacle, which he equated with politics, noting that, to get attention, the artist needed to present the work aesthetically (Thompson, 2015). In this way, relational art practices assumed a new form of power and increased capacity for social transformation, particularly through activism.

Activism, resistance, and politics

Bishop (2006a) claimed that SEAP necessarily involved contention and resistance, while others questioned whether they necessarily thrived on antagonism (Miller, 2016) and ambivalent interests and identities (Kester, 2004). There were many ethical questions centred on the artist's intention, the purpose of the artwork, and whose interests it served. Socially engaged practice can be associated with activism because it often deals with political issues (Tate.org.uk).

Thompson (2011) associated the growth of relational practices with the rise of neoliberalism and the internet as a radical platform for resistance, while Rasmussen (2017) saw the politicisation of art as embedded within relationally antagonistic works that raised questions about the appropriateness of aesthetic responses to social ills. One example of the artist-provocateur was Santiago Sierra, whose performative works, like *160 cm Line Tattooed on Four People* (Sierra, 2000; to view images and a video from this work go to www.santiago-sierra.com/200014_1024.php) demonstrated an absence of ethical concern for participants within his practice. In this artwork, he hired four prostitutes, who agreed to be tattooed for the price of a shot of heroin (12,000 pesetas or USD85) far more than they charged for their services, e.g., between 2,000 and 3,000 pesetas (USD14–21) for fellatio.

Miller (2016) believed that Sierra exploited the inequalities between himself as the artist and those participating in his artworks. He perceived an absence of "democratic participation" and "dialogue" in Sierra's work, where the focal point was the exploitative nature of the exchange between the artist and his participants. The antagonism in Sierra's work promoted the myth that the relational was essentially good. However, Sierra intentionally highlighted that, in their relationships, humans frequently dehumanised and exploited one another. Sierra was not interested in discourse, engagement, or collaboration per se; rather, he was interested in *the reproduction of social ills as spectacle* in the pursuit of critical awareness in the viewer. Did Sierra intend his work to be socially transformative? There is no clear indication that this was the case and perhaps the only transformative act is to draw is the viewer's attention to "hierarchies of power and exploitation" (Twyman, 2018, n.p.) and the tension in the choice made by the participants between their addiction and economic circumstances.

Miller (2016) was critical of the idea that *antagonistic* relational art practices were "impervious to ethical analysis" (p. 170), simply because they were works of art: "It cannot be the antagonistic gesture *per se* that counts as an aesthetic virtue – it matters *what kind* [original emphasis] of antagonism it entails" (p. 177). He argued that Sierra's work should not transcend ethics even if its goal of critical awareness was offered as moral justification: "Art that evokes sensations of unease and discomfort rather than belonging has aesthetic value only in relation to the presumed ethical value of raising consciousness by means of these sensations" (pp. 172–173). He did not see ethical merits in "aesthetically rendered exploitation" (p. 173). The shock value of a work or the "uncritical valuation of confrontation for its own sake" (p. 174) did not exclude it from ethical critique. Further, antagonism was not the only way to raise awareness. There were "democratically productive forms of social engagement" (p. 174).

For Miller (2016), the same principles held with *agonistic* art practices that highlighted "disagreement and difference" (p. 174) and fomented dissent to make social issues that the dominant consensus tended to obscure and obliterate visible. Whether antagonistic or agonistic, the "second-order ethical imperative for critical awareness [did not trump] . . . first-order ethical concerns about the nature of aesthetic relations" (p. 173). The utilitarian end of critical awareness-raising should not override deontological concerns about the ethics of aesthetic relations.

Creative rewards of collaborative activity

Still unanswered was the question of whether artists who engaged in relational practices were more interested in a relational aesthetic than the "creative rewards of collaborative activity" (Bishop, 2006a, p. 1). Socially engaged art offered a "palpable aesthetic experience – the joy, bursts of imagination, self-knowledge, insight beyond surfaces, and temporary experience of . . . a connecting spirit" (Cohen-Cruze, 2016). Most writers saw aesthetic concerns as central to the theory and practice of early incarnations of relational art. Beyond aesthetics and collaboration, relational works embraced diverse concerns, among them oppression, marginality, otherness, ecology, popular culture, the impact of technology, radical politics, feminism, privilege, and power (Lacy, 1995). Bishop's (2006a) questions about collaborative activity arose, in part, from Kester (2004, 2011), whose work indicated that relational artists were "less concerned with aesthetic innovation and formal sophistication than engaging in concrete collaborations with an outside community" (Rasmussen, 2017, p. 2). In framing art as collaborative, Kester (2011) proposed that artists, like Suzanne Lacy, offered context but were devoid of content against which the work might be analysed and evaluated. His critique of these practices attempted to create an art historical and aesthetic framework against which to assess SEAP. Within this frame, Kester (2011) did not explicitly address the so-called "creative rewards of collaboration" (Bishop, 2006a, p. 1). Rather he argued that, aggregated, these practices disclosed the history of modern art and the "current political moment" (Kester, 2011, p. 10). Collaboration, for Kester (2011), involved "united labor" (p. 1), though he acknowledged its shadow side and counter meaning of betrayal or treasonable cooperation. Nevertheless, Kester (2011) believed that "the most pressing political and ethical questions of our time" (p. 2) sat at the centre of collaborative art projects.

Kester (2011) perceived increasingly porous boundaries between art and "other zones of symbolic production, urbanism, environmental activism, social work, etc." (p. 7). He saw a movement away from textual modes of production, where the artist created an object or event and presented this for the viewer, toward process-based, participatory experiences ranging from "neo-conceptual through to activist works" (p. 7) that dissolved boundaries between avant garde, mainstream, and relational art practices; this made it increasingly difficult to discern one from the other. Kester (2011) identified three areas of significant transformation in contemporary art practice:

1 Increasingly collaborative complicated "conventional notions of aesthetic autonomy" (p. 10) by which he meant the artist had less autonomy in making the work.
2 It raised important ontological questions regarding what constituted "art" and its defining conditions as borne out of the nexus between aesthetic and ethical criteria related to the evaluation of the artwork.
3 The hermeneutic implications of collaborative practice involving dialogical processes that "suggest a model of reception and a set of research methodologies" (p. 10), which differed from object-based art practices and were more closely aligned with the social sciences.

Thus, Kester's (2011) transformational concern rested with the nature of contemporary art practice rather than social change per se.

For Helguera (2011), collaboration lay at the centre of critical and artistic practice and served to mobilise cultural practice. Here, "artistic practice is defined through, not in advance, of collaboration" (Papastergiadis, 2006, pp. 198–199) and, in return, collaboration socialised artistic practice. In socially engaged art, the artist set the collaborative tone and acted as conceptual director of the project. The role the artist took defined the nature of collaboration (Helguera, 2011, p. 51). Helguera (2011) argued that successful collaboration required the articulation of accountability between artists and collaborators. The nature of the collaboration became critical: Was decision making within projects collective or controlled by the artist to the point that it barely resembled collaboration? The work of Santiago Sierra falls into this latter category.

Discussions on collaboration highlighted the nature of relational encounters and the potential for the aesthetic to challenge conventional viewpoints that led to the discovery of new ways of being together. This, Kester (2011) argued, distinguished dialogue and collaboration in an artwork from that in social work or political activism. However, others have argued this boundary was blurred and porous (Schubert & Gray, 2015; Thompson et al., 2004).

Context or location of engagement

Thompson (2011) argued that, despite common critiques of socially engaged artworks, they remained complex with each project informed by its context or location of engagement, which generated a dance among multiple publics, media, pedagogy, political actors, local conditions, receivers, and audience.

Bishop (2006a) highlighted the interdisciplinary nature of relational practices within "pre-existing communities" and "one's own interdisciplinary network" (p. 2). She ignored the ambiguous nature of the term "community" and the position the artist assumed as an insider or outsider of a community in this kind of work. She stated that SEAP "are less interested in a relational aesthetic than in the creative rewards of collaborative activity – whether in the form of working with pre-existing communities or establishing one's own interdisciplinary network" (Bishop, 2006a). Kwon (2004) argued that this ambiguity was consistent with slippages occurring with terms like "audience", "site", and "public" (p. 94) also being relevant to considerations of disciplinary location. She explored this question extensively and noted the depiction of community-based art as "aesthetic evangelism" (p. 142), which she equated with the practice of social workers and reformers, who viewed personal transformation and growth as pivotal in addressing social problems. Kwon (2004) distinguished among three paradigms: art in public places, art in public spaces, and art in the public interest. She located relational practice in the latter category. Suzanne Lacy's art practice was one example of the latter, as shown in Figure 16.2.

In Suzanne Lacy's (1991) *Cancer Notes* (images of this work can be viewed at www.suzannelacy.com/cancer-notes/), the relationship extended beyond the participant to include reciprocal relationships among venue, content, and approach. Lacy undertook a seven-day performance addressing cancer, relationality, and death within a New York cancer research hospital. Meeting one person an hour for eight hours a day, Lacy interviewed patients and staff, spontaneously recorded notes, and made diagrams that formed large drawings, mapping connections, creating shared meaning with participants, and portraying the workings of a hospital. This temporary installation included discussions with participant on their observations and experiences, while the artist documented the project through her graphic representations. Lacy (1991) saw empathy as "a service artists offer to the world" (pp. 174–175). She suggested there was "no quick fix for some of our most pressing social problems, [and] there may be only our ability to feel and witness the reality taking place around us" (pp. 174–175). Thus, it would appear that Lacy viewed her work as having the potential to develop shared meanings, work across disciplines, and connect with community; it had limited potential for long-term social transformation. While Lacy (1991) struggled to measure the outcomes of this project, her work was the antithesis of the kinds of works Bishop (2006a) inferred in her "artistic gestures of resistance" (p. 2) and politicisation of art within these resistive gestures.

In the "Safe at Home" project, Schubert (2012) overtly attempted to transform community attitudes toward domestic and family violence using art as her medium (see Figures 17.1 and 17.2, which provide examples

Figure 17.1 Panel 100 (the centrepiece) of the Snakes and Ladders mosaic created as part of the "Safe at Home" project

Source: Mel Gray.

Figure 17.2 Panel 48 of the Snakes and Ladders mosaic created as part of the "Safe at Home" project

Source: Mel Gray.

of key anti-violence messages and images developed with participating community members that were integrated into the artworks. For further details of "Safe at Home" please see Schubert, 2012; Schubert & Gray, 2018). Taking into consideration the key ideas related to SEAP – relational aesthetics, collaboration, context, interdisciplinarity, resistance, and the politicisation of art – discussed earlier in this chapter, "Safe at Home" further incorporated feminist ideals. It was based on a belief that art in social work was an instrument of social change (Rapoport, 1968) and a process of "making special" (Dissanayake, 1988, p. 126). By this Dissanayake (1988) meant it enabled transformation through recognition of – and entry into – "an alternative [or imagined] reality" (p. 99). At the very least, art could "promote a climate of change" (Kaplan, 1968, p. 163) given the social benefits of art inhered in their transformative potential (Matarasso, 1997). Using an arts-based community development approach, "Safe at Home" incorporated a Freirean transformative focus on empowerment, community action, and social change. It acknowledged the political nature of art, which could be "about politics" and "political" in and of itself by providing "a context within which others [could] take action" (Purcell, 2007, p. 114). Finding new ways to raise awareness about domestic and family violence in a community context using art constituted a political act.

While the community members involved were supportive of "Safe at Home" and what it tried to achieve, art was not able to draw most of the adult community members into active project participation due to their concerns about feeling unsafe with their neighbours. Substantial arts-based community transformation required the building of trust over time and long-term funding to ensure the project did not end just as trust was beginning to develop. This dilemma served to challenge sustainable change when ongoing funding was not secured.

Ultimately, the "Safe at Home" project found that art was not an effective short-term intervention for transforming awareness of – or attitudes toward – domestic and family violence. However, it raised the need for long-term research to examine such interventions, particularly in relation to health promotion and early intervention. What art successfully achieved in the "Safe at Home" project was the generation of hope and possibility within the community.

Conclusion

This chapter examined six important ideas underpinning the expanded field of relational practices: relational aesthetics, collaboration, context, interdisciplinarity, resistance, and the politicisation of art. It showed that artistic quality and social impact, rather than railing against each other, were part of a complex of factors socially engaged art practice entailed. It intertwined impact, quality, aesthetics, collaboration, context, resistance, politics, and interdisciplinarity. The examples drawn from the art practice of Leanne Schubert, Suzanne Lacy, and Santiago Sierra stood in varying degrees of opposition and illustrated the extremes of opposing intentions and ethical stances possible in socially engaged art practice. The viewer's response would reflect his or her ethical stance. In conclusion, two streams of practice emerged along the clef of an ethical divide – the antagonistic and agonistic – and transformative intent that the work of Sierra at one end and Lacy and Schubert at the other reflected. It seemed that philosophy, theory, and art criticism continued to lag the ever-expanding field of relational practices in a socio-political context demanding ever-more-detailed measurement and evaluation of works produced through socially engaged practices.

References

Badham, M. (2010). The case for "socially engaged arts": Navigating art history, cultural development and arts funding narratives. *Legitimation: Local-Global*, 84–99. http://prodmams.rmit.edu.au/8nn22vgkb7pwz.pdf

Barber, B. (1997). *Paragraphs on littoral art*. www.brucebarber.ca/index.php/paragraphs

Barber, B. (1998). *Sentences on littoral art*. www.brucebarber.ca/index.php/sentences

Basualdo, C., & Laddaga, R. (2009). Experimental communities. In B. Hinderliter, V. Maimon, J. Mansoor, & S. McCormick (Eds.), *Communities of sense: Rethinking aesthetics and politics* (pp. 215–238). Durham, NC: Duke University Press.

Belfiore, E., & Bennett, O. (2008). *The social impact of the arts: An intellectual history*. London: Palgrave Macmillan.

Bishop, C. (2004). Antagonism and relational aesthetics. *October*, *110*, 51–79.

Bishop, C. (2006a). The social turn: Collaboration and its discontents. *Artforum*. www.artforum.com/html/issues/200602/new

Bishop, C. (Ed.). (2006b). *Participation*. Cambridge, MA: MIT Press.

Blanche, R. (2014). Towards a shared responsibility for quality in participatory arts: Key insights into conditions underpinning quality. *Journal of Arts & Communities*, 6(2&3), 145–164.

Bourriaud, N. (1998). *Relational aesthetics*. (Simon Pleasance, Fronza Woods, & Mathieu Copeland, Trans.). Collection Documents Sur L'art. Dijon-Quetigny: Les presses du reel.

Clements, P. (2007). The evaluation of community arts projects and the problem of social impact. *International Journal of Art and Design Education*, 26(3), 325–335.

Cohen-Cruz, J. (2016). *The imagination and beyond: Toward a method of evaluating socially engaged art*. Centre for Artistic Activism. https://artisticactivism.org/wp-content/uploads/2016/02/The-Imagination-and-Beyond_Toward-a-Method-of-Evaluating-Socially-Engaged-Art-©-Jan-Cohen-Cruz.pdf?x35829

De Bruyne, P., & Gielen, P. (Eds.). (2011). *Community art: The politics of trespassing: Antennae*. Amsterdam: Valiz.

Dissanayake, E. (1988). *What is art for?* Washington: The University of Washington Press.

Foster, V. (Ed.). (2016). *Collaborative arts based research for social justice*. New York: Routledge.

Gablik, S. (1991). *The reenchantment of art*. New York: Thames and Hudson.

Habermas, J. (1984). *Theory of communicative action. Volume One: Reason and the rationalization of society*. (T. A. McCarthy, Trans.). Boston, MA: Beacon Press.

Helguera, P. (2011). *Education for socially engaged art: A materials and techniques handbook*. New York, NY Jorge Pinto Books.

Holmes, B. (2012). Eventwork: The fourfold matrix of contemporary social movements. In N. Thompson (Ed.), *Living as form: Socially engaged art from 1991–2011* (pp. 72–85). New York: Creative Time Books.

Kaplan, S. (1968). Discussion of Lydia Rapoport's creativity in social work. *Smith College Studies in Social Work*, *18*(3), 162–168.

Kester, G. H. (2004). *Conversation pieces: Community and communication in modern art*. Los Angeles, CA: California University Press.

Kester, G. H. (2011). *The one and the many: Contemporary collaborative art in a global context*. Durham, NC: Duke University Press.

Kwon, M. (2004). *One place after another: Site specific art and locational identity*. Cambridge, MA: MIT Press.

Lacy, S. (1991). *Cancer notes*. www.suzannelacy.com/cancer-notes

Lacy, S. (Ed.). (1995). *Mapping the terrain: New genre public art*. Seattle, WA: Bay Press.

Lingwood, J. (2013). *Entanglements: Artists and places*. Sydney, NSW: Carriageworks in partnership with the Museum of Contemporary Art Australia.

Matarasso, F. (1997). *Use or ornament? The social impact of participation in the arts*. Stroud, Glos: Comedia.

Miller, J. (2016). Activism vs. antagonism: Socially engaged art from Bourriaud to Bishop and beyond. *Field: A Journal of Socially-Engaged Art Criticism*, *3*, 165–183.

Papastergiadis, N. (2006). *Spatial aesthetics: Art, place and the everyday*. London: Rivers Oram Press.

Purcell, R. (2007). Images for change: Community development, community arts and photography. *Community Development Journal*, *44*(1), 111–122. doi:10.1093/cdj/bsm031

Rapoport, L. (1968). Creativity in social work. *Smith College Studies in Social Work*, *18*(3), 139–161.

Rasmussen, M. B. (2017). A note on socially engaged art criticism. *Field: A Journal of Socially-Engaged Art Criticism*, *6*, 1–11.

Schubert, L. (2012). *Art, social work and social change.* Callaghan, NSW: University of Newcastle.

Schubert, L., & Gray, M. (2015). The death of emancipatory social work as art and birth of socially engaged art practice. *British Journal of Social Work, 24*, 1349–1356.

Schubert, L., & Gray, M. (2018). Safe at home: A community intervention to address domestic violence through the Arts. *Social Dialogue, 19*, 4–7. https://socialdialogue.online/volume/19/read/#page=6

Sierra, S. (December, 2000). *Línea de 160 cm tatuada sobre 4 personas El Gallo Arte Contemporáneo. Salamanca, España. Diciembre de 2000 [160 cm Line Tattooed on 4 People]* a video documenting an action that took place at El Gallo Arte Contemporáneo in Salamanca, Spain in December 2000. www.santiago-sierra.com/200014_1024.php

Thompson, N. (2011). *Nato Thompson on socially engaged art outside the bounds of an artistic discipline.* Vimeo: Creative Time.

Thompson, N. (2015). *Seeing power: Art and activism in the 21st century.* London: Melville House.

Thompson, N., Sholette, G., Thompson, J., Mirsoff, N., & Chavoya, O. C. (Eds.). (2004). *The interventionists: Users' manual for the creative disruption of everyday life.* North Adams, MA: MaSS MoCA.

Twyman, J. (2018). *Santiago Sierra: Walking the line.* Art Exchange, University of Essex, Colchester. www.artexchange.org.uk/event/santiago-sierra-walking-the-line/

18 The art of making public

The politics of participation in participatory art practices

Siebren Nachtergaele, Tine Vanthuyne, and Griet Verschelden

In recent years, many social work and art practices developed at the intersection between the cultural turn in social work and the social turn in the arts, with participation as a central constitutive element of their practice (Bishop, 2012; De Bisschop, 2009; Jans, 2014). We call these practices participatory art practices, which are

> a form of artistic research, in which artists together with citizens seek the right artistic format that allows alternative voices and interpretations to be heard. The artists understand their artistic work as the driving force behind wider processes, rather than as the creation of a preconceived artistic product. Their participatory way of working aims to make mechanisms of power and exclusion transparent, and to make people aware of the real conflicts.
>
> (Trienekes & Hillaert, 2015, p. 5)

Participatory art practices are quite often seen as radical democratic practices (Kester, 2003) or as an answer to social and economic alienation (Gruber, 2013) and polarization in the society. They are seen as practices with a clear social agenda (Bishop, 2012; Schubert & Gray, 2015). But are participatory art practices really democratic? Do they transform society? Do they need to transform? And if so, in which way? Can we pinpoint the democratic moments they realize (Biesta, 2011; Biesta et al., 2013)?

The aim of this contribution is to scrutinize the participatory processes of participatory art practices and reflect on their political or agonistic potential. How, in which ways, and why do participatory art practices seek to foreground the sociopolitical in their work and connect or participate in public and political debate? What are the traces that affect and condensate these practices in the art of making public?

DOI: 10.4324/9781003105350-19

Figure 18.1 "Fake Calligraphy"

Source: © Manoeuvre

The question on the politics of participation in participatory art practices is part of a broader research on the social impact of participatory art practices. We investigate how participatory arts practices affect people and society on an individual and collective level. In our research we see impact as an open-ended concept and as an individual and collective meaning-making process. This differs from an evidence-based, economically rationalized understanding of impact, measuring assessment in terms of numbers and other logics of profit, benefit, growth, and expansion (Bala, 2019; Belfiore & Bennett, 2008). Our notion of impact needs a critical interpretative research approach combined with an action-oriented approach. We examined twenty-one participatory art practices (see Figure 18.1), using participatory observations, interviews, and document analysis. Two of these participatory art practices were involved in an action-oriented trajectory for a longer period of time (Nachtergaele et al., 2021 – www.impakt.gent)

At the cutting edge between the social turn in the arts and the cultural turn in social work

Participatory art practices are a growing field within the arts, with a social component that is at the heart of the aesthetic and cultural practice. These practices are scrutinized separately in the art field, captured as the social turn in the arts. In the social field these practices are described as part of the cultural turn in social practices.

Claire Bishop (2006, 2012) describes the growing numbers of engaged artistic creations since the nineties. These art works focus on participation as the core of their aesthetics. They hold a social engagement and focus on participation as an artistic concept in their work. Addressing the public (even if without actors at all, i.e. immersive arts) and breaking the boundaries between art and context are the main aesthetic principles of performance today. Erwin Jans describes this development in the mission statement of the State of the Arts in Flanders as "this points out to a broader trend in the arts to engage audiences in a different way and to engage them more as active partners in processes of creation and meaning-making" (2014, p. 10).

Furthermore there is a tendency in social sciences and social work to work with a growing interest in cultural and artistic practice. Since the nineties, there have been more and more artistic and creative practices developing in the social field (quite often therapeutic, social, and creative activities but also community arts related with community development). Historically the linkage with artistic practice was part of the critical and emancipatory work in the social field. Mel Gray and Leanne Schubert (Schubert & Gray, 2015) criticize this lack of critical engagement in the current social practices, overwhelmed by a bureaucratizing tendency of assessments and dealing with clients instead of human beings. Participatory art practices are inspiring for social work (or the social field) today because they can broaden the social-political horizon and create alternatives in the imaginary third spaces they create with their artistic work.

In this chapter, we consider participatory art practices from an interdisciplinary perspective, bridging both the social and cultural turn which are influencing these practices. This implies an approach of participatory art practices as cultural–artistic and social practices. These practices are branched out and entangled in a network of artistic and cultural actors and are culturally and historically imbedded, which means that participatory arts are part of a broader cultural practice. At the same time, these participatory art practices are also social practices, embedded in society and in interaction with actual social and cultural developments and actors. In our research, we scrutinize participation not only as a social concept but also as an artistic and cultural concept.

So we see participatory art practices as *hybrid*, on the intersection of the arts and the socio-cultural, and at the cutting edge of different mediums, disciplines, backgrounds, etc. Furthermore we see participatory arts as *practices* (Reckwitz, 2002), which means we unravel these art projects/collectives as practices with both a social and artistic component in their artistic work.

Pitfalls of participation

The notion of participation in participatory art practices is well contested. Several respondents in our study refuse even to talk about their practice in terms of a participatory practice. They even refuse to apply for funding by the Decree for Fine Arts in Flanders (Belgium) because they don't agree with the interpretations of the concept of participation made by the Flemish Government (Pourcq et al., 2017).

> I don't have a problem with the concept: "participation", but this doesn't mean everything we are doing can be covered under this umbrella term. Then art becomes a kind of vehicle for social work. I don't think that is a good idea. That's why we don't call this a socio-artistic practice. But a social and an artistic place or practice. We do not want the former to instrumentalize the latter. These are two things that coexist with and through each other.
>
> (R3; interviewees are listed with R and a number)

We distinguish several pitfalls or "nightmares" (Miessen, 2010). First, characteristics in the description of participation are based on target groups, functions, methods, and goals. This is a functional view on *what* and *how*, diverting the attention from the *why* questions of these practices and without consciousness on the social and artistic value of the work.

> A bit of my problem with participation is that you immediately read [in policy documents] what it will serve for, what the intention is. The standards are often very high, are often formulated separately from some knowledge of the practice, of the people you work with, and it is just strange that you already connect objectives and standards of participation and social impact in advance. You often have the feeling that it serves to support the policy and to work on a kind of sugar coating of the policy choices.
>
> (R1)

Second, there is a problem of instrumentalization of the art practice when these practices are seen as part of a political or economic agenda (De Bruyne & Gielen, 2011). This points to a broader discussion, in which the increasing attention to participation in the arts resonates with an economic logic that creeps into the arts. Art practices are seen as a part of the experience economy, where goods and services are exchanged for personal experiences. This implies, according to Claire Bishop (2012), a form of instrumentalization of the arts in function of policy and economic agendas. Think, for example, of a place temporarily used for a cultural intervention that is simultaneously used to increase the economic value of this cultural hotspot, in order to subsequently be able to keep the value of the houses that are being built there sufficiently high (Steel et al., 2012). This is where the "use(er) value" of the artistic work becomes more important than the artistic value (Wright, 2014).

> Everyone is very sorry that those things happen, but we are going to watch the show [at the theater] and we go outside and think: oh gosh, it will be fine. There was a politician at the show, who said: the whole performance is very beautiful, the images and so on, but everything else: the views you take on urban renewal [gentrification], that is not your job. Then I think: participatory practices, I don't know well.
>
> (R1)

Bishop (2006) critiques the self-evident fact that participatory art practices would break the status quo, while at the same time they can be an instrument of market mechanisms or government programs that are drawn by top-down process and do little good or can be, de facto, anything but participatory. Participatory art practices can maintain the current social order or tendencies instead of questioning them, confirm cliché images about certain population groups rather than adjust them, or merely be used as an instrument where governments fail in their social responsibility.

At the same time, we can also see the criticism of the so-called instrumentalization of art in function of policy and economic objectives (external to those of the artist) as a critique of instrumentalization of art in function for social purposes, "to instrumentalize art in compensation for some perceived social lack" in Bishop's words (2006, pp. 178–183).

> The aesthetic for Rancière therefore signals an ability to think contradiction: the productive contradiction of art's relationship to social change, which is characterised by the paradox of belief in art's autonomy and in it being inextricably bound to the promise of a better world to come. While this antinomy is apparent in many avant-garde practices of the last century, it seems particularly pertinent to analysing participatory art and the legitimating

> narratives it has attracted. In short, the aesthetic doesn't need to be sacrificed at the altar of social change, because it always already contains this ameliorative promise.
>
> (Bishop, 2012, p. 29)

In regard with this problem of instrumentalization, respondents in our research point out some little advantages when local governments take possession of their art practice:

> The title of the book "Do you speak Sint – Gillis?" has been taken over in a new call for project funding from the local government. That is wrong, because on the one hand your idea is taken over by the civil service, but on the other hand it also means that something has already changed, and that the project reached some impact.
>
> (R5)

In the same participatory debate, An Van den Bergh (2016) points out the distinction between instrumental and fundamental participation:

> Instrumental participation is based on a static and rational concept of the arts. Experts determine what a good theatre performance is, for example. Participation is then an instrument to introduce as many people as possible to their own programming. Perhaps there are barriers that the public must overcome in order to achieve this. All kinds of methods and formats can help with this: a reduced ticket price, a pre- or debriefing, a tour behind the scenes, a targeted communication or the choice of a more accessible or accessible presentation place. . . . But in order to realize an open, diverse and democratic arts field, it is not enough to just ask ourselves who visits our halls or museums and how we can make this audience more diverse. We must dare to question the entire art scene itself – from creation to distribution. This requires fundamental participation.
>
> (pp. 3–4)

These pitfalls of participation refer to a broader discussion on the conflict between two paradigms in cultural policy: the *democratization of culture versus cultural democracy* (Evrard, 1997). The approach to participation is predominantly motivated by a cultural policy aimed at democratization of culture, as a cultural marketing strategy, which aims to disseminate cultural supplies to an audience (as large as possible) that does not have ready access to them, for lack of financial means or knowledge. This idea of democratization of culture implies a *Bourdieu-esque* notion of hierarchy of cultural value, as a result making this democratization a question of accessibility to culture (Morató & Valenzuela, 2018, p. 187). But the approach to participation is not so much aimed at cultural democratization (Bonet & Négrier, 2018), in the sense of questioning the cultural canon itself, including the existing hierarchies in the cultural and artistic landscape and widening the range of voices heard. In this approach the starting point is that there is not one culture but that there are different cultures and that they are equal to each other, and therefore everyone has the same right to cultural development (Deceur, 2017). Ciska Hoet states, "However, anyone with any experience in participation knows that anyone who wants to enter into new relationships with their audience and wants to make that audience more diverse cannot avoid questioning their own standards, nor from opening up the programming" (Hoet, 2016, p. 3).

When do participatory art practices become political and when might they contribute to transform society?

With regard to these pitfalls, the question remains: how and in which ways do participatory art practices seek to foreground the sociopolitical in their work, and how they connect to public and political debate? How can we conceive participatory processes which are doing justice to all subjects involved and overcome existing inequalities in groups, communities, and society? Our research shows that participatory art practices have political and agonistic potential when they are about commoning, when they build on a cultural and artistic workplace, when they are about shareability, when they are situated in space and place, when they are about role fluidity, when they participate in the public discourse, or when they question, redistribute, and break through existing power relations.

Commoning, about the process of making something mean (good)

Commoning comes from the word "common". Commoning is about the process of making things or commodities communal. Making it communal means making the good or the goods collective or common. A commoning practice wants to organize itself as horizontally and as collaboratively as possible. A process of commoning is driven by a common goal, in which strategies of alienation (i.e. intervening at the appropriate time and bringing in something new) are used to bring the work forward. The process stands and falls with a collective and shared concern for the common good.

> I want something collective. I work in the theater and think that the scene is still a public space. . . . For me, co-creation, co-production with those people, is a way to make the scene a public place again.
>
> (R1)

> We notice the great tension between the individual artists and the type of collective process where artists take the lead, or even almost disappear from the project or become invisible. This is a field of tension because full support in the art world is only provided by the individual artist(s). . . . So there is a challenge for the policy to adjust their frameworks to how the practices really take place. Because there are a lot of collaborations between activism, urbanity, art practices that mess with each other without fitting into one box.
>
> (R3)

Building on a cultural and artistic workplace

The workplace is the space where artists and culture workers and other collaborators create the artistic work and shape the cultural practice. This is a physical or virtual place, which is formed in and through a ritual of gestures and actions. These ritual gestures and actions intensify the process of collaboration and creation and initiate a relational and collective (learning) process. The workspace gives special attention to (traditional) making and collaborating on this. This creates a collaborative or experimental, co-creative space, where you can contribute and collaborate through different "entrances" (different perspectives, expertise, and abilities). Thinking is situated in doing and doing in thinking. The material consciousness, the collectively created ritual, and the temporality of working together in the workspace make connections possible.

> We made a work at a colloquium. And then everyone could participate, and sitting at the table there, which is nice. . . . In the meantime, the words are running, we work that way. Together we actually come up with ideas in the making, we talk to each other, you listen, you invite people. . . . We don't show, we are and we do the work. Our workplace itself is also part of the artwork, it participates.
>
> (R13)

Shareability, about becoming part of the work and creating a shared resonance space

Shareability is about making the work public and presenting it. Enabling shareability means sharing the work with an audience, a context and the wider world. The rules of the game are opened up. This allows one to become part of the work and to bear or acquire shared responsibility and ownership. This also points to knowledge and expertise sharing in a horizontal way, with attention to both dry knowledge (theoretical and institutional knowledge) and wet knowledge (i.e. lived knowledge: knowledge in our hands and bodies). This allows a plurality of voices, narratives, and perspectives to connect and fertilize each other. In this way, the shared work triggers meaningful exchanges and interactions. These vibrant and meaningful exchanges create a shared resonance space.

> Now we say that we work with an artistic core . . . and that we have a wider artist community around us with performers, but also writers, activists etc. . . . There are those who are directly involved, who also guide our conversations. Around this there is a circle with actively involved participants. They have participated in conversations, which participate more often, which also invite us to organize something together.
>
> (R9)

Situated in place and space, about site involvement and anchoring the work

The place where the artistic work is made gives meaning to the art practice. The resonance of the work and the broader practice is determined by the way in which the work is grounded in the space. The artistic and cultural work is made in one place and is driven by a commitment to the place: they work "in" the place and also "with" the place. This does not mean that the meaning only resonates in and on the place but that it does resonate from and through the place to the environment and the world around it.

> It's not like you go to a place to pick up material to make the performance somewhere else. You do something in that place that has meaning for that place. In my opinion, theatre is a medium that first has to sort out the place itself, and then tell about the whole circumstance outside of it. Where you know that you will never be told everything.
>
> (R1)

Role fluidity, about making roles liquid and divisible

There are no strictly or rigidly defined roles in participatory art practices. A collective work or creation process liquefies the roles. It concerns the roles of the participants or of the participants, players/co-creators, and the broader group of people involved. These roles can shift during the work process (including the role of the person responsible). In this way, shared responsibility can arise. Role fluidity implies hybrid profiles, roles, and processes, but it does not mean that there are no specific responsibilities in a collective work and making process.

> The premise of intersubjectivity as a practice not only redefines the role of the initiator, curator or architect, but at the same time shifts the role of the viewer and the role of the installation as such. These shifting roles can be seen as a crucial precondition to think of a shift on the level of the embodied experience. It's about the shift in responsibility from object to subject where the difference can be made. I believe it is (t)here that societal impact can be formulated and the active potential can be found.
>
> (R4)

Participation in the public discourse

Many participatory art practices create their own critical discourse or consciously intervene in the art and culturally critical discourse. In this way, they weigh in on the debate and discourse that is developing around one's own practice, as well as around the broader cultural sector and pressing themes. Think of the debate that developed around and corona measures that affect the cultural sector. Breaking into the discourse is therefore also connected with questioning and possibly breaking through current power relations in the wider society.

> A final point that I see as participation is that we make performances that get resonance outside the theater walls. For example, to write an open letter after a performance. To be invited to the radio appointment or to allow the public to debate afterwards. That we even provoke this to a certain extent. In that sense, there is also a form of participation in the public debate. . . . As a way of creating an opposing/contra discourse. For example, in the performance Amnesty/Amnesia. . . . This performance was about children of Syria fighters and children of collaborators and Eastern fronters (during WW2). That was very sensitive at that

> time, because there is a great consensus not to bring these children to Europe. In that sense you are trying to develop a counter-discourse. You actually give a megaphone to those who don't have a megaphone at the time.
>
> (R14)

Questioning, redistributing, and breaking through power relations

Questioning power relations is the starting point of many participatory art practices. People often work this out as a vision and action framework and apply this in their own operation and broader practice. This (micro)political act can be a counterexample to the current, unequal social structures. Introducing counter-objection is characteristic here, to play upon what is "normal", "evident", or "generally behaved" (i.e. the consensus or status quo) with symbolic means. This is politicizing, implicit or explicit. One thematizes and highlights things that otherwise remain under the radar.

> A lot of people in the artistic and cultural field assume that we are the powerful as artists or cultural practitioners, because we have the so called expertise, as white middle class people. It's the idea that I am the professional, who will collaborate with non-professionals. On the contrary, I have the feeling that I am the non-professional there, because I do not know the context very well. I am very dependent on the local knowledge, with the residents, to better understand the place where I'm working in and with.
>
> *(R2)*

The art of making public

As we argued earlier, the idea of democratization in the field of culture has always entailed multiple ambiguities and contractions. Discussions about inclusion and exclusion, social imagination and social change (Rutten et al., 2018), cultural democratization versus democratization of culture, and between the individual and the collective or between the private and the public are central in these practices (Bishop, 2012; Deceur et al., 2016).

Our research shows that the political dimension in participatory art practices and its potential for social transformation is linked to the balance of power relations within practices and between practices and the broader society. It is about recognizing and

Figure 18.2 "Publieke Spanning", maneuver and participating audience @ Ham, sorry not sorry, Gent, 2016

Source: © Manoeuvre

acknowledging cultural forms of expression or symbolic languages, which cultural groups and communities create and share. These art practices have a metapolitical character. They make visible and sensible what is in the shadow. They listen to and offer a stage for voices that are not audible or visible. This does not mean that these practices always express themselves (explicitly) socially critically, in the sense that artistic work is made with explicit political messages. The political points in the first place to the broadening of meaning and interpretation horizons. This idea refers to the work of Chantal Mouffe (2008), in which she elaborates on the aspect "dissensus" as the essence of artistic intervention in public space (Rancière & Corcoran, 2010). In line with this, she argues that the distinction between political and non-political art does not matter. Art will always play a role in the establishment, maintenance, or undermining of a certain symbolic order. After all, art is not neutral and will always take a stand. Either art will confirm the existing order, or art will help create new "agonistic" public spaces.

References

Bala, S. (2019). What is the impact of theatre and performance? In M. Bleeker, A. Kear, J. Kelleher, & H. Roms, (Eds.), *Thinking through theatre and performance* (pp. 186–199). London, UK: Methuen Drama.

Belfiore, E., & Bennett, O. (2008). *The impact of the arts: An intellectual history*. London: Palgrave Macmillan.

Biesta, G. (2011, February 17). Learning in public places: Civic learning for the 21st Century. Inaugural lecture on the occasion of the award of the international Francqui professorship to Prof. Dr. Gert Biesta, Ghent.

Biesta, G., De Bie, M., & Wildemeersch, D. (Eds.). (2013). *Civic learning, democratic citizenship and the public sphere*. Dordrecht, the Netherlands: Springer.

Bishop, C. (2006). The social turn: Collaboration and its discontents. *Artforum*, *44*(6), 178–183. www.artforum.com/print/200602/the-social-turn-collaboration-and-its-discontents-10274

Bishop, C. (2012). *Artificial hells: Participatory art and the politics of spectatorship*. London: Verso Book.

Bonet, L., & Négrier, E. (2018). Introduction. In L. Bonet & E. Négrier (Eds.), *Breaking the fourth wall: Proactive audiences in the performing arts* (pp. 12–26). Kunnskapsverket: Elverum.

De Bisschop, A. (2009). *Community Arts als discursieve constructie* [Community arts as a discursive construct]. Doctoral thesis, Faculty of Psychology and Educational Sciences, Ghent University.

De Bruyne, P., & Gielen, P. (2011). *Community art: The politics of trespassing*. Valiz.

Deceur, E. (2017). *Sociaal-cultureel werk als democratische arena : de inzet van participatieve praktijken in stedelijke contexten* [Socio-cultural work as a democratic arena: The use of participatory practices in urban contexts]. Doctoral thesis. Faculty of Psychology and Pedagogy, Ghent University.

Deceur, E., Roets, G., Rutten, K., & De Bie, M. (2016). "A singer is a group": Creating a "researcher template" to uncover complexities in the participatory arts project rocsa singers. *Critical Arts-South-North Cultural and Media Studies*, *30*(3), 357–375.

Evrard, Y. (1997). Democratizing culture of cultural democracy. *The Journal of Arts Management, Law and Society*, *27*(3), 167–175.

Gruber, C. (2013). *InterActions: Performing actual and virtual spaces as stages of inter-est*. Marburg: Tectum Verlag.

Hoet, C. (2016). *Het grote participatiedebat*. Rekto: Verso. https://s3-eu-west-1.amazonaws.com/rektoverso-resized/sites/default/files/downloads/Onderzoekspresentatie%20Ciska%20Hoet.pdf

Jans, E. (2014). *Visietekst Participatie – Landschapstekening kunsten*. VTI, Muziekcentrum Vlaanderen en BAM. http://bamart.be/files/Visietekst_participatie.pdf

Kester, G. (2003) *Conversation pieces: Community and communication in modern art*. London: University of California Press.

Miessen, M. (2010). *The nightmares of participation*. Berlin: Sternberg Press.

Morató, A. R., & Valenzuela, R. (2018). Real democratization: Involving audiences with different cultural capital. In L. Bonet & E. Négrier, E. (Eds.), *Breaking the fourth wall: Proactive audiences in the performing arts* (pp. 178–184). Elverum: Kunnskapsverket.

Mouffe, C., & Stichting Kunst en Openbare Ruimte. (2008). *Art as a public issue: How art and its institutions reinvent the public dimension*. Rotterdam: NAi Publishers.

Nachtergaele, S., Vanthuyne, T., & Verschelden, G. (2021). *Grammatica van impact*. Gent: HOGENT. www.impakt.gent

Pourcq, L., Matthys, V., Van Eeckhaut, M., & en Van Reeth, I. (2017). *Onderzoeksrapport – Onderzoek naar de functie participatie in het Kunstendecreet* [Research report: Research into the function of participation in the Arts Decree]. Antwerpen: Karel de Grote Hogeschool.

Rancière, J., & Corcoran, S. (2010). *Dissensus: On politics and aesthetics*. London: Continuum.

Reckwitz, A. (2002). Toward a theory of social practices: A development in culturalist theorizing. *European Journal of Social Theory*, *5*(2), 243–263.

Rutten, K., Van Beveren, L., & Roets, G. (2018). The new forest: The relationship between social work and socially engaged art practice revisited. *The British Journal of Social Work*, *48*(6), 1700–1717.

Schubert, L., & Gray, M. (2015). The death of emancipatory social work as art and birth of socially engaged art practice. *The British Journal of Social Work*, *45*(4).

Steel, R., Van Eeghem, E., Verschelden, G., & Carlos, D. (2012). *Reading urban cracks: Practices of artists and community workers*. (R. Steel, E. Van Eeghem, G. Verschelden, & C. Dekeyrel, Eds.). Ghent, Belgium: University College Ghent: School of Arts & Faculty of Education, Health and Social Work, and MER. Paper Kunsthalle.

Trienekens, S., & Hillaert, W. (2015). *Kunst in transitie: Manifest voor participatieve kunstpraktijken* [Art in transition: Manifesto for participatory art practices]. Brussel, BE www.demos.be/kenniscentrum/publicatie/kunst-in-transitie-manifest-voor-participatieve-kunstpraktijken

Van den Bergh, A. (2016). *Inleiding het Grote Participatiedebat* [Introduction to the great participation debate]. https://demos.be/sites/default/files/inleiding_het_grote_participatiedebat_an_van_den_bergh.pdf

Wright, S. (2014). *Toward a lexicon of usership*. U Museum of Arte Útil & Van Abbemuseum, Eindhoven, 7th December 2013–30th March 2014, laatst geraadpleegd op 5 april 2019. http://museumarteutil.net/wp-content/uploads/2013/12/Toward-a-lexicon-of-usership.pdf

Attachment 1

Participatory art practices involved in the research (see also www.impakt.gent)

Lucinda Ra Simon Allemeersch
Elly Van Eeghem
de Koer Tim Bruggeman
TAAT Breg Horemans & Gert-Jan Stam
Constant vzw Peter Westenberg
Peter Aers
Frascati theater Berthe Spoelstra & Heske van den Ende
The Turn Club Merlijn Twaalfhoven
Building Conversation Lotte van den Berg
Seppe Baeyens
Decoratelier Jozef Wouters
Mestizo Arts Platform Tine De Pourcq
Manoeuvre Chris Rotsaert
Action Zoo Humain Chokri Ben Chikha
Homelands Sergio Roberto Gratteri
Benjamin Verdonck
Recyclart Stephane Damsin
Globe Aroma An Vandermeulen
KVS Gerardo Salinas
Radio Marie Christine & Caravane La Lea
Samenwerking tussen Bravvo asbl en Atelier Graphoui Lionel Galand

19 Evaluating arts projects and programmes designed for social impacts

The need for improved methods

Diana Betzler and Oto Potluka

It is now widely recognized that the arts and creative sectors (ACS) include social impacts such as cultural value and innovation as well as economic, educational, and learning effects (Ezell & Levy, 2003; Wright et al., 2006). An early definition describes the social impacts of the arts as "those effects that go beyond the artefacts and the enactment of the event or performance itself and have a continuing influence upon, and directly through, people's lives" (Landry et al., 1993, p. 50). It includes the effects of artistic expressions and arts-based activities on social issues, including equality, livelihoods, mental health, poverty, justice, social inclusion, and education.

Due to the complexity of the field, Belfiore and Bennett (2007) asked whether it is at all possible to investigate the "intricacy and complexity" of the aesthetic experience – given its specificity – and whether any meaningful generalizations can be made about the social impact of the arts in a complex world. Some would even argue that social value is an argument that has prevailed in the ACS over the last decades to help cultural managers and policymakers to broaden their scope and thus their funding opportunities (Belfiore & Bennett, 2007). The conviction that arts have social impacts has prevailed in politics and has been boosted throughout Europe with the EU's Culture 2000 program. In this program, cultural participation is a core tool to foster social cohesion. Thus, in the past decade, social value development has become a cultural policy goal that is regularly evaluated for achievement and impact.

The field of social impacts in arts and culture is well researched (Belfiore, 2010; Belfiore & Bennett, 2007; Crossick & Kaszynska, 2016; Galloway, 2009; Gilhespy, 2001). However, there is not a systematic literature review on the different types of projects and project objectives (targets), approaches in implementation (processes and inputs), evaluation criteria (measurement) and achieved results (outcomes), and mid- and long-term effects and impacts.

DOI: 10.4324/9781003105350-20

This chapter aims to carry out a structured investigation using a selection of deliberately chosen examples and literature sources. We aim to contribute to a better understanding of the methodological approaches to evaluating social impacts in cultural projects and programmes. First, we discuss central insights and challenges that arise in evaluating programmes and projects in which artistic-creative interventions aim at social impacts. These challenges lie both in the intangible nature of the artistic work and in the equally elusive social objectives. In these projects, evaluators often find themselves blocked by the limits of their existing methodological tools. They are often met with a lack of understanding by the actors in the cultural scene. With our small investigation, we hope to uncover the essence of these programmes and projects and elucidate the potential they have to improve mutual understanding between evaluators and those evaluated.

State of the art

In many countries, an increasing emphasis on accountability is stated in cultural policy. This has led to the emergence of a small, specialized arts evaluation industry. Those who are part of the industry conduct impact studies in the arts and cultural sectors and these studies are commissioned by funders. These evaluators then advise cultural organizations to monitor their performance by providing specific toolkits and advisory platforms for them to use. Simultaneously, debates between economic and humanistic justifications for the arts prevail (Miller, 2006) and permanently challenge evaluators to question and re-justify their approaches and methods.

Evaluation of cultural policies, programmes, and events includes some challenging tasks. The complex, small-scale, undirected production and delivery structures as well as the intangible nature of cultural products and activities make their long-term impacts methodologically difficult to measure (Donovan & O'Brien, 2016). Evaluators search for measurable variables, and thus they tend to convert intangible to tangible concepts. That is why economists are reaching their limits when it comes to evaluating artistic quality and impacts; as Morson and Schapiro put it in their blog article: "in their passion for mathematically-based explanations, economists have a hard time in three areas: accounting for culture, using narrative explanation, and addressing ethical issues that cannot be reduced to economic categories alone" (Morson & Schapiro, 2017). In recent decades, therefore, a methodological turn has taken place, where evaluators have realized that the immeasurable cannot be measured in a simplified way and have increasingly turned their focus to the use of more theory-based (Galloway, 2009), qualitative, and interpretive evaluation approaches.

The social value of arts and culture has received much scholarly attention in recent years (Belfiore, 2010; Belfiore & Bennett, 2007; Brown et al., 2015; Crossick & Kaszynska, 2016; Galloway, 2009; Gilhespy, 2001). Social impact dimensions of arts and culture can be observed on society, individual, and community levels (Sandell, 2003; Vermeulen et al., 2019). They encompass social integration and cohesion of groups, identity, and communities. Moreover, they promote democracy and civic engagement, like cultural participation and engaged citizenship (Crossick & Kaszynska, 2016). On the individual level, the arts promote the ability to reflect on individual and social issues, foster empathy and understanding of foreign cultures, and contribute to talent and identity development (Goddard, 2009; Van de Vyver & Abrams, 2018). Social impact evaluation studies are found in the fields of health and mental health, education, criminal justice, regeneration, and social inclusion (Cohen & Pate, 2000; Ezell & Levy, 2003; Fleuriet & Chauvin, 2018; Ford et al., 2018; Galloway, 2009).

Authors generally agree that the multidimensional, social effects in the ACS are complicated to measure (Belfiore & Bennett, 2010). The evidence base of social-impact research is assessed as weak in several instances (Galloway, 2009). For example, previous literature reviews note that the studies in this area measure only easy-to-collect-output such as visitor numbers, willingness to pay, or revenue generated (Vermeulen et al., 2019). Furthermore, the literature falls short in assessing the non-intended effects and the long-term social impacts such as changes in tastes, attitudes, and behaviour (Galloway, 2009). Economic valuation standards are in use as in the case with Cost-Benefit Analysis (CBA) and Social Return on Investment (SROI). These standards are widely applied in social evaluation. Simultaneously, these methods are subject to considerable scepticism in the cultural sectors (Galloway, 2009). The cultural and creative products can be seen as non-marketed goods encompassing various intangible social values that are difficult to measure in monetary terms (Donovan & O'Brien, 2016). Proven concepts and scales from the social sector should be used sensitively (e.g., the wellbeing indexes). When it comes to the intangible effects of artistic-creative products and work, elaborate measurement concepts and scales are often missing (Donovan & O'Brien, 2016). Some exceptions exist, e.g., tailored logit models found in fields like arts schools (Kishchuk, 2014) or the "Neighbourhood Arts and Culture Impact Assessment" (NACIA). Out of the need to take into account better the specificity and complexity of the ACS, various authors have formulated a call for more theory-based evaluations and refer to approaches of cultural sociologists, such as Bourdieu's social status theory (Galloway, 2009; Newman, 2013).

Various authors note that, in addition to the significantly lower evaluation budgets in contrast to other policy fields, little expertise is available to measure social value by the standards of current evaluation methodologies (Galloway, 2009; Newman & McLean, 2006; Secker et al., 2011; Throsby, 2003, 2012; Vermeulen et al., 2019). Moreover, lack of methodological expertise may lead to an overemphasis of methods (Sanderson, 2000) and a failure to address fundamental questions of "orientation" and "logic of enquiry" (Galloway, 2009). By critically analysing selected cases, we take a closer look at the aforementioned methodological challenges of social impacts measurement in the arts and cultural sectors.

Cases

It was a challenge to find empirical work and qualified cases of evaluation in arts and culture in the current research literature, despite the proximity between evaluation and empirical science. This challenge may be due to the confidentiality of many evaluations related to counselling practice or the scarcity of cases in this field.

We researched the internationally recognized journals in arts (International Journal of Cultural Policy, Cultural Trends, and International Journal of Art Management, Law, and Society) and the relevant evaluation journals (Evaluation Review, Evaluation, and American Journal of Evaluation). We searched for documented cases of evaluations in the cultural sector using keywords such as "evaluation", "arts", "social", or "social impact".

In total, we evaluated 57 cases. Of these, 13 cases fulfil the criteria for analysis, i.e. they comprised evaluations of identified arts projects and programs. Two cases are from the field of arts education in schools (Epp, 2008; Wright et al., 2006); two cases concern work with the elderly (Fleuriet & Chauvin, 2018; Ford et al., 2018); three cases are from the field of mental health and disability (Hendriks et al., 2019; Onyx et al., 2018; Secker et al., 2011); two cases are from the field of criminal justice (Brewster, 2014; Ezell & Levy, 2003); one case is from the field of inclusion (Vermeulen et al., 2019); and three cases concern the community building (Grisolía et al., 2010; Jackson & McManus, 2019; Lee, 2013). The selected cases cover a wide range of fields in which art is exerted to achieve social impacts. All cases' characteristics were collected in terms of their project objectives, inputs/activities, outcomes, evaluation criteria, and applied evaluation methods (Table 19.1).

Table 19.1 Overview of the cases investigated

	Project/policy objectives	*Cultural processes/ activities*	*Evaluation criteria/ questions*	*Evaluation methods*	*Outcomes*
Wright et al. (2006)	NATIONAL ARTS AND YOUTH DEMONSTRATION PROJECT: Change in art skills, change in prosocial skills, change in emotional problems, and social integration of young people (9–15 years old) from low-income communities.	After-school nine-month arts program focused on theatre (also included visual arts and media arts).	(a) To determine if arts organizations can successfully recruit, engage, and sustain youth, (b) assess youths' progress in artistic and social skills, (c) ascertain if programmes improved psychosocial outcomes, and (d) explore the perspectives of the participating youth and parents.	Attendance records, observational data in the form of a behaviour checklist and interviews with parents and youths. Propensity score matching to have a control group.	Positive effect on art skills, development of prosocial skills, and a decrease in emotional problems.
Secker et al. (2011)	OPEN ARTS aims to provide relaxing, welcoming art groups, combating social exclusion. The project works with people at risk of mental illness, health issues and isolation and recovery from mental health problems.	Introductory art courses aiming to provide relaxing, welcoming art groups: Courses run for 10–15 weeks with sessions in various media.	The aim is to illustrate the value of participant feedback in shaping the development of OPEN ARTS covering: expectations of the course; first impressions; settling in; course organization, venue, and program; levels of support provided; individual gains; and suggestions for improvement.	Focus groups and interviews, the Warwick – Edinburgh Mental Well-being Scale (WEMWBS), is a validated measure consisting of 14 statements.	Improvement in wellbeing and social inclusion.

Hendriks et al. (2019)	UNFORGETTABLE PROGRAM in museums: Aiming to improve social engagement and quality of life of people with dementia.	90-minute visit for a person with dementia with an accompanying person in 1,212 Dutch museums.	(a) What are the characteristics of participants? (b) How do participants experience and appreciate it? (c) Are the experience and appreciation of the program reflected in mood changes after the guided museum tours? (d) Are the experience, appreciation, and change in mood related to specific characteristics of the participants?	Comparison of questionnaires before and after the intervention, data collected from people with dementia and their caregivers.	Positive findings: Better mood, more talkative, having a better appetite, social connections. Negative findings: Technical problems, poor accessibility of a toilette. Attendance of informal caregivers is essential and has an instrumental role.
Ford et al. (2018)	ART IN HEALTH PROGRAM for patients, their families, and staff in a dedicated acute care medical inpatient unit for the elderly: Benefits for quality of life and wellbeing for older patients and ways nurses perceive improved care.	Art activities for patients: Art making, customized music and song, snapshot, enlivening the space.	(a) Explore the impact of the arts activities for patients and their families, including their engagement, participation, and enjoyment; (b) the impact from the perspectives of staff; and (c) the influence of the program on the physical environment.	Semi-structured interviews, qualitative data in the form of transcripts and field notes, focus groups for staff.	Positive evaluation of environment transformation, increased engagement and enjoyment of patients, calming and settling of some patients, enhanced communication between patients and staff.

(*Continued*)

Table 19.1 (Continued)

	Project/policy objectives	*Cultural processes/ activities*	*Evaluation criterial/ questions*	*Evaluation methods*	*Outcomes*
Fleuriet and Chauvin (2018)	SENIOR THEATRE PROGRAM: Improve emotional intelligence, self-confidence, self-esteem, memory, social engagement, verbal skills of participants.	Eight-week SENIOR THEATRE PROGRAM sponsored by The Playhouse San Antonio: Older adults acting and practice similar to what actors followed for a show.	(a) To document the impact of the senior theatre participation on self-confidence and self-esteem, emotional intelligence, memory, social engagement, and self-rated physical and mental health, and (b) to document organizational and pedagogical variables that could encourage intended outcomes of the SENIOR THEATRE PROGRAM.	The survey, focus group interviews, participant observation, and focus group.	Creative engagement in participatory art can enhance wellness, notably in-group relationships, health and wellbeing, and learning and creativity, except memory-related cognitive functions.
Grisolía et al. (2010)	REGIONAL THEATRE: ASSESSMENT of the degree to which a typical regional theatre engages with society. Evaluation of an institution.	Shows of a regional theatre in Newcastle (comedy, drama, family, and Shakespearian productions): No specific interventions were analysed.	Criteria: Social representation or engagement, differences of attendance in occupation, education, Interacting variables: Age, gender, ethnic minorities.	It uses postcodes from theatre booking to compare people's socioeconomic profiles from these regions with other regions. Discriminant analysis is used to identify the socioeconomic factors associated with theatre and non-theatre attendance. More than 7,000 postcodes were linked with National Statistics Socioeconomic Classification.	Education factors as determinants of attendance, with occupational categories being important; lower socioeconomic groups were less likely to engage with theatre. Social engagement and factors determining attendance varied by type of show.

Jackson and McManus (2019)	Art gallery: Use of the social return on investment (SROI) methodology to describe and measure the Turner Contemporary art gallery's social impacts in Margate. Evaluation of an institution.	Work and communication strategies of a gallery: No specific interventions were analysed. Mediation and sale of art.	Social return on investment (SROI), according to its principles.	SROI methodology. The stakeholders themselves identify the outcomes (the primary stakeholders are visitors to exhibitions, participants in formal education, and participants in lifelong learning), typically using interviews, focus groups, and workshops, with analysis being undertaken to identify dominant themes and patterns in the data (three-stage-approach); e.g., causality chain of outcomes for lifelong learners, quantified factors, determination of a key figure/ratio.	Participants became more open-minded and confident. They strengthened their social networks, and they enhanced their knowledge and skills.
Onyx et al. (2018)	ARTS AND PEOPLE WITH DISABILITIES: Establish a method of assessing the potential social impacts of arts and disability projects, application on ten projects, main target groups are professionals, community.	Twelve programmes of arts and disabilities, different art forms: visual, multimedia, audio, performance.	Social impacts instrument development: Four stages: (a) Welcoming organization where members belong, (b) social and citizenship values, (c) actions: skills and networks, (d) Contributions for others. Three factors per stage, analysis of qualitative case studies.	Case studies research: In-depth interviews and focus groups, further data gathering. Modelling: Iterative research process, scoring, and case comparison.	Confirmation that there is a profound and positive social impact on the participants, both individually and collectively.

(*Continued*)

Table 19.1 (Continued)

	Project/policy objectives	*Cultural processes/ activities*	*Evaluation criteria/ questions*	*Evaluation methods*	*Outcomes*
Lee (2013)	Peace Project (GUERNICA PEACE MURAL PROJECT (GPMP)), Columbus, Ohio: Exploring how community arts generate social capital to promote intergroup cohesion.	Eighteen graduate students (seven graduated arts teachers), twenty Somali children, in a summer program: Use of participatory and collaborative arts, high level of interactions, authentic personal interactions, informal setting, non-hierarchical relationships or equal partnerships.	Social Capital Indicators: Increased understanding of Somali people and Somali culture, tolerance of difference, friendship, empathy, mutual trust, mutual respect, sense of oneness, solidarity, cohesion.	Participatory observation, interviews, survey questionnaire, online postings, follow-up after one year.	Exposure to and understanding of relationships, solidified connections, bridge-bonded social group.
Brewster (2014)	PRISON ARTS PROGRAMMES: Measurement of attitudinal and behavioural changes in inmates who participated in theatre, visual arts, poetry, and writing courses.	Theatre, visual arts, poetry, and writing courses in prisons.	Personal effectiveness: Life Effectiveness Questionnaire measuring time management, social competence, achievement motivation, intellectual flexibility, emotional control, active initiative, and self-confidence.	110 participants from 4 prisons were evaluated, quantitative, control-groups, descriptive analysis, ANOVA, t-tests.	A reduction in disciplinary reports and greater participation in academic and vocation programmes.

Epp (2008)	Arts Therapy for School-Age children: The study examines the effectiveness of a social skills therapy program for school-age children ages 11 through 18.	Super Kids therapeutic model: Weekly group therapy using cognitive-behavioural strategies, arts activities to broaden and deepen the techniques to help children with social developmental disorders to improve their social skills.	Social skills: cooperation, assertion, self-control, and responsibility. Problem behaviour: externalizing problems (aggressive acts and poor temper control); internalizing problems (sadness and anxiety); and hyperactivity (fidgeting and impulsive acts).	Pre- and post-test instruments were distributed to parents and children. Social Skills Rating System (SSRS) (Gresham & Elliott, 1990) questionnaires for parents and teachers. Two sections, social skills and problem behaviours.	Scores revealed a significant improvement in assertion scores and decreased internalizing behaviours, hyperactivity scores, and problem behaviour scores in the students.
Vermeulen et al. (2019)	INCLUSIVENESS IN MUSEUM: Cultural participation activities to strengthen the legitimacy and a valuable contribution to society, to attract migrant audiences, to add value to lives of the target group, to improve cultural participation, to build a research framework for other cultural organizations.	Visits/tours for students with migrant backgrounds: Half of the students visited a guided museum tour; the second half used an interactive multimedia guide. The approach is to evoke emotions through the direct tone of voice and quotes from Van Gogh's letters.	Characterization of the respondents: Educational level, identity, sex, and age, the impact of family Cultural Participation: Active versus receptive cultural participation, motivation, perceived values, social inclusion (SIS scale).	A research framework combines the level of participation and ways to engage the target group. A mixed approach was used to analyse the secondary school vocational students' visit to the museum, blending qualitative and quantitative methods (survey) – baseline study.	Vocational educational students prefer to participate in active cultural activities. The Van Gogh Museum can positively impact specific factors that result in social inclusion amongst the students in the research sample.

(*Continued*)

Table 19.1 (Continued)

	Project/policy objectives	*Cultural processes/ activities*	*Evaluation criteria/ questions*	*Evaluation methods*	*Outcomes*
Ezell and Levy (2003)	A CHANGED WORLD (arts program for youth in prison) aims to inculcate cultural and community awareness; to lessen the risks of inappropriate behaviour; to develop skills that will motivate and assist the student in searching for employment; to reduce the likelihood to re-offend after release.	The youth were involved in the workshops when planning the film, including (a) the script and filming; (b) the musical score; and (c) the catalogue that accompanies the film.	(a) Do students learn new academic and vocational skills from the art workshops? (b) Does the institutional behaviour of program participants improve during their workshops? (c) How does the recidivism rate of program participants compare to nonparticipants?	An open-ended survey, observation, monitoring.	Among the participants, 60% learned new vocational skills, 70% reported positive feelings, 17.6% feelings of accomplishment, the number of incidents decreased by 63%, 16.7% recidivism within the six-month follow-up period.

Observations

Based on the critical examination of these cases, we have identified three commonalities. First, there is no existing universally accepted tool for evaluating social impacts in the arts. Some studies have used pre-existing know-how from the best practices in the social and health sectors. For example, Secker et al. (2011) used the Warwick-Edinburgh Mental Well-being Scale (WEMWBS) to evaluate the impact of introductory arts workshops on mental health. Jackson and McManus (2019) applied the SROI method to an art gallery evaluation. Epp (2008) used the Social Skills Rating System SSRS to evaluate art therapy for school-age children. All other cases used self-tailored instruments. Although these instruments capture the specific subject of the evaluated case best, they might hinder comparability and transferability within the arts field. Onyx et al. (2018) realized this shortcoming and developed a social impacts instrument for arts interventions in people with disabilities. Lee (2013) used the cultural sociological theory of Bourdieu to measure cultural capital and, in doing so, developed a specific approach for their evaluation of a community arts project to foster peace.

Second, our impression is that many of the underlying evaluations are subject to scarce resources. Some evaluations pragmatically use existing data. Grisolía et al. (2010) used postcodes and social data from theatre bookings to analyse differences in social involvement between theatre visitors and non-visitors. Several studies used focus group interviews, which allow for the efficient collecting of the research participants' experiences (see Fleuriet & Chauvin, 2018; Ford et al., 2018; Jackson & McManus, 2019; Secker et al., 2011), but the standards of reporting seemed to be insufficient or too costly for evaluation of these studies. Thus, methodological challenges were not addressed in these cases, probably to avoid costs and time-consuming methods.

Several case studies in our chapter used qualitative research (Epp, 2008; Ford et al., 2018; Hendriks et al., 2019; Lee, 2013; Onyx et al., 2018). Here, limitations in resources may lead to rather superficially evaluated qualitative interviews. A methodologically more permissible method is developing self-evaluation tools, but none of the case studies analysed made use of this option. Due to limited affordability in some cases, smaller samples were selected (Ezell & Levy, 2003; Fleuriet & Chauvin, 2018; Wright et al., 2006). The consequence of the rather limited funding is a narrow scope of evaluation: evaluators are driven to focus primarily on the treated groups and pay little attention to control groups (Ford et al., 2018; Hendriks et al., 2019). Brewster's study represented an exception with consideration of control groups (Brewster, 2014), as was the study conducted by Wright, who applied quasi-experimental methods (Wright et al., 2006).

Third, we found that all studies critically reflected on the outcomes and impacts of their studies. We also observed an awareness of the use of limited and thus unsatisfactory methodological approaches. However, recommendations based on the outcomes and impacts identified in the studies and directed to cultural practitioners, programme leaders, and policymakers have often been missing and not made explicit. We also expected to find more reflection on the methodological approaches used and how they can be improved and optimized in the future in each of the studies. A consolidated presentation of the consequences on practice and cultural policy, together with an open, adaptive approach to evaluation methods and tools would be a useful tool in order to increase the acceptance and value of evaluation studies in the ACS. This type of report could even help to find support for performing more follow-up studies and scaling up evaluation in the future.

Discussion and conclusion

The inventory in this chapter has shown how diverse the evaluation of artistic-creative interventions can be in terms of their social effects. Artistic-creative intervention measures are applied in the cultural system and other areas such as health, justice, social affairs, youth, and education. Likewise, artistic-creative intervention measures have pursued different goals and achieved different effects. Thus, we value all methods as relevant, regardless of whether they are quasi-experimental methods, SROI, interviews, surveys, or observations. Their specific application depends on the concrete evaluation goal(s), the evaluation object, and other framework conditions such as actors, type of artistic intervention, and the like. There is no such thing as "the" social impact, so we have always used this word in the plural (see also Belfiore & Bennett, 2007).

Despite this diversity, social impacts analysis in the ACS can advance in some respects. In our view, there is a need for a stronger exchange of results and evidence, concepts and approaches, methods and projects. We call for closer collaboration among evaluators and practitioners from the arts scene. In this way, instruments and models could be tested for their replicability, and expertise could be built up to a greater extent. Concerning selected policy and programme objectives such as participation and inclusion, we can learn from existing approaches, test new ones, and apply proven models.

The connection to evaluation research should be further strengthened and advanced. There has been little interest in evaluating cultural programmes and policies in evaluations-oriented journals and vice versa. Contributions in arts-and-culture-oriented journals should use more rigorous methodologies. Collaboration between these two communities should be fostered to enrich each other and achieve valuable and rigorous evaluations of cultural programmes and policies.

Evaluations in the field of arts and culture are needed. However, they should be performed only with adequate funding in order to be able to achieve methodologically well-grounded results.

References

Belfiore, E. (2010). Art as a means of alleviating social exclusion: Does it really work? A critique of instrumental cultural policies and social impact studies in the UK. *International Journal of Cultural Policy*, *8*(1), 91–106. doi:10.1080/102866302900324658

Belfiore, E., & Bennett, O. (2007). Rethinking the social impacts of the arts. *International Journal of Cultural Policy*, *13*(2), 135–151. doi:10.1080/10286630701342741

Belfiore, E., & Bennett, O. (2010). Beyond the "toolkit approach": Arts impact evaluation research and the realities of cultural policy-making. *Journal for Cultural Research*, *14*(2), 121–142. doi:10.1080/14797580903481280

Brewster, L. (2014). The impact of prison arts programs on inmate attitudes and behavior: A quantitative evaluation. *Justice Policy Journal*, *11*(2), 1–27.

Brown, J. L., MacDonald, R., & Mitchell, R. (2015). Are people who participate in cultural activities more satisfied with life? *Social Indicators Research*, *122*(1), 135–146. doi:10.1007/s11205-014-0678-7

Cohen, C., & Pate, M. (2000). Making a meal of arts evaluation: Can social audit offer a more balanced approach? *Managing Leisure*, *5*(3), 103–120. doi:10.1080/13606710050084810

Crossick, G., & Kaszynska, P. (2016). *Understanding the value of arts & culture, report commissioned by the arts and humanities research council's cultural value project*. London: AHRC.

Donovan, C., & O'Brien, D. (2016). Governing culture: Legislators, interpreters and accountants. *Critical Perspectives on Accounting*, *37*, 24–34. doi:10.1016/j.cpa.2015.10.003

Epp, K. M. (2008). Outcome-based evaluation of a social skills program using art therapy and group therapy for children on the autism spectrum. *Children & Schools*, *30*(1), 27–36.

Ezell, M., & Levy, M. (2003). An evaluation of an arts program for incarcerated juvenile offenders. *Journal of Correctional Education*, *54*(3), 108–114.

Fleuriet, J., & Chauvin, T. (2018). "Living other lives": The impact of senior theatre on older adult well-being. *Journal of Applied Arts & Health*, *9*(1), 37–51. doi:10.1386/jaah.9.1.37_1

Ford, K., Tesch, L., Dawborn, J., & Courtney-Pratt, H. (2018). Art, music, story: The evaluation of a person-centred arts in health programme in an acute care older persons' unit. *International Journal of Older People Nursing*, *13*(2), e12186. doi:10.1111/opn.12186

Galloway, S. (2009). Theory-based evaluation and the social impact of the arts. *Cultural Trends*, *18*(2), 125–148. doi:10.1080/09548960902826143

Gilhespy, I. (2001). The evaluation of social objectives in cultural organizations. *International Journal of Arts Management*, *4*(1), 48–57.

Goddard, S. (2009). Heritage partnerships: Promoting public involvement and understanding. In D. Therond & A. Trigona (Eds.), *Heritage and beyond* (pp. 141–148). Strasbourg: Council of Europe Publishing.

Grisolía, J. M., Willis, K., Wymer, C., & Law, A. (2010). Social engagement and regional theatre: Patterns of theatre attendance. *Cultural Trends*, *19*(3), 225–244. doi:10.1080/09548963.2010.495277

Hendriks, I., Meiland, F. J. M., Gerritsen, D. L., & Dröes, R.-M. (2019). Evaluation of the "Unforgettable" art programme by people with dementia and their caregivers. *Ageing and Society*, 1–19. doi:10.1017/s0144686x19001089

Jackson, A., & McManus, R. (2019). SROI in the art gallery: Valuing social impact. *Cultural Trends*, *28*(2–3), 132–145. doi:10.1080/09548963.2019.1617937

Kishchuk, P. (2014). *Evaluation of the school of visual arts: Findings synthesis.* https://yukon.ca/en/evaluation-school-visual-arts-2014

Landry, C., Bianchini, F., Maguire, M., & Worpole, K. (1993). *The social impact of the arts: A discussion document.* Bournes Green, Stroud: Comedia.

Lee, D. (2013). How the arts generate social capital to foster intergroup social cohesion. *The Journal of Arts Management, Law, and Society*, *43*(1), 4–17. doi:10.1080/10632921.2012.761167

Miller, T. (2006). Screening citizens. In M. S. Campbell & R. Martin (Eds.), *Artistic citizenship: A public voice for the arts* (pp. 97–114). New York: Routledge.

Morson, G. S., & Schapiro, M. (2017). *Why economists need to expand their knowledge to include the humanities.* www.weforum.org/agenda/2017/08/why-economists-need-to-expand-their-knowledge-to-include-the-humanities

Newman, A. (2013). Imagining the social impact of museums and galleries: Interrogating cultural policy through an empirical study. *International Journal of Cultural Policy*, *19*(1), 120–137. doi:10.1080/10286632.2011.625419

Newman, A., & McLean, F. (2006). The impact of museums upon identity. *International Journal of Heritage Studies*, *12*(1), 49–68. doi:10.1080/13527250500384514

Onyx, J., Darcy, S., Grabowski, S., Green, J., & Maxwell, H. (2018). Researching the social impact of arts and disability: Applying a new empirical tool and method. *VOLUNTAS: International Journal of Voluntary and Nonprofit Organizations*, *29*(3), 574–589. doi:10.1007/s11266-018-9968-z

Sandell, R. (2003). *Museums, society, inequality.* Abingdon: Routledge Publishing.

Sanderson, I. (2000). Evaluation in complex policy systems. *Evaluation*, 6(4), 433–454.

Secker, J., Loughran, M., Heydinrych, K., & Kent, L. (2011). Promoting mental well-being and social inclusion through art: Evaluation of an arts and mental health project. *Arts & Health*, *3*(1), 51–60. doi:10.1080/17533015.2010.541267

Throsby, D. (2003). Determining the value of cultural goods: How much (or how little) does contingent valuation tell us? *Journal of Cultural Economics*, *27*, 275–285.

Throsby, D. (2012). Heritage economics: A conceptual framework. In G. Licciardi & R. Amirtahmasebi (Eds.), *The economics of uniqueness* (pp. 45–72). Washington, DC: The World Bank.

Van de Vyver, J., & Abrams, D. (2018). The arts as a catalyst for human prosociality and cooperation. *Social Psychological and Personality Science*, *9*(6), 664–674. doi:10.1177/1948550617720275

Vermeulen, M., Vermeylen, F., Maas, K., De Vet, M., & Van Engel, M. (2019). Measuring inclusion in museums: A case study on cultural engagement with young people with a migrant background in Amsterdam. *The International Journal of the Inclusive Museum*, *12*(2), 1–26. doi:10.18848/1835-2014/CGP/v12i02/1-26

Wright, R., John, L., Alaggia, R., & Sheel, J. (2006). Community-based arts program for youth in low-income communities: A multi-method evaluation. *Child and Adolescent Social Work Journal*, *23*(5–6), 635–652. doi:10.1007/s10560-006-0079-0

20 Human Rights Tattoo

A Zoom conversation between Sander van Bussel, Maria Kint, and Eltje Bos about the Human Rights Tattoo project. 21 December 2021

Sander van Bussel, Maria Kint, and Eltje Bos

ELTJE: We will start this conversation which will describe a unique project, with a statement from the project website, "We are free to live, love, work, dance, laugh, write, speak, vote, travel, and debate. We are equal no matter what our age, nationality, gender, ancestry, skin colour, sexual orientation, or political preference is. Freedom and equality are, in short, the cornerstones of what it means to be human". The web site is available at www.humanrightstattoo.org/

And now, welcome Sander and Maria, we are in this online meeting to learn about and reflect on your project of Human Right Tattoos. Who are you, what kind of project is it, and how did it come about?

SANDER: As a social artist and lecturer at St. Joost School of Art and Design I worked on many community art projects, such as connecting people in a community by their "under the shower songs"; we asked people to record their singing as they took a shower; we taped it and through the specific structure of pits/drains in the streets we "broadcasted" the songs in the streets through the pits/drains as a part of a cultural walk through the city of Tilburg in the Netherlands.

MARIA: I see myself as a cultural entrepreneur, consultant, teacher, and activist. Coming from a background of activism and training in Southern Africa, HRT was a great project to sink my teeth in once I was "retired" and living back in The Netherlands.

SANDER: In early 2012 a Kenyan social artist, whom I befriended and was working with in my workshop in Tilburg, was murdered in the

DOI: 10.4324/9781003105350-21

slums of Korogocho, Kenya. I was shocked. There was no police investigation, nothing. To me it is totally unacceptable that someone, a link, was taken out of the chain of living before his time.

I felt I had to do something, to react to this. The idea for Human Rights Tattoo came like a pure and instant emotional reaction. A way of reacting as an artist as well. The idea came as a way of uniting people as an unbreakable chain, something like a talisman that can protect us, a chain where no link can be missed. I worked from my intuition, that's what I do as an artist. It is just what I can contribute as social artist; I am not a lawyer or politician; I have to work with my imagination. It just seemed right to me, to share and to keep these rights alive and to unite people in their moral values, because of what or where they are.

I felt human rights could be shared and kept alive by a tattoo art project, where the bodies of people serve as a canvas and at the same time connect them by doing so.

Our body is what makes us human, our vehicle that carries us through our time and physical space. I thought it to be a strong idea to invite people, worldwide, to carry one letter of the Universal Declaration of Human Rights as a tattoo on their skin, as a sign, a statement, that one carries on the outside of the body, on the skin, and it also has an impact on the inner life, on feeling and thought. It is a permanent commitment, for life.

For some people it is a courageous decision; in some countries, it really takes courage because of the political circumstances. We have been in 26 countries over the last years.

To make this declaration truly universal, I felt we had to make this a worldwide project. We announced our tattoo sessions and shared the stories of the participants, and it worked! We now have had over 60 tattoo events in 26 countries and we connected 4,600 people from 77 different countries, the last one for now being the E for Daniela from Mexico – from the line: *Everyone has the right to rest and leisure.*

So we are well on our way as the Universal Declaration of Human Rights consists of: 1 text, 30 articles, 6.773 individual letters *www.humanrightstattoo.org/*

MARIA: The online part of this project enables us to stay connected as a community even though the last two years have been during the Covid pandemic. Whenever it was possible we organised events, in Mexico at the ITESCO University, during their cultural week, in Brussels at the BXL festival, in "Schauspielhaus Wien", a theatre in Vienna, and in the Mauritshuis museum in the Hague. Just before the outbreak of Covid we were in Cape Town (Wetopia academy), we were in St. Petersburg during the Queer festival, and in Nepal, celebrating International Wheelchair Day. The map below shows where we have been.

ELTJE: How do the tattoo events work in practice?

SANDER: The idea spreads itself, with people talking about their tattoo in real life or sharing it online, and requests to join come in every day, from all over the world. The tattoo events are then coproduced with local organisations; with local tattoo-artists, communication, and a venue that can provide a space to meet with the necessary hygienic arrangements.

We send out a call online and people can sign up for the event to get a letter tattooed. People can choose from several fonts, but the letter itself will be the next letter in the declaration.

ELTJE: I see you offer a design for what a workshop should look like in terms of physical space, to be sure it isn't too cramped, and that it is clean.

MARIA: Yes, the hygiene is important. We collaborate with local tattoo professionals. We ask the participants for their motivation, we want people to be sure about their decision to get a tattoo and not to regret it. Also, people tell us why they decided on a HRT tattoo; each one has their own story. We ask them whether we can publish their story on the website; if you click you see the number of the letter in the text and the letter in the text fragment with a picture of the person carrying that letter and her or his motivation or story. By looking at the site people can share their stories and see how they are connected.

ELTJE: How do you see the impact of this project?

MARIA: There are various levels of impact. First of all, some people do it to make a statement for themselves or to support others. As I look on the website I can read what some have written: *I wanna have a tattoo because I want to be free* (Danny, Malawi). *I just wanted to remember it, and keep doing it in the ordinary life* (Reka, Hungary). *I am not a human rights lawyer or anything, but I am human, and I should be aware of my rights. Getting this tattoo is great for me because it will be part of a greater movement world-wide. In a way, I will have made my mark on the human rights declaration!* (Cecilia, Zimbabwe). *I make this statement for those who do not have the rights to make it* (Sharon, Netherlands).

I felt when I was at the events/gatherings that it gave me a feeling of being included, most people participating are younger than I am; nonetheless we have had lively and fundamental conversations. Somehow the hierarchy between people seems to disappear. Also the atmosphere is friendly, some people are just curious, step in and want to know more and in the end decide not to get a tattoo, and that's fine. A guard in Russia, after serving at his post an entire day by a queer festival and listening to the people coming in, decided in the end of the day he also wanted to support the project and got his tattoo.

SANDER: At the events people are physically connected; they meet and discuss why they participate, and every letter is the beginning of a story and a new connection. People who live in difficult circumstances, like political and LGBTQA-activists, feel supported and recognised in their struggles, knowing there are many others in this community. In this way we unite the world in ink, with people making 1cm of their skin available for one of the letters. We document everyone on site, with a portrait, a photo of the tattoo, and their motivation, to make a visual representation of this community.

There also are other aspects of impact, like the Mauritshuis in Netherlands, making it an issue because of the reframing of museums in the context of the history of slavery in the Netherlands.

We are thinking of expanding the impact a bit more: to work closer together with museums, perhaps with an exhibition of photos and participants' stories, and we could engage in online meetings with the people who already participated.

ELTJE: How are you doing financially?

MARIA: the project is made possible by private donations and with the help of project funding, by foundations and some local and provincial government support. Amnesty International annually funds some projects like the upcoming event in Marseille. There the HRT event will be part of an Art Festival but with a focus on the LGBTQ+ community and refugees. And we are exploring possibilities for funding by international funders as the Soros and Gulbekian foundations

And in the near future, on 1 March 2022 we will have an online event, celebrating the International Wheelchair Day, with our partners the Jawalakhel Wheelchair Sports Club from Nepal. Our last pre-pandemic event was in Nepal celebrating this day together. We had a film made then; now we will have the premiere

HUMAN RIGHTS TATTOO
spreading hope since 2012

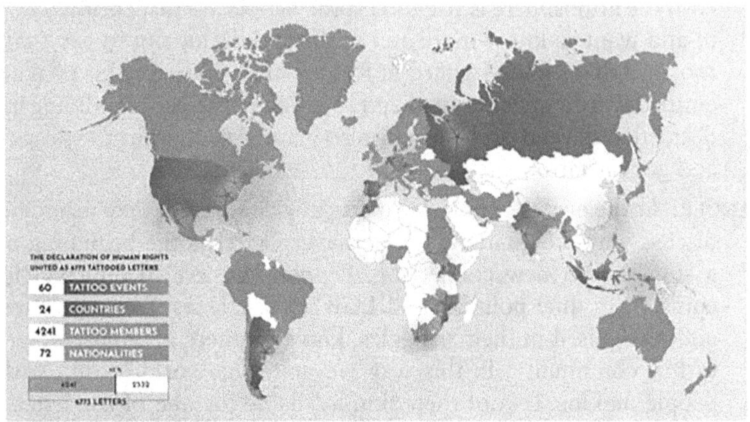

Figure 20.1 Human Rights Tattoo: spreading hope since 2012

screening of the film "Bharat BC, letter 4221: R". A short video portrait by Mari Sanders of Bharat BC, a young man who against all odds overcomes being stuck in a wheelchair in rural Nepal and manages to get a master's degree.

Eltje: Thank you so much for your time and for telling about this wonderful project. This project works through the online possibilities we have to connect people so beautifully. And I am sure many people look forward to your next events.

Literature

www.un.org/en/about-us/universal-declaration-of-human-rights

General assembly resolution 217A

www.un.org/sites/un2.un.org/files/udhr.pdf

Article I: All human beings are born free and equal in dignity and rights. They are endowed with reason and conscience and should act towards one another in a spirit of brotherhood.

Article 2: Everyone is entitled to all the rights and freedoms set forth in this Declaration, without distinction of any kind, such as race, colour, sex, language, religion, political or other opinion, national or social origin, property, birth or other status. Furthermore, no distinction shall be made on the basis of the political, jurisdictional or international status of the country or territory to which a person belongs, whether it be independent, trust, non-self-governing or under any other limitation of sovereignty.

Index

Page numbers in *italics* indicate a figure on the corresponding page. Page numbers followed by 'n' indicate a note.

For Product Safety Concerns and Information please contact our EU representative GPSR@taylorandfrancis.com
Taylor & Francis Verlag GmbH, Kaufingerstraße 24, 80331 München, Germany

www.ingramcontent.com/pod-product-compliance
Lightning Source LLC
Chambersburg PA
CBHW060153280326
41932CB00012B/1739

* 9 7 8 0 3 6 7 6 1 5 1 8 5 *